I0605837

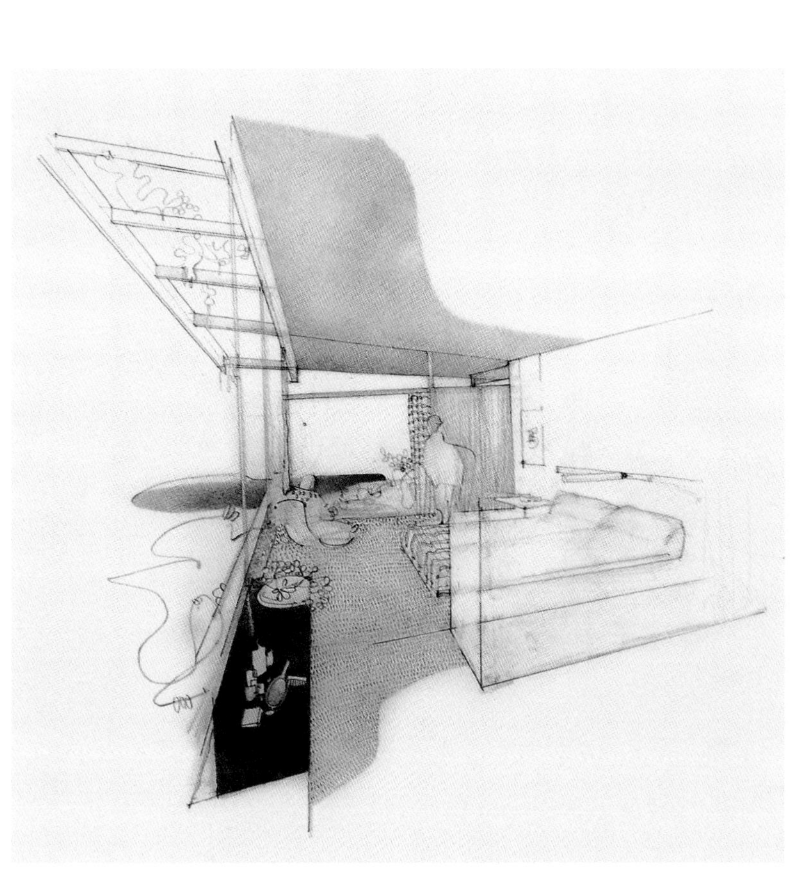

Principal Photographer

Julius Shulman

NEUTRA

Texts by Barbara Mac Lamprecht
Editorial Assistance by Dion Neutra
Edited by Peter Gössel

TASCHEN

CONTENTS

HISTORY AND THE MILIEU OF SOCIAL CRITIQUE

Travel sketch, Serbia, 1916, when Neutra served in the Austro-Hungarian Army.

Born into that remarkable crucible, fin-de-siècle Vienna, the career of Richard Joseph Neutra (1892–1970) paralleled Modernism's own exploding arc of ascendancy as it redefined 20th-century art and architecture. The city was filled with restless, gifted figures, so monumental that any list of their names is both familiar and incomplete: cultural critic Karl Kraus; author of *The Man without Qualities* Robert Musil; Arnold Schönberg, who conceived 12-tone music; the poet Peter Altenberg; and other giants such as painters Gustav Klimt, Oskar Kokoschka, Egon Schiele; architects Otto Wagner, Adolf Loos, Josef Hoffmann, Joseph Maria Olbrich. All were involved in exposing and uprooting what they believed to be a decadent culture riddled with a myriad of middle-class hypocrisies. The dialogue among these individuals was daily, fierce, and intimate.

This atmosphere of cultural upheaval was the air Neutra breathed and moved in. His family were agnostic, long-assimilated Jews with important cultural connections, the same kind of people who disappeared into World War II. Their careers straddled the arts and sciences, as Neutra's own work would do. His father owned a foundry; his grandfather and brother were doctors (as is Richard's son Raymond); the Neutras and Freuds were friends. Wilhelm, his older brother, became a psychiatrist in Freud's circle, and wrote *Rational Psychology*, a 1935 study of anxiety neuroses; his other brother Siegmund was a violinist who mingled with Schönberg's musical circles; Neutra's sister was courted by a Russian nihilist before marrying Arpad Weixlgärtner, a highly respected art curator, who introduced Neutra to art history as well as contemporary artists such as Klimt.

Neutra was acutely sensitive to his surroundings, it appears, from the first. His earliest recollections record not so much memories of people but rather recollections of sensations and surfaces, such as the feeling of refuge hiding underneath a grand piano with a thick drape thrown over it, a "splintery parquetry floor" or "licking the brass hardware of my cupboard."

In describing his decision to become an architect, Neutra tells two stories in his autobiography *Life and Shape* that exemplify his own fusion of science and art. The first describes the consequences of a lethal *physical* environment: writer Emile Zola and his wife suffocated in their Paris bedroom in 1902 because of the fumes of a defective flue, horrifying the ten-year-old Richard. The second deals with a visual impact: at about the same age, Neutra often ran up and down the new railway stations and bridges designed by Austria's leading civic architect, Otto Wagner. Wagner's own search for a modern architecture struggled to address newly urgent theoretical questions about how buildings are conceived. His formal solutions, so startling to the contemporary eye, made a sharp impression on the young Richard.

Layers of Influence: Philosophical

Architects Otto Wagner and Adolf Loos were huge figures in Vienna's intellectual milieu. Visually, Neutra's architecture has little to do with theirs, but he absorbed their values and their questions about ethics in architecture. Loos insisted that ethics were expressed in buildings which were to be *beyond* time, to be timeless, and therefore exempt from the concerns of "fashion," while Wagner required that a building be "*of* its time," no longer mimicking the past but

Arpad Weixlgärtner (1872–1961), Richard's older brother-in-law, 1931

exploiting and expressing new construction technologies. In 1894, two years after Neutra's birth, Wagner was appointed as the imperial professor of architecture at the conservative Vienna Academy of Fine Arts. At the same time he began writing the first of four editions of his book *Modern Architecture*, a sweeping and comprehensive break with architecture's (as well as his own) eclectic past. It is filled with declarative writing, such as "something impractical cannot be beautiful" and "*Artis sola domina necessitas*": "necessity is art's only mistress." Wagner celebrated the "straight line and smooth surface" of the machine, proclaiming that the modern eye had become accustomed to less varied images, to long, straight lines and plainer silhouettes.

Wagner's ideas were part of a much larger debate on theory which also addressed the architectural implications of the new fields of experimental psychology, perception, and Darwin's theory of natural selection. Theorists such as Hermann Muthesius proposed "a far more rigorous architecture based on 'scientific objectivity', abstaining from decoration, and unconditionally correlating form and purpose." Words like "Architecture" were to be dropped altogether, having too many corrupt associations with the word "style," and replaced by "Baukunst," the art of building. Wagner agreed. The title of the last edition of his manifesto, published in 1914, was not "Modern Architecture" but *Die Baukunst unserer Zeit*, "The Art of Building in Our Time." Richard Neutra's own first book (1927), based on his fresh observations of new construction techniques of America, is not "How America Designs" but "How America Builds" (*Wie baut Amerika?*).

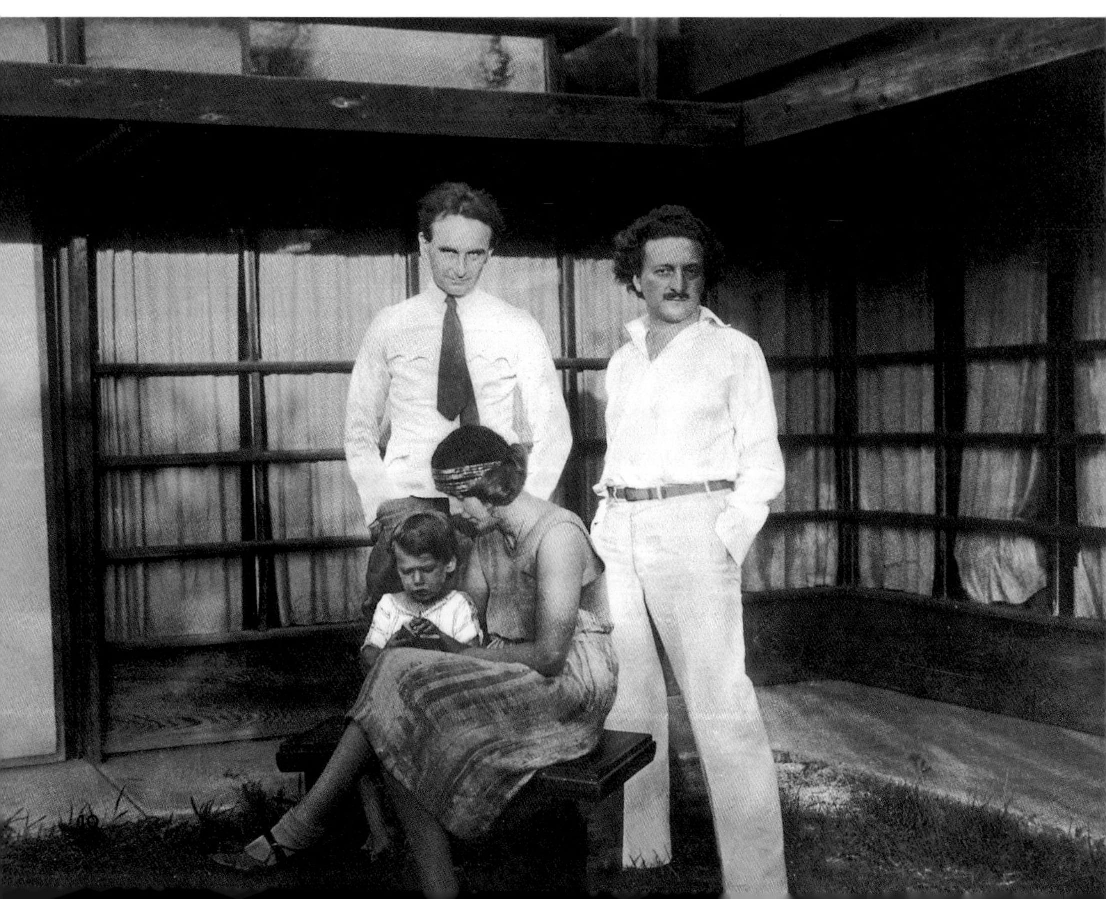

Under Hannes Meyer, the Bauhaus changed its department of architecture to the department of building.

Neutra followed Wagner's footsteps when he chose to enter the Technical University in 1911. His architectural education was interrupted when World War I broke out in 1914. He enlisted as an officer, and was promptly dispatched to the Balkans. Thus he had no chance to attend Wagner's famous "master classes," which, over the years, included such protégés as Joseph Maria Olbrich, Jože Plečnik, Jan Kotěra and Josef Hoffmann, the founders of the Secession, as well as Rudolph Schindler, Neutra's partner in the early Los Angeles years.

Adolf Loos, Neutra's other mentor in values, never shared Wagner's social success or prestige. He embodied the outsider in Viennese architectural circles. Loos even called his short-lived newspaper *Das Andere*, or "The Other." His close friend Karl Kraus was his kindred Jeremiah, peeling away facetiousness in newspaper language riddled with meaningless ornament in its gush of adverbs and adjectives, aiming polemic after polemic at anyone who breached his ideal of absolute personal integrity. Using language like a raised sword, Loos too sought purification, in his case to cleanse architecture of any vain association with art, and to rid Viennese culture of what he considered almost hysterically illegible ornament, damning it as a "violence perpetrated on the material in order to make it tell a lie."

Neutra characterized his beloved friend best: "Loos was a violent attacker, a reformer of ruthlessness and at the same time a most calm, almost whispering, quietly smiling philosopher of wrath." He loathed anything to do with style, and praised the utilitarian in craft. Loos also championed the anonymous, ancient masterbuilders, those who renounced the narcissism of

Above: Richard Neutra, ca. 1930

Opposite: Richard and Dione with Dion, the middle son, and Rudolph Schindler, ca. 1929

the self in favor of the larger process of history itself. Instead Loos proposed the quality of "lastingness," of casting off anything superficial. That was his greatest philosophical legacy to Neutra. A Neutra building is deceptively, apparently, neutral, like a blank canvas, except that his "canvas" has been carefully primed as a backdrop for human endeavor. (Even Neutra's chairs and tables, built to last forever, have an anonymous quality to them, with no egocentric gestures, yet so comfortable one is unconscious of them.)

Neutra met Loos while at university, and he spent long evenings drafting for him before World War I, talking with other Loos cronies around his café table or leaning over the marble countertop at the tiny American Bar in the Kärntner Strasse. This one small room is the world's most sensual

Adolf Loos, American Bar, 1907, Vienna, Austria

bar, rich in leather, marble, and brass. Its intimate low lighting glimmers through perfect martinis. Here the materials, as Loos intended, glow with their own beauty. Just above head height, where the burnished rosewood paneling ends, he placed mirrors high up on three sides of the room, so that the coffered ceiling goes on into infinity. Neutra, too, used mirrors high on the wall to stretch space, but in a more sophisticated way based on his own research into a mirror's impact on animal behavior.

Most Loos houses are stripped-down configurations of cubes. Windows and openings are deep punch-outs. Their interiors express Loos' famous *Raumplan* theory, which assigns a room's hierarchy through its height and then packs each room, like a piece in a vertically oriented, three-dimensional puzzle, into a rigidly defined enclosure. These different heights were meant to induce disparate emotions. Loos, too, was affected by the new research on perception when he wrote that an architectural effect is "the sensation that the space produces in the spectator; which may be fear or fright, as in a prison; a sense of warmth, as in his own house ... The effect is achieved by means of material and form." Loos was talking about feelings generated inside a house. Given his disdain for Viennese society, it is not surprising that Loos houses are aggressively private, almost hostile to the vapid society beyond the door.

Schindler and Neutra

In different ways Loos' *Raumplan* influenced both Neutra and his Viennese compatriot Rudolph Schindler, for whom Loos was also a seminal influence. Neutra took the *psychological* idea of the *Raumplan* which related material and form to emotional qualities, but added nature as a critical third ingredient in evoking that emotional, or psychological response. That mandated that the outdoors be available to the inhabitants, so that the house had to be a membrane, not a shield. In contrast to Neutra, Schindler embraced the *architectural* promise of *Raumplan*. On the same open Southern California landscape on which Neutra designed, Schindler's spaces reach out horizontally as well as vertically, and are far more animated in section, in general, than Neutra's dwellings. Schindler played great attention to spatial flow and continuity while Neutra built specific relations among rooms and outdoor views. Schindler's work also engages the wall as a monolithic mass. In contrast, Neutra uses distinct layers of materials and colors which are clearly applied as planes, or veneers, to a structural skeleton.

Schindler was five years older than Neutra, and attended both the Vienna Academy of Fine Arts under Wagner and the Technical University, where he met Neutra. Schindler found the first-year student closely examining Schindler's final student project. "He was the first to understand exactly what I was after," Schindler said later. Schindler left Vienna for Chicago right after he graduated, weeks before the Austrian Archduke Francis Ferdinand was assassinated on June 28, 1914. By 1918 he was working for Frank Lloyd Wright in Wisconsin. Neutra, meanwhile, was caught up in war chaos, getting his first taste of total immersion in foreign cultures. Remaining longer in Europe, he witnessed the rise of the Bauhaus and De Stijl schools.

This need to re-establish order after such chaos may be one of the reasons why Neutra was so interested in creating a system that excluded any sense of the "arbitrary." Schindler certainly thought so: the work of the Bauhaus schools, he said, was "an expression of the minds of people who had lived through World War I, clad in uniform, housed in dugouts, forced into utmost efficiency and meager sustenance, with no thought for joy, charm, warmth." Their viewpoints on architecture could not have been more different. The medium of Schindler's architecture was the manipulation of space itself. For him it was a delicious problem that he solved uniquely in each project. Neutra's primary building material, as he often said, was the human being, whose life could be improved by humane systems which effectively exploited technology.

Schindler worked for Wright from 1918 to 1921, while Neutra only did a four-month stint with Wright from late 1924 to early 1925. When the Neutras arrived at Schindler's hand-built concrete and wood house in Los Angeles, now a landmark in American architecture, Neutra and Schindler worked on and off together for the next few years. They briefly taught together, but their entry to the 1926 League of Nations competition is the only example of what a unified vision between the two might look like. Each made his international reputation designing houses for the same clients, Philip and Leah Lovell.

Adolf Loos, Tristan Tzara House, 1927, Paris, France

Schindler and Neutra were doomed to become Southern California's favorite architectural couple, Schindler playing id to Neutra's superego; Neutra's Apollo to Schindler's Dionysus; the former the verbose go-getter, the latter an articulate hippie; Schindler the collarless shirt, Neutra the wearer of ties; Schindler as shaper of space, Neutra the architect of systems; Schindler finding Eden, Neutra creating Utopia.

Layers of Influence: Architectural

In its implications for the organization of a building, its relationship to its site, and in how a building appeared in elevation, Wright's early work, published as two sets of portfolios by Ernst Wasmuth in Germany in 1911 and republished by Wasmuth and others in the 1920s, stunned the European architectural community.

Here Wright introduced the asymmetrical and "free" or pinwheel plan, which abandoned the conventional 19th-century rectangular enclosure of the box and reached into the landscape. Vis-à-vis the elevation, toward the end of his introduction to the portfolios, Wright flatly declares, "The horizontal line is the line of domesticity," perhaps thinking of the strongly vertical skyline rearing up in Chicago, defined by the skyscrapers his former employers Dankmar Adler and Louis Sullivan, among many others, designed. He also justifies the use of the horizontal line in his elevations as a line taken from the horizon itself, a line that becomes an abstracted *genius loci* of the low rolling prairies of southwest Wisconsin.

He writes that in "considering the forms and types of these structures, the fact that they are nearly [all] buildings for the prairie should be borne in mind ... the great levels where every detail of elevation becomes exaggerated; every tree a tower above the great calm plains ... All unnecessary heights have for that reason and for other reasons economic been eliminated ... and more intimate relation with out-door environment sought to compensate for loss of height." This quality of horizontality was often echoed in buildings through ribbons of stucco alternating with "fenestration in strips rather than fenestration in spots." It can readily be seen, for example, in the 1909 Gale House (Oak Park, Illinois). In any case, henceforth the Modernist single-family house was indeed imbued with horizontality, whether in France or in Southern California, though whether that quality can be attributed to Wright alone is open to debate.

Neutra, who saw the portfolios in 1914 just before he left to fight, was struck by Wright's "ability to be both serious and monumental without stressing symmetry." Later, Neutra learned of Ludwig Mies van der Rohe's Project for a Brick Villa of 1923, whose drawing of opposed discrete lines of varying length is not so much a plan of a building as a diagram of intent. Along with the De Stijl movement in Holland and Constructivism in Russia, these sharp, deep shifts in architectural thinking were part of the European atmosphere of social and tectonic critique with which Neutra sailed to America.

Neutra's Vision of America

Schindler and Neutra came to America because Frank Lloyd Wright pulled them and because Adolf Loos pushed them. Loos had a thoroughly romantic notion of America based on a three-year stint in the mid-1890s, when he had worked as a laborer in poor but apparently deliriously happy circumstances. Along with Erich Mendelsohn's admiration of American industrial buildings, Loos' worship of America with its fresh nature geared to mechanization and industry spurred Neutra west 30 years later.

While Loos loved the individual image of the humble anonymity of the American "man in overalls," the America in Neutra's mind was one huge benevolent experiment: "This country would foster modern architecture as no other could: not only did it have ingenuity and the machines to service a new auxiliary production of broadly adaptable fabricates, but above all it had biological success at its disposal because consumption could be, had to be, widely and sharply observed; it had the distribution system, it had the mail-order houses, and their pattern of distant control. From diet to man-made microclimate in our abode, biology could win."

Apart from his professional agenda, Neutra had a personal reason for coming to California. On December 8, 1919, he wrote in his diary: "I shall never live with fewer worries, never have time to develop ideas. I wish I could get out of Europe

Rudolph Schindler, Lovell Beach House, Newport Beach, California, 1926

and get to an idyllic tropical island where one does not have to fear the winter, where one does not have to slave, but find time to think and, more importantly, to be a free spirit." He was right. He never lived with fewer worries, but he made time to develop his ideas. The dream was graceful contemplation; the reality was frantic activity and agonizing self-doubt. His work day began at dawn, and in later years after his first heart attack his bed became a second work station. Here he redlined the previous day's work by his architects and draftspersons, or color-rendered presentation drawings pinned to cardboard, whose internal ribbing is obvious in his chalk drawings. He would call on the intercom that the drawings were ready for assistants to deliver to the office for the morning's work. He had already been working for hours. His wife Dione once described him as "my white tornado," referring to his shock of thick white hair and unceasing animation. He became internationally famous in his early thirties, and was on the cover of *Time* magazine on August 15, 1949, where a sun in the background shines through the blueprints behind his portrait, a graphic demonstrating his architectural intentions of light, transparency and serenity.

Richard's ashes lie next to Dione's in a quiet place under a Chinese elm tree in the courtyard at the Neutra VDL Studio and Residences. He died in Germany on April 16, 1970, Dione died on September 1, 1990.

TECHNOLOGICAL INVESTIGATIONS

In his 1930 book *Amerika: Die Stilbildung des neuen Bauens in den Vereinigten Staaten* Neutra labels one structure that to him represents the promise of American technology. It is not a steel skyscraper or a Frank Lloyd Wright house or a grain silo. It is the circus tent, and it fitted all his requirements for lightness in construction: "In North America, one can view the gigantic tent of the multiple ring circus of Barnum and Ringling Brothers around the middle of the 19th century as America's most characteristic architectural production. Developed for erection, dismantling, and rail transport almost in the span of hours, in whose framework are arranged stairs, folding seats for many thousand spectators as well as electric and water installations ... [the way that] the constructive members, such as covers and ropes, function only as mere tensile stresses, and therefore are of minimal dimensions, imparts to the tent also in other ways prototypes for our era which views lightness of construction as an architectural duty and dear to its heart ..."

Above: Circus tent, sketch, Aspen, Colorado, 1952

Opposite: Beard House, 1935, a vertical section shows a hollow steel wall that allowed hot air to rise and escape, cooling the interior.

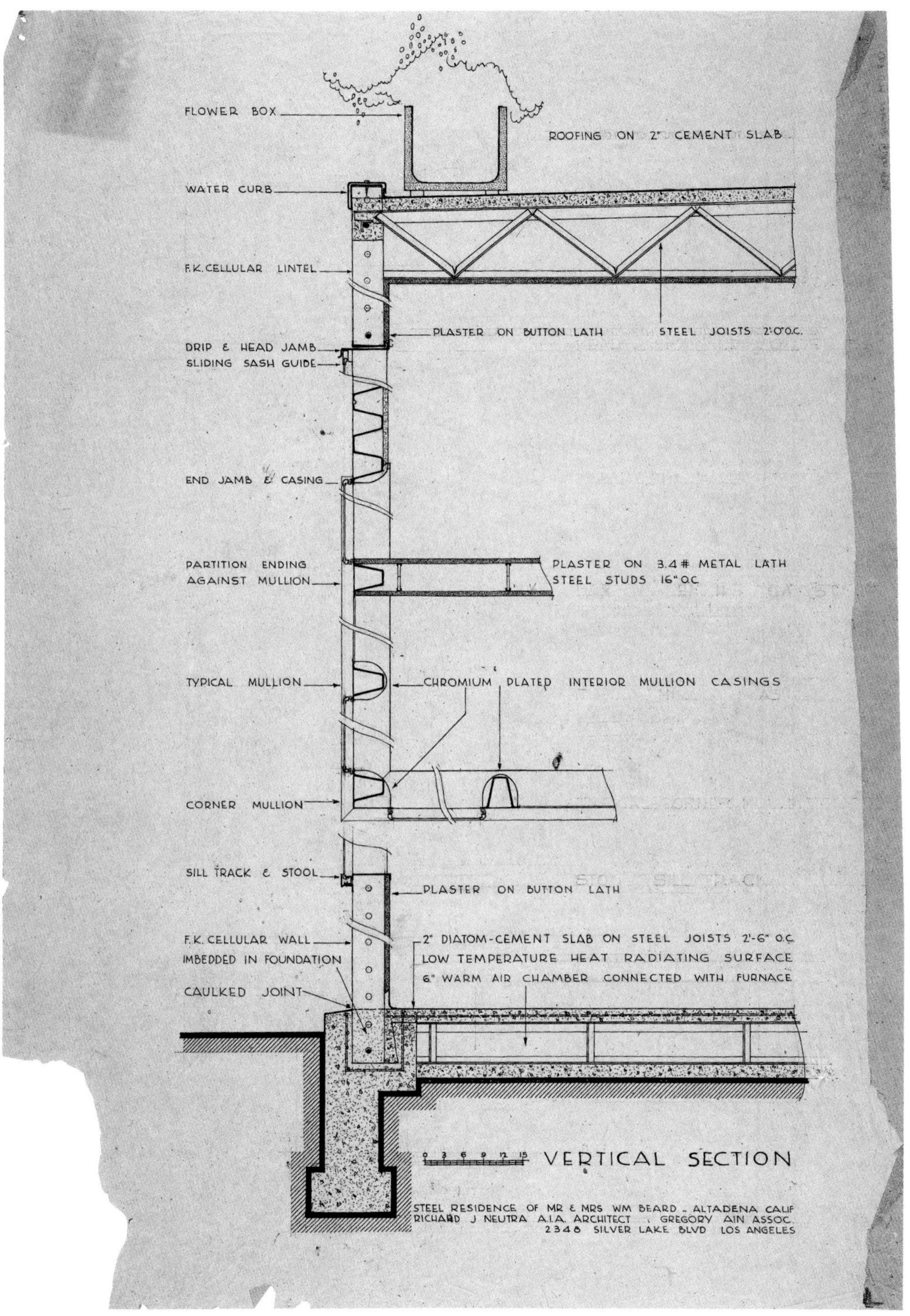
FLOWER BOX
ROOFING ON 2" CEMENT SLAB
WATER CURB
F.K. CELLULAR LINTEL
PLASTER ON BUTTON LATH
STEEL JOISTS 2'-0" O.C.
DRIP & HEAD JAMB
SLIDING SASH GUIDE
END JAMB & CASING
PARTITION ENDING AGAINST MULLION
PLASTER ON 3.4 # METAL LATH
STEEL STUDS 16" O.C.
TYPICAL MULLION
CHROMIUM PLATED INTERIOR MULLION CASINGS
CORNER MULLION
SILL TRACK & STOOL
PLASTER ON BUTTON LATH
F.K. CELLULAR WALL
IMBEDDED IN FOUNDATION
CAULKED JOINT
2" DIATOM-CEMENT SLAB ON STEEL JOISTS 2'-6" O.C.
LOW TEMPERATURE HEAT RADIATING SURFACE
6" WARM AIR CHAMBER CONNECTED WITH FURNACE
0 3 6 9 12 15
VERTICAL SECTION
STEEL RESIDENCE OF MR & MRS WM BEARD – ALTADENA CALIF
RICHARD J NEUTRA A.I.A. ARCHITECT . GREGORY AIN ASSOC.
2348 SILVER LAKE BLVD LOS ANGELES

Above: Beard House, 1935. A welder is shown connecting steel elements.

Opposite: Beard House, 1935. East-west section diagramming open web steel joists for the decking.

With its light loads supported by the center post, the circus tent is a dramatic example of membrane architecture. Neutra used this strategy only once, for one of his unbuilt housing "prototypes," the overlooked but intriguing Diatom House. Though he never tried anything as acrobatic as that again, he experimented with other building systems that suggested the same potential for light, fast, cheap construction. That meant steel, and *Wie baut Amerika?*, his first book, is really a paean to the Chicago skyscraper and its designers, led by Louis Sullivan. Neutra writes as a true believer.

While working on the huge steel-framed Palmer Hotel in Chicago while a draftsman for Holabird and Roche in 1924, Neutra immersed himself in understanding steel's every characteristic. To Neutra's disappointment, his hero, Wright, who had developed his "textile concrete block" system first used at the Millard House in Pasadena (1923), a system which Neutra drafted in his precise hand, and then at the Ennis House a year later (1924), did not share Neutra's zeal, despite Wright's 1926 project for a steel cathedral. Neither did Rudolph Schindler, who had recently completed the poured-concrete 12-unit Pueblo Ribera Courts in La Jolla when Neutra arrived in Los Angeles in 1925. To Neutra, the material represented what he had left behind in Europe: heavy mass. Schindler's new courts did not persuade him otherwise. To build his walls at the court, Schindler used concrete that was poured sequentially in movable forms. Though his innovative approach is now a standard building technique, then it seemed to Neutra to be a finicky process. Problems with water infiltration in conjunction with friable concrete developed quickly; Wright's concrete block houses in Los Angeles have not fared well either.

In *Amerika*, Neutra contrasts the precision of prefabricated steel with the "costly dead loads" of concrete, which was further subject to "the honesty of the concrete mixing contractor." (Apparently he had great faith in steel workers.) Concrete was also inflexible in renovation, too, he argued, and thus prone to obsolescence. Nonetheless, always eager to learn, he devotes a good deal of both books to the work of Schindler, Wright and California architect Irving Gill, examining their building methods in detail. By the late 1940s Neutra himself began using concrete again, most notably for the Treamaine House.

Neutra's attitude toward technology changed in the four years between the first book and the second. Technology and its social impact were no longer infallibly innocent. There are, he wrote darkly, "unaccountabilities" and "mass production without exactness." He studied the way American commercial buildings were put up – looking functional but "given to an obsolescence driven by … the unusually accelerated power of money." For Neutra that did not mean abandoning technology, but harnessing it. Despite his unease at technology's direction, he also saw huge opportunities to use standardization (technique) and steel (material) to create flexible spaces and structures whose steel members were reusable, thus achieving that Loosian quality of "lastingness."

Domesticating the Skyscraper: Steel as Frame

The Lovell Health House (1927–29) ushered in Neutra's most intense period of innovation. The home was designed for Philip and Leah Lovell, a well-to-do couple who promoted active, healthy lifestyles. It was the first all light-steel-framed house in America. Thousands of visitors, flanked by breathless publicity, descended. The

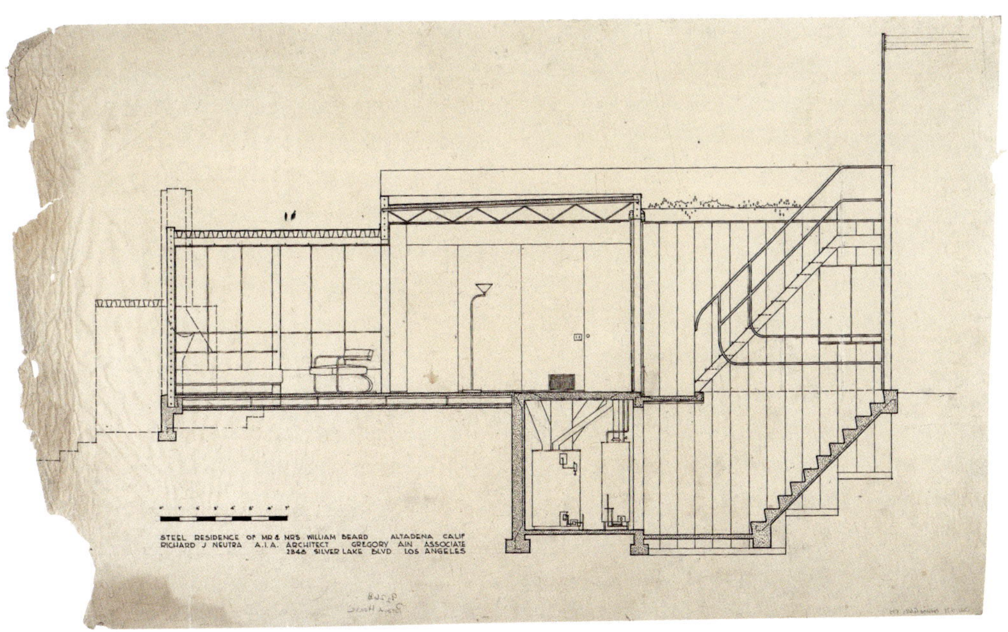

glass, steel, and white concrete house lent itself easily to photography, secured Neutra his international reputation, and earned him a place in the now-iconographic 1932 modern architecture exhibition at the Museum of Modern Art in New York. Yet it is also a house that addresses the art of living in Los Angeles, a city of wide, flat valleys interrupted by canyons and hills, where coyote and deer disregard human territorial "rights." Like Wright's Falling Water, the Lovell Health House is just below the peak of one of those hills, seeming to hover against it. Neutra described the taut, filigreed presence of the house as a bird's nest in the landscape.

The house "was the frame ... the frame was the house." There are two grids in the frame. The secondary grid consists of steel sash casement windows in gangs of three, which were slipped into the larger column-and-beam grid system. This required hand craftsmanship: Neutra writes in *Amerika* that he "transferred the full-scale unit lines from drawing board onto the difficult site on stretched cloth between 4x4 posts." The frame went up in 40 work hours, and Neutra acted as general contractor to save money, rising before sunrise to oversee the bolt holes and as many as 70 subcontractors and laborers. Nonetheless, the project cost about $65,000, including Neutra's 10 percent fee, an expensive house for its day.

In contrast to Le Corbusier's concept of the façade freed of load-bearing responsibilities, Neutra's frame is indeed load-bearing, but the house still achieves a weightless quality. Asymmetric horizontal white bands seem to arbitrarily interrupt the framing grid, shifting and sliding against each other, sometimes acting as walls, other times as balcony enclosures. Neutra terminates some of these planes with thin, up-ended parapets, which are higher than the bands. Because they are higher, they not only hide the sloped roof, they also start to read as independent planes, an idea that Neutra fully realized in later work. The bands are Gunite, a lightweight concrete sprayed onto expanded metal mesh with long hoses, a technique Neutra might have learned from Schindler, who used Gunite on a concrete substrate at the Packard House in Pasadena in 1924. A swimming pool in its own concrete cradle forms the bowels of the house so that a swimmer swims out straight from its depths into the daylight and the valley, then returns to the darkness, as though tracing the long horizontal line of the house. The one great vertical gesture is the grand staircase, where one is led from the street across a bridge before descending to the low, long living room amidst a flood of sunlight. This lower floor hints at the flowing but tightly disciplined spaces of other Neutra work, though the upper street-level floor is a warren of awkwardly connected rooms, lacking his typical ordering of long, logical spines in plan.

In a sense the house is a homage to Sweet's Catalog. Architect Harwell Hamilton Harris, who worked for Neutra from 1928 to 1933, once wrote: "For Neutra, Sweet's Catalog was the Holy Bible and Henry Ford the Holy Virgin ... Neutra continued to marvel that out of this one book, Sweet's (then a single volume) he could design an entire building." In a salute to Ford, the Lovells' staircase is embedded with a Ford headlight (there was another at the von Sternberg House), and is one of the few witticisms in Neutra's sober buildings.

Steel as Panel System

Whether Neutra was inspired by circus tents or by Buckminster Fuller's 1927 Dymaxion House with its central supporting mast, he used a similar

"Cantilever Chair," patented in 1936. The curved, "springy," flat bar responds kinetically to the body.

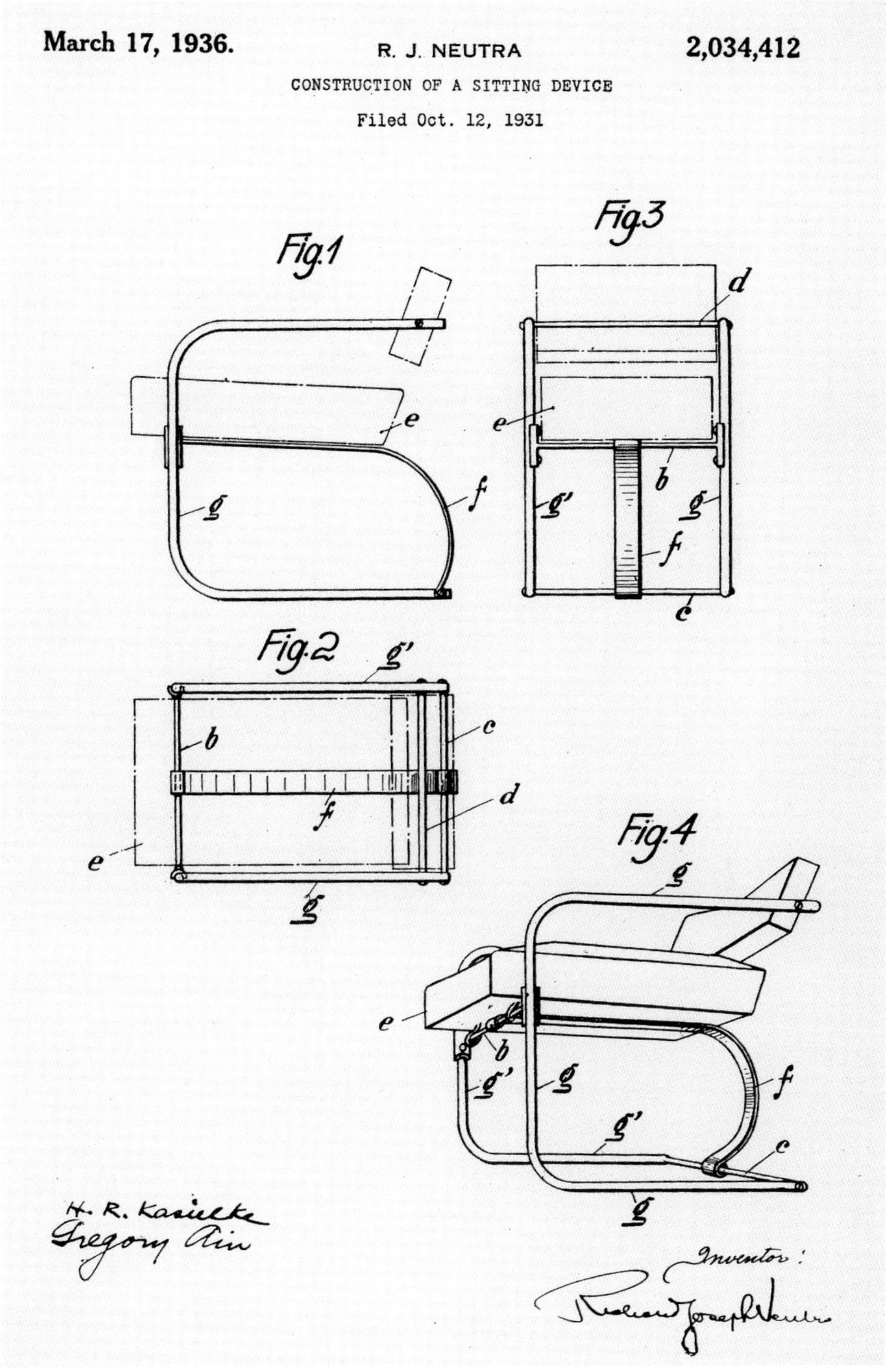

March 17, 1936. R. J. NEUTRA 2,034,412

CONSTRUCTION OF A SITTING DEVICE

Filed Oct. 12, 1931

Fig.1

Fig.2

Fig.3

Fig.4

H. R. Kasielke
Gregory Ain

Inventor:
Richard Joseph Neutra

strategy in one version of the Diatom House, a series of prototypes designed in the 1920s and 1930s. (The word "diatom" comes from the algae that create seashells which are then crushed; in the 1920s and 1930s Neutra believed diatomaceous earth was the key ingredient in creating "steam-hardened earth" akin to lightweight concrete, which could then be made into prefabricated panels used for walls and floors. The additive eventually proved to be too soft and crumbly.)

There were several variations on the Diatom House, which became a valuable tool not only for technological questions but also for probing what modern tract housing might look like and how the car could be inserted into the program. The type called "One-Two," based on the circus tent, is an additive approach to building in which one unit (a room) could be connected to a larger box of roughly 1,000 square feet; a third unit was the roof garden above a garage. The short walls were solid while the long walls were primarily glass from end to end, so it felt bright, open and loft-like. A prefabricated kitchen and bathroom made up the central mechanical core. The roof was suspended with tension cables from a series of masts whose center steel columns were set in contrived, prefabricated steel footings set into the ground, thus eliminating what Neutra believed were "over-dimensioned" concrete footings. The steel footings were to be adjustable and portable, so they were just as mobile as a circus. (He was granted a patent for this in 1948 along with others in the 1930s and 1940s with the help of his brother, a patent lawyer, but it was never manufactured.)

Frame and Sheathing as One

Neutra came west to seek new technologies, and he found a highly promising one right in his backyard being developed by a local Los Angeles builder. Fascinated by its potential, he immediately employed it in what became one of his most memorable "prototypes," the 1934–35 Beard House in Altadena. The Palmer system, as it was called, was similar to the Lovell Health House only in that both were steel load-bearing wall systems. This time the steel was not an open skeleton that required a stucco skin, but a panel system in which folded sheet metal decking was clad with silver-painted steel panels on the exterior. He told a U.S. Navy symposium that "the sheet metal sections were meant to play their role as floor decks, but I used them with other enthusiastic collaborators as wall sections, quickly assembled and fitted together with their ceilings (either the same decking or open web steel joists for areas where spans were longer). As this was a hollow section, I pushed up electrically hot air ... to heat the interior space from all sides." Conversely, holes in the bottoms and tops of the walls, which Neutra placed in the parapets extending beyond the roof to hide the sloping roof, were to set up convection currents so hot air would escape up and out. That was theory – the system never seems to have worked.

Because the exterior panels were steel, Neutra could eliminate a time-consuming step: the "wet" step of the messy application of concrete or stucco. Diatomaceous concrete was used for the radiantly heated floors, consisting of a sandwich of concrete separated by a honeycomb of air cells. According to his widow Dione, this was the first project in which he introduced sliding glass doors, one on the west leading to one patio and one on the north, part of a glass-and-steel wall leading out to the garden, a roof deck and the mountains beyond. The steel columns separating the glass wall are covered with shiny, polished cadmium-plated steel in a smooth parabolic shape, part of Neutra's effort to "dematerialize" the wall.

There are many treatments in the Beard House that became quintessential Neutra, such as the radiant floor heating and the cleverly placed built-in lighting made to do "double duty" by illuminating interior and exterior paths at the same time. Exterior light strips in the roof overhang soften the transition between indoors and outdoors at night; doors extend floor to ceiling and are framed without surrounding casements so they become invisible in the wall plane. Large, dark Masonite panels, typically a cheap material that looks cheap, are transformed when rubbed with wax. These softly glowing panels do not run the wall's full height: a band of white plaster runs above them, a characteristic of traditional interiors he saw on his 1930 visit to Japan. The house is relatively closed off to the street and open to nature in the rear, another typical Neutra characteristic in suburban dwellings.

On the exterior, Neutra sets up a lively dialogue among three different "rhythms" of steel: the vertical cells of the exterior paneling, the close ribbing of the sheet metal fascia capping the roof, and the exposed corrugated decking on the underside of the porch overhang. This shimmering, changing surface, in turn, complements the overall composition of interlocking volumes. In evening light, the exterior looks as though Neutra handled light as though it were paint at the end of a dry brush, selectively pricking out the horizontal and vertical outlines of the house.

When the house won a national award in the small house category in the *Better Homes in America* competition, Neutra must have felt that popular acceptance and his dream of systems building was very close. He in fact did use Palmer's system again for two other projects, the California Military Academy and the much more lavish estate he designed for the Hollywood director Josef von Sternberg (both 1935), as though eagerly testing the viability of the system in varied settings. But like the Lovell Health House, the Beard House was a highly custom building: even the distances between the steel columns in the living room vary slightly. It is clearly not a "systems" building but points to it.

At the same time Neutra explored plywood, which had just been introduced with waterproof glues. In the Plywood Model Demonstration House (1936), built for a building exhibition, steel frames hold each plywood panel in place. As Neutra had envisioned, the building proved to be portable, and later was moved to a nearby site and reassembled.

The Evans Plywood Building (1940) in Oregon also demonstrated plywood's versatility. The overall composition is a mild nod to Le Corbusier's Villa Savoye in the curve of the second-floor balcony rail and roof fascia, here rendered in plywood.

One Building, Multiple Experiments

The original VDL Research House (1932), the Neutras' family home in Silver Lake, was Neutra's third building in America. On a surprise visit to Los Angeles, the Dutch industrialist Cornelius (Kees) van der Leeuw loaned him $3,000 to help build the house, which cost under $8,000. Since Neutra could not afford to build in steel but wanted the effect of uninterrupted ribbon windows, he altered standard wood construction by replacing conventional wood stud construction with larger 4x4 wood posts on a module of 3′ 3½″, which, as at the Lovell Health House, was based on the space required for the steel casement windows he used there. He persuaded manufacturers to donate materials, and coaxed Libby-Owens-Ford to fabricate a sandwich panel of aluminum and glass to reflect heat in bathrooms. Aluminum foil was also used to insulate all exterior walls, which were either stucco or painted pressboard.

Resilient cork floor, rubbed Masonite and exterior soffit lighting were incorporated. Prefabricated concrete joists with a suspended slab provided a fire-retardant support for the first floor. Industrial steel and glass folding doors led to the outdoor sleeping porch, and gorgeous dark-blue enameled steel panels were used for the porch's wainscoting. Even with all its devotion to function, there was a sensual quality to VDL 1, with its low black leather settees ringing the outdoor porch, and in its dark colors and silvery tones.

But while both the first and second VDL houses were virtually materials-testing laboratories, they were both by far more important as spatial experiments. The lot, between Silver Lake and a rear street, is a tight 60′ x 70′. The question was how to bring in nature, provide privacy, and also create quarters for two families, guests and a fully-staffed office. The easy livability of this compound of buildings is unexpected, given its small spaces and lack of open plan. Neutra managed this by first shrewdly taking advantage of the ambiguity of early zoning codes, building the house out to the street line in front and to its full 60-foot width. He created a quiet, private courtyard embraced by the main and the guesthouse, which was built in 1939. These two were linked to each other by a ground-floor "bridge" of small rooms for Neutra's newly arrived youngest son Raymond. Neutra elected to devote more of the 2,100 square feet in the house to public rather than private functions, so the bedrooms were designed as compact ship's cabins with built-in furniture. In the Neutra VDL Studio and Residences, co-designed by Dion Neutra, the high captain's beds could be rolled away from the wall so beds could be made easily, sill heights were reconfigured, and a small reflecting pool was added in the front of the house. Dion Neutra introduced a wide range of energy-saving and other innovations, as his father did in the original. Later in his career, Neutra no longer used entirely new building systems that challenged existing paradigms, even as Case Study architects such as his former employee, Raphael Soriano, began a second, fresh generation of experimentation in steel. It was expensive, and remained a highly custom alternative for the exceptional circumstance. Instead, Neutra confined his technical innovations to materials and their applications. Despite the efforts of his generation and the next, wood framing was overwhelmingly America's favorite way to build. Neutra accepted that he could not change the convention. Instead he leavened it with his own rigorous systematic detailing in a post-and-beam wood frame and developed his own private conventions, thus ensuring consistent quality control.

VDL Research House, 1932, Los Angeles, California, living room

However, his overall optimism in the idea of standardization never wavered. In 1957, Neutra was invited to speak at a symposium sponsored by the U.S. Navy. The topic was how to use creative design to reduce construction costs; he spoke on prefabrication. He interrupted his speech at one point to add this personal note: "I must show you right now that I am really in love with the thing. No matter what I am going to say next, I am in love with it ... I am married to this prefabrication idea for 34 years ..." But Neutra also made it clear in the same speech that technology, industrialization, prefabrication, standardization were not the end, but a means to an end: "There will always be a lot of new patents for new materials [as Neutra would know, having been granted several] but the greatest progress of all must be in those research papers which deal with the newest in human biology ...

SILVER PAINT, THE DUTCH, AND JAPAN

Above: Brinkman and van der Vlugt, Kees van der Leeuw House, Rotterdam, Netherlands, 1929. Neutra was a guest at the house in 1930.

Opposite: VDL Research House, 1932, winter solarium. The glass wall faced southwest for solar gain.

Silver paint was the one constant in Neutra's palette of materials. He specified it for hundreds of wood window sills, wood posts, roof gutters and galvanized metal fascia, whether the building was residential or commercial, 1935 or 1965. The office joke ran: "Mr. Neutra, what is the best material to use for a steel house?"

The question implies a mild deceit. If he was indeed making wood look like steel, Neutra was "dishonestly" aligning himself with the heroic new machine age of prefabrication and new technologies. Faux steel was better than no steel. And the joke was in character. Neutra constantly doctored photographs. (As photographer Julius Shulman tells, he even had to send an irritated editor a second, clean photograph because Neutra's grease pencil had made the image of the first unintelligible.) He introduced instant "mature" landscape on the raw hillsides below the Lovell Health House. With drafting tape, he "removed" the traditional Dutch row housing inconveniently attached to the strange new Schröder House so it appeared to be a free-standing building. He thoughtfully "thinned down" his wife's upper arm for a 1960s publicity photograph. On a real building, the Jardinette Apartments' dark-painted horizontal lines insinuated continual strips of ribbon windows, an act for which he was roundly scolded as "a trick of design that was hardly frank." In other words, Neutra manipulated reality just as matter-of-factly as anyone armed with a computer today.

These are great dinner party stories that propel a convenient stereotype, but they do not lead to the more subtle and humane reasoning of the man behind the silver paint, reasoning based on a shrewd hypothesis grounded in biology and psychology. Neutra did indeed intend to deceive, but his objective was not to mask materials. Structural "honesty" and being "frank" were words better left to the realms of human behavior, and had little to do with his architecture. The object of his deceit was the human eye itself. His agenda was physiological: since silver reflected and diffused light, it reduced an element's visual impact so the eye was less likely to be deflected from its trajectory out to nature, to landscape and sky. That was his imperative. In Neutra's work, it is usually apparent how loads are transferred to the ground, but sometimes far more difficult to see the source for a cantilever support.

Except for entire houses such as the steel Beard and von Sternberg houses (which would rust in any case without a protective coating), Neutra restricted the silver color to thin planes and lines. The silver appears only in those places where the sightline is affected. The substrate

Above: Richard and Dione Neutra, ca. 1930

Opposite: Sutemi Horiguchi, Kikkawa Residence, Tokyo, 1930, cited by Neutra in *Die Form,* September 15, 1931.

could be wood or steel or aluminum – the material was immaterial, so to speak, as long as its surface performed its work vis-à-vis the human eye.

In a letter to clients Sidney and Sonia Brown dated June 9, 1954, he suggested that the living room posts leading to the terrace, as well as a prominent interior column, be clad in stainless steel and rubbed to a fine finish "like a real jewel" to "dematerialize" them. In later houses, such as the Clark House in Pasadena, the interiors of the wood trim are silver while the exteriors are a dark brown, because it was the view out that mattered. In another letter, dated October 10, 1962, airborne to Hamburg, Neutra was still anxious about the visual impact of the double-height staircase glazing at the Lovell Health House, 33 years later. The faithful Dione writes home to the office in "Letter #9" that "RJN told me verbally the window frames could be painted silver-gray in order to more obliterate the many division bars which were necessary in 1928 but which he would avoid now. Window frames should have as nearly as possible glass color to blend in ..."

The joke about Neutra also exhibits some Southern California parochialism. By 1930, when Neutra lectured abroad as part of his round-the-world trip after the completion of the Lovell Health House, Europe had long since embraced the issues of dematerialization and light, qualities exhibited by many new Modernist buildings. Among them was the house of Neutra's future patron, wealthy industrialist Cornelius (Kees) van der Leeuw, a fanatical devotee of functionalism and an owner of the huge Van Nelle fortune and the trading company based in Rotterdam. He and Neutra shared similar passions for new materials and hopes for Modernism. They were almost the same age and even looked alike then, greyhound lean, dark-haired, blue-eyed, with intense, fervent expressions.

When they met while Neutra was lecturing in Basel, the new Van Nelle Factory had just been finished, its sweeps of glistening glass and white and articulated volumes contradicting the flat landscape and gloomy Dutch weather. Van der Leeuw took Neutra under his wing, arranged for him to speak throughout Holland and introduced him, as Neutra recalled in his autobiography *Life and Shape*, to "all the modern leaders in architecture." He seized every opportunity to not only meet them but hurl himself into their milieux. He wandered through Josef Hoffmann's lavish new Stoclet House with none other than Le Corbusier. Neutra taught at the Bauhaus for six weeks at Mies van der Rohe's invitation, who heard the émigré speak in his role as the American delegate to the third CIAM, the International Congress for New Building, in Brussels. The organization's annual symposia, each with a different topic on Modernism, invariably attracted what are now the greatest names in 20th-century architecture. So late one evening when Neutra received a telegram from Van der Leeuw inviting him and Dione to his new Rotterdam home, they did not hesitate but immediately agreed by return telegram. The house coincidentally shared its completion date (1929) and its framing material (steel) with the Lovell Health House, but Neutra saw much there that he coveted, a word used here because when a new work of architecture speaks directly and deeply to an architect seeing it for the first time, sometimes a kind of profound internal resonance occurs, a kind of wanting and finding at the same time, a quality that finds its way into the viewer's own work with a new voice. As avant-garde as his own Los Angeles design was, with as much praise as the Lovell had received, even so Neutra called the "other VDL" the most modern house he had ever seen.

The Rotterdam house was an essay in light in all its incantations. On the exterior, silver-painted trim offset the white stucco. On the interior, silver-colored drapes and nickel and chrome finishes were softened by tones of green and yellow. The house bristled with so many advanced technical innovations that it was really a machine for living. Given what Neutra had already designed, it appears that the Van der Leeuw house didn't point the way so much as confirm his direction, just as his time in Japan earlier that year reinforced his ideas on the integration of nature and architecture. Certainly the house in Holland

Tetsuro Yoshida, Baba Residence, Tokyo, ca. 1930, cited by Neutra in *Die Form*, March 15, 1931.

shared many similarities to Neutra trademarks and to his own house in Silver Lake.

Both houses, complete with simple rooftop penthouses, overlooked a tranquil view of a lake located in the densely populated suburbs of a large city. The similarities continued on the interior. Here architect Van der Vlugt included several kinds of indirect lighting via clerestories, above interior soffits, or through translucent glass. The house opened up to the landscape with its double-height "winter garden" with its long, low south-facing planter and first-floor rear terraces that reached out to the garden. Along with the built-in or tubular-steel furniture, all elements worked together to increase lightness, whether defined as mass or as illumination. Other qualities of the house shared Neutra's sensibilities about privacy. The Van der Leeuw façade was closed to the passerby except for a long, bold ribbon of windows on the first floor, which provided a panoramic view of the lake, and a narrow strip of clerestory windows on the ground floor. The rear of the house was almost entirely glass, with a huge glass "garage door" that was precisely counterbalanced so that it could be pushed up with one finger to instantly connect the interior to the garden.

If the original "VDL" House spoke about light, nature and technology, the Schröder House by Gerrit Rietveld spoke about the art of composing space through line and plane, instead of arranging space within a six-sided box with holes in it. On the same trip, and again arranged by Van der Leeuw, Neutra stayed at the famous house. Already six years old, it was the three-dimensional embodiment of the De Stijl movement.

While Neutra's own designs were less busy, it is hard not to credit the ideas expressed by this house with having some impact on Neutra's thinking akin to historian William Curtis' observation on De Stijl art: "Controlled asymmetry and the enlivened contrast of hovering planes seem to have taken on an almost sacral meaning for De Stijl artists as the correct mode for revealing the nature of the emergent epoch."

Neutra once acknowledged Mondrian's explorations into relationships between lines and plane and the idea of non-symmetrical balance on his own sense of composition. "Piet Mondrian was no false saint," he remarked. Neutra appreciated those same qualities of "controlled asymmetry" in the Japanese architecture he saw earlier that summer on the Oriental leg of his trip. In Tokyo, Kyoto, and Osaka he lectured and toured new and old architecture, and was shocked at the cheering audiences who greeted him. Before he sailed east to Japan (to go round the world the other way would have cost him an extra $150), Neutra wrote a short note to a friend about his expectations: "To see some glimpse of the Orient, before arriving in Europe, will help me to find the right proportions of values." His guess proved accurate.

At the 17th-century Katsura Imperial Villa in Kyoto he discovered a "relaxed asymmetry" in the gardens and delighted in how the Japanese gave nature such a prominent place in the overall scheme. It was a mystery, he mused later, "how traditional Japanese houses fuse with their gardens, gardens so spontaneously free of the shackles of dry geometricity." But Neutra's attention to the physiological aspects of design was never very far away from his critiques on composition. "Even the vestibular sense of the inner ear busily records for us our turns, accelerations, and retardations when, following a magical paving pattern, we haltingly walk the irregular windings of a carefully planned, non-repetitious path or tread the willful zigzag of simple planks bridging a lotus pool," he added.

Neutra admired the contrast of thin paper walls with heavier, more permanent post-and-beam framing (these translucent shogi screens performed two functions, not only keeping weather at bay but also permitting the play of light and shadow on the interior); flexible, minimal spaces with plain, built-in furniture; nuanced entrances from exterior to interior, the importance of water, seen in Katsura's dark pools. Like medieval European buildings or the Viennese interiors of Adolf Loos, the Japanese also placed dark wood against white walls, a contrast Neutra often invoked. He reflected on the vigilantly maintained yet anonymous sense of timelessness of Japanese building, the same attributes that Loos mandated in his own concept of an ethical architecture.

Many of these same elements can be seen in Neutra's work, not only in residential applications but in urban planning as well. The year before, Neutra sent a paper to the second CIAM conference held in Frankfurt in 1929, while he stayed in Los Angeles to complete the Lovell Health House. The topic was the *Existenzminimum* (minimum habitation); his paper theoretical. In witnessing Japan in 1930, he said, he now had living proof that a "tightly massed civilization need not spell the defilement of the natural scene but can mean its glorification." Japan was a miracle of land economy, he wrote, in that such complex unity could be "accomplished on the most diminished scale."

Katsura, the Bauhaus at Dessau, Kees van der Leeuw's house, CIAM: 1930 was a pivotal year for Neutra. It exposed him to new ways of thinking and affirmed his own.

BIOREALISM: BODILY SUBSTRATE OF THE MENTAL LIFE

Lovell Health House, Los Angeles, 1929

"An architect can be your low-brow henchman and blow up your marriage – any marriage – by daily irritations he piles up unsuspected."

The outstanding quality of Richard Neutra's buildings is usually considered in terms of architectural form-making, as superb in composition, as elegant in style. He was a Modernist's Modernist. But the stuff that drove that form-making – an obsession with the human as architecture's raison d'être – has been largely ignored. His endless curiosity about his fellow human, rather than an endless search for form, was his life's work. Neutra argued for over half a century that not only could architecture have a profound impact on society but that it did, and did so irrevocably. This granted, or burdened, the architect with an inescapable responsibility for human well-being, and the practice of architecture itself with a terrible urgency. He or she cannot arbitrarily indulge in self-expression but rather is a learned doctor who must understand *Homo sapiens* thoroughly – the very physicality and anthropology of the animal – before commencing treatment.

So, Neutra would also get to know his fellow animal – as species and as individual. He would determinedly verbally interrogate his clients, asking questions such as: "When you give a dinner party, do you wash dishes right away? Is it important that they are not visible to guests?" Husbands and wives submitted independently written essays ("with no consultation with each other, please") on their background and daily lives, along with informal photographs of themselves and dimensions for any furniture they expected to use in the new home.

A Background in Science

Two fields of science, one rooted in the 19th century and the other in the 20th, were fundamental to Neutra, and led him down a different path from all his contemporaries. The first is based on the ideas of the now-obscure German philosopher Wilhelm Wundt, the second is Gestalt theory.

According to his widow Dione, Neutra discovered the writings of Wilhelm Max Wundt (1832–1920) in the library of the Technische Hochschule in Vienna, where he was a student. He was drawn to the title of one of Wundt's most widely known works, *Principles of Physiological Psychology*, first published in 1874. Its introduction is entitled "Bodily substrate of the mental life," which sounds like a definition of Neutra's own approach to architecture, an architecture linking body and mind, the physical and the psychological. Wundt and physicist/ philosopher Gustav Theodor Fechner (1801–87), whom Neutra also read, are considered the founders of experimental psychology. Wundt's work laid the groundwork for those measuring physical sensation and stimulus by emphasizing experimentation and observation. The book catalyzed a lifetime of reading in the sciences and associations with figures as diverse as Albert Einstein and behaviorist Konrad Lorenz. Neutra came to believe that the human environment must address the role of the senses. He defined his approach to design as "biorealism": "bio" from the Greek word *bios*, meaning life, and "realism" because architecture had to take its cue from how humans really behave and how they evolved: a blend of historic anthropology, psychology and physiology. Some of what he believed is outdated or crude compared with recent advances, but "conceptually he was 40 years ahead of his time," according to environmental psychologist James Wise.

Neutra accepted the hypothesis that the human genetic code evolved on the savannas of East Africa, which were open plains with occasional groups of trees. That hypothesis had dramatic consequences for design. More than anything else, humans had to be able to orient themselves in their surroundings, and they needed all their senses to do that. Flat horizons and distant mountains, for example, provided a sense of boundary and the ability to gauge distance. The theory explained why people need physical contact with nature and the outdoors, why they need to feel the breeze, see water and moving clouds, even why people have an innate but strong sense of the horizontal. Not surprisingly, Neutra's architecture responds to many of these concerns. The title of one of Richard and Dion's books sums it up: *Senses and the Setting*. A house was not a house; it was a "sensorium."

Embracing such a hypothesis was also one of the reasons why Neutra came not just to America but specifically to Southern California. Just as he saw the nation as a giant experiment in technological innovation, so Southern California manifested the same climatic traits as those of East Africa, and thus was a perfect "Petri dish" for experiments in biorealism. As he said, "I felt that Southern California was a godsend. It was an instructive new subtropical country ... climatically it favored the launching of new architecture, quite a little closer to biological requirements, a new mode of living. And so I tried my best to launch it."

Neutra was a highly sophisticated inductive, not deductive, thinker. He did not wait for hard data but followed his intuition. Although his architecture is systematic, his writings are not. He does not offer a "Five Points of Biorealism" or a "Biorealistic Pattern Language." Exemplified by books such as *Survival Through Design* and *Nature Near*, his thousands of pages, published and unpublished, are a sustained cry for research that could transform architecture into the art of "applied biology." Neutra never argued that employing science by itself would create good architecture. He never implied that applying biorealistic principles would produce architecture like his. Nor was he so naive as to believe that such research would always be put to benevolent ends. But Neutra rightly suspected that future research would confirm his suspicion that the senses were far more sophisticated than anyone imagined.

Thus, even though Neutra's architecture is often portrayed as being a "machine in the garden," there is another way of looking at it. For Neutra the real machine in the garden – albeit a highly sophisticated one – is the human, whose daily experience could be exquisitely calibrated by his or her environment. In turn, the environment itself could be considered as alive, as organic, as supple as a living being. Architects who could pick up the tool of science and wield it skillfully could create a kinetic equilibrium between the two. They would be 20th-century shamans indeed: "Quite simply, our habits, moods, efficiency, and health are intimately related to our habitations. Lawyers are not independent of the courtrooms in which they plead their cases ... workers certainly are not independent of the factories and plant and ships where all manner of deficiency can demean or maim them ... [the resolve of hospital patients] to get well can depend on how cheerful, warm and reassuring those settings are ..." "In a courtroom, justice is conditioned by changes in the air, characteristics of the room and from soporiferous butyric acid and body odors."

For Neutra, the true "International Style" was this fascinating biological repertoire of human needs, beyond history and geography. In contrast to those contemporary urbanists and developers who dress their houses in historical styles to project old "traditional" values, Neutra intentionally ignores history and/or culture when it is exploited as an architectural determinant. Instead he fixes his gaze on the human, that messy package of genetic code and physical and psychological needs enriched by the peculiarities of anthropology. Neutra is unquestionably a Modernist in that he does not seek to soothe a society anxious for its future by delivering the traditions of the past, since he sees no need to retreat from it. Rather, one needs to be equipped for the future by the designer acting as the professional "midwife" Neutra so often called himself.

Gestalt and the Bauhaus

In addition to discovering Wundt, Neutra was also familiar with Gestalt theories of perception, which informed his sense of composition. Founded in 1910, Gestalt (meaning shape or configuration) theory addresses the perception of the dynamic interplay of parts and whole, or the relationship between figure and ground. Gestalt

Tremaine House, Montecito, California, 1948. Landscaping by Lockwood de Forest and Ralph Tallant Stevens.

Neutra Office Building, Los Angeles, 1950, rear view; Dion Neutra, project architect. The building also served as Neutra and (Robert E.) Alexander's practice in the mid-1950s.

theory was already the rage at the Bauhaus in 1930 when Neutra made his six-week stay there. He spent many hours with "the masters" such as Josef Albers and Paul Klee, who taught the *Formlehre* class, the study of form and composition. Klee invited Gestalt psychologists to lecture on the new theory; in turn, Peter Behrens, teacher of Walter Gropius, and Marcel Breuer were hired by famed Gestalt psychologist Kurt Lewin to design his home and interior.

Neutra used Gestalt ideas in many ways to inform his compositions. He made walls recede (dark) or project (light). For example, one of the theory's laws is "dynamic self-fulfillment," so small gaps in a line are visually disregarded. In the second VDL House, Dion and Richard Neutra "join" the water on the roof's pool with Silver Lake beyond, so that someone sitting on the roof perceives one seamless body of water (and is also cooled by the microclimate). Since space was a matter of perception and biology, formal symmetry for its own sake alone made no sense to Neutra in biorealistic terms. That was "empty geometricity." He argued that perception could supersede reality, particularly in making small houses feel expansive. "My own work has been geared to the stretching of space too but not just geometrically," he wrote. To that end, the same floor or ceiling material continues from indoors to out. Glass corners elongate space through diagonal vistas; they also allow a wider scope for peripheral vision, in turn empowering the inhabitant. If there was no real nature, faux nature would do: at the Beckstrand Medical Clinic, located in a busy urban area, Neutra installed wall-length photographs of an ocean scene and a mountain scene, each composed to include a foreground, middle ground, and horizon line, thus relieving stress by acknowledging our "savanna heritage."

At the end of his career, Neutra *père et fils* finally had the opportunity to apply their biorealistic principles to large-scale work. On February 27, 1970, the Neutras, along with Wesley Woodson, a pioneer in the field of human factors engineering, published a draft proposal with an extraordinary title, "An Activity Analysis of Family Group Behavior in Functional Home Living Spaces Leading to Human Engineering Recommendations for the Design of Universally Adequate Mass Housing." If it had gone forward, Richard would at last have had his chance to bear down with intelligence, with quantitative data in hand, on his most beloved building type, mass housing. He died seven weeks later.

Mirrors for the Middle Class

Neutra was fascinated by legends, like Cinderella, that linked hand mirrors with the treachery of an evil queen. He was also taken by their role in history as status symbols, with huge mirrors signifying the brilliant and infinite reign of the French aristocracy. It wasn't until the Industrial Revolution that mirrors and their magical powers were available to everyone.

Neutra used mirrors almost as often as he used silver paint, a fact usually ascribed to his love of shiny surfaces such as glass, metal and water. That may be, but for Neutra mirrors were also fabulous medicinal tools for the 20th-century architect. They really did have a magical ability – to change the destiny of a species: "Mirrors gave the insects the illusion of increase in numbers and this caused the insects to grow wings ... Pigeons, in isolation, do not lay eggs. Here also mirrors were used to give the illusion of numbers, and the laying of eggs was stimulated. So architecture can have biological consequences. Loneliness causes humans, like seagulls, to be less fruitful ..."

However, the indiscriminate use of mirrors was equally bad. If placed where they could reflect the movements of too many people, the room would fill "with visual and auditive noise, for eye and ear, so that it appears psychosomatically crowded and irritatingly tight." He often placed mirrors in places above head height at right angles to a window to bounce views of treetops and moving clouds. The point was to use the right biorealistic tool effectively.

A common critique of Neutra's work can be summed up as: "If you have seen one Neutra house you have seen a thousand." In a way the critique is correct. Neutra's work is a methodical search for a supple, organic algorithm for living, not a series of one-off solutions. If you have seen one Neutra house, good; if you have experienced one, you have witnessed a hypothesis being tested.

Neutra's architecture is an equation, a methodology refined to respond to three variables: the site, the client, and the budget. Of course there are shifts and developments in a career that began with a small but telling wooden hut, the Officers' Tea House (ca. 1915) in Trebinje, and ended with his last buildings in the late 1960s before his death in 1970. Some dwellings express a coalescence in thinking more profoundly, such as the notable Kaufmann Desert House in Palm Springs. But the image of that house also colludes in its fame as an icon. It is memorable in part because photographer Julius Shulman sensed the potential in walking away from the house and away from Neutra to capture

Above: Kun House #1, Los Angeles, 1936, rear view, sited below Kun House #2, 1950, across the street, for the same client.

Opposite: Perkins House, Pasadena, California, 1955

a breathtaking image. Here the variables indeed had changed: a highly sophisticated department store magnate, a desert site, a generous budget. However, there are potential moments such as this in many houses: Bucerius, Cole, Chuey, Oyler, Perkins, Rados, Singleton, Taylor, Kemper ... the list goes on. There is a shorter list for houses, many never published, which are singularly disappointing in their curiously awkward internal plans as originally designed, such as the Brown House in Bel Air, but even these houses typically achieve outstanding moments.

One cannot understand Neutra's intentions for his system without understanding his view on nature. Humanity is not something "other" than nature, but one aspect of it. As he writes in *Nature Near*: "The universe of which we are a part is a dynamic continuum. It extends from the most distant galactic systems into our atmosphere, biosphere, and terrestrial mantle, wafting even deeper into an energetic array of molecular and subatomic events that configure all matter, motion, and mind. Our skin is a membrane, not a barricade, and these universal processes reach through it, locking into our innermost vitals. The most remote contours of the cosmos are not just 'out there somewhere' but causally interlaced with the nearest and deepest folds of our interior landscape."

For Neutra, the architectural implications of that belief were profound. His self-assigned task was to understand the human in order to build a "shell" robust enough to respond to a human's complex needs: "When designing in limestone or in forged iron, nobody in his senses would think that it was an 'extraneous chore' to consider their intrinsic properties ... Therefore, if the architect's primary and most important material is human nature ... he will certainly have to cherish and understand it in relation to his work ..." To stretch the analogy to snails and their shells, one human did not require a habitat much different than another's. In his 1930 round-the-world tour, Neutra observed that in Japanese architecture a house for royalty or peasantry shared similar characteristics. Later in that same tour, when he taught at the Bauhaus, he made the observation again when he noted that Gropius, too, had apparently made the same assumptions in designing housing for the Bauhaus masters: "Here were practically standardized and identical abodes, accommodating the most diversified people who were certainly not convergent as artists! ... These people could indeed live in identical dwellings, when we worry whether or not one can frame habitations for quite ordinary families of coal miners or steel workers in Pittsburgh or East Germany! What a demonstration! What a fascinating, persuasive deed of Walter Gropius! And a typical characteristic of the Bauhaus at that!" This view was idealistic or even

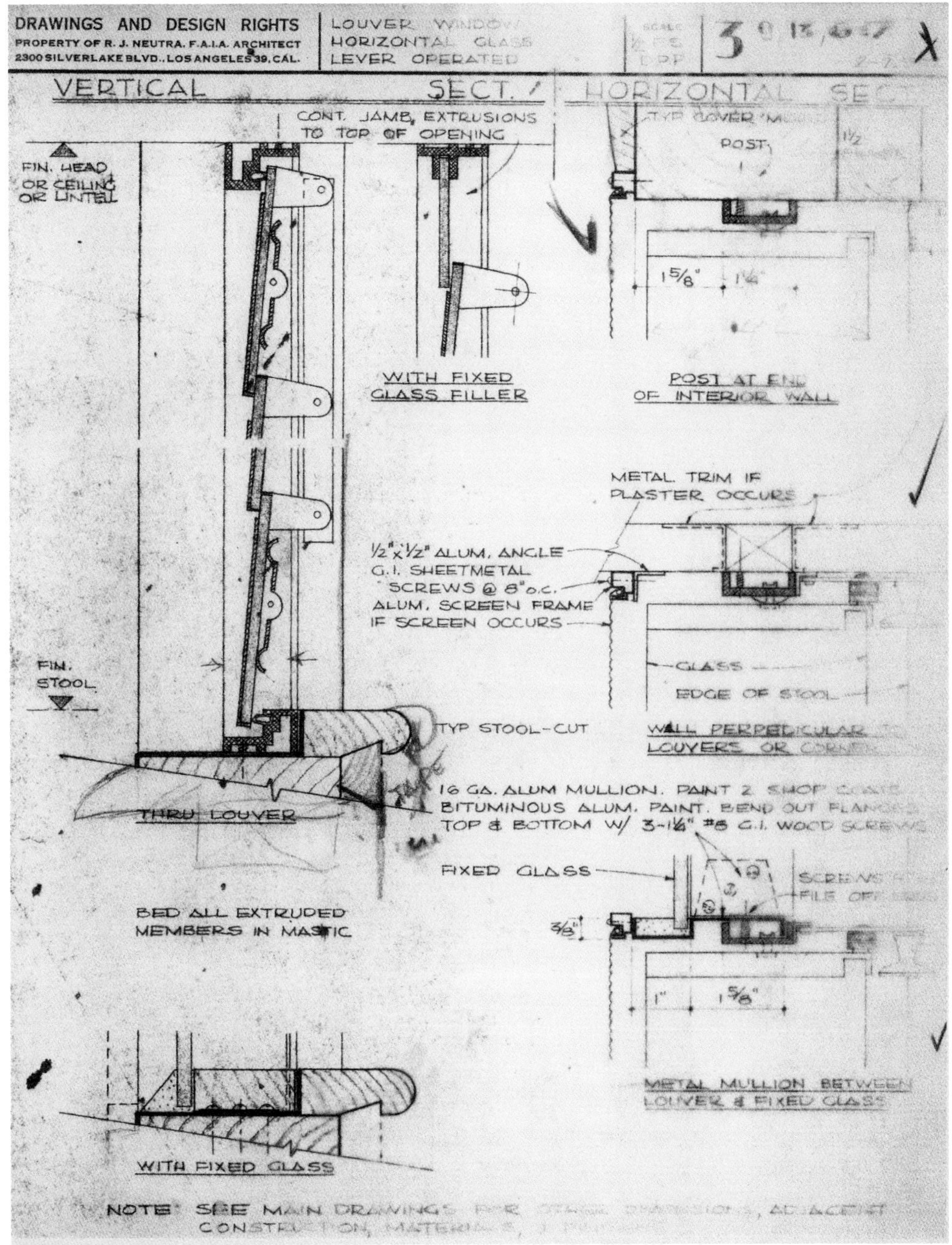

Opposite: Miller House, Palm Springs, California, 1937. Cutaway sketch shows Grace Lewis Miller at her Neutra-designed vanity.

Above: Hendershot House, Los Angeles, 1962, section, louver window

Nesbitt House, Los Angeles, 1942

naive. Though the masters were indeed eclectic, talented and volatile individuals who battled ferociously, they were also essentially united in their goal to propel "the new sensibility." Japan was relatively isolated when Neutra visited it, and in many ways remains a homogeneous, closed culture. Still, for Neutra, the true "International Style" was this biological repertoire of human needs, beyond history and geography, enriched by the peculiarities of anthropology.

Sacred Places in the Home

Besides providing him with a rationale for building a "generic" dwelling, Neutra's view on nature also had other important consequences for dwelling. Frank Lloyd Wright's architecture emphasized the hearth as the nucleus of the home. If there is a comparable sacred spot in a Neutra house, it is the terrace, preferably a terrace with radiant heating, so that the relationship between indoors and out becomes charged with ambiguity. The conventional opaque boundary between indoors and out must be reduced to a thin plane of glass so nothing can interfere in that potent and primal relationship, whether set in the benign landscaping of suburbia or the terrifying grandeur of the Swiss Alps. Neutra even shifts fireplaces away from the center of the room and to the outdoors, as though the fireplace, too, seeks to aid the shift out toward the site itself. Fireplaces are often placed at right angles to the glass, so nature is always at the periphery of one's eye. He often cantilevers the fireplaces so they float: the fire is acknowledged, but it is untethered to the ground or to nature, and closer to the body.

His concept of linking indoors and out may also explain why in his later work Neutra often used a uninterrupted standard eight-foot ceiling that flowed past the glass wall to become a deep overhang. This accomplishes three things: the overhang pulls the site in, it permits outdoor living, and the standard dimension cuts construction costs. Depending on its direction and angle, a sloped roof can accomplish this too, and despite his reputation for flat roofs, Neutra designed a surprising number of buildings with shed roofs undisguised by his parapets.

Rather than designing a *place*, he created *transitions* between site and building. That does not mean that Neutra's dwellings have "no sense of place." He always talked about the important human need for "soul anchorage" and for harnessing each site's *genius loci* in creating it. To Neutra's thinking, like any other creature, we humans must know where home is, but because humanity is not in opposition to nature but part of it, "home" is more of an area: a constellation of planets rather than a single sun. A Neutra house may indeed be formally "pure" compositionally, but it is that partnership with its site, that "exultant dance of interconnectedness," that gives both the house and the site a richer meaning.

Neutra's view on nature had another impact on his architecture: since humans (and therefore their built environment and technology itself) were part of nature, there was no need to sentimentalize it, tame it, or romanticize it by pretending that buildings were "grown": "We know children were not brought by the stork. Buildings stand on waterproofed foundations poured in concrete forms from details dimensioned according to engineering computation and contained in a set of blueprints stamped by the building department. Any pretense that buildings are rooted, or draw nourishing chemicals or moisture from the soil into their circulation of sap ... is poetic metaphor at best and misleading at worst," he said.

Neutra's buildings meet the ground cleanly, with no pretense of roots or transitions. In contrast, Frank Lloyd Wright believed building and ground needed a more literal relationship. He said (as though speaking to Neutra): "Any building for humane purposes should be an elemental, sympathetic feature of the ground, complementary to its natural environment ... But most 'modernistic' houses manage to look as though cut from cardboard with scissors ... in a childish attempt to make buildings look like steamships, flying machines, or locomotives."

In contrast, Neutra expected people to relish the dialectic between constructed buildings and the rest of nature. For example, at the Tremaine House (1948) he notes the juxtaposition of "thrillingly" fragile, "huge sheets of polished plate glass set against the rough bark of the oak trees." When he uses materials such as brick and wood at the Nesbitt House (1942), they are always "brought to a much finer finish than Nature's outdoor surfaces," emphasizing the contrast between one element of nature, human artifice, and another, the landscape. The contrast is dramatized further at the Kaufmann Desert (1946) and Miller (1937) houses, both sited in the harsh desert climate of Palm Springs, where irrigated grass runs abruptly to the edge of desert landscaping, with only broken pavers serving as a transition. Landscape and its myriad of rich, green textures are treated as major interior design elements, another reason Neutra generally, though not always, preferred neutral interior colors. In a letter to clients Dr. and Mrs. Earl Brod he urged them not to go with the busy bright red and green interior they envisioned. A strong green, he said, would "devour and pale out" all the green of the vegetation beyond the glass.

The dialogue between these two aspects of nature, human and non-human, is also evident in his presentation renderings for clients, but in an expressionistic way that recalls the anguished linework of Viennese artist Egon Schiele. The sky dominates the scene completely, writhing and twisting as though possessed, while the houses are almost generic, one easily substituted for another. It is perhaps not surprising that Neutra often worked with painter Roberto Burle Marx and Garrett Eckbo, both brilliant 20th-century landscape architects. Their work, playful, painterly, yet self-assured when they employed curves and diagonals, often dynamically enhanced Neutra's rectilinear shapes.

Generic Details for Unique Dwellings

Neutra refined a family of details over decades. Some details, such as metal casement windows, remained a permanent element in Neutra's kit-of-parts, and were used for lavish homes or modest ones, in the 1930s or 1960s. Early in the 1950s, he used aluminum casement windows, although he regularly restricted them to more private parts of the house such as kitchens or bedrooms, using much larger sheets of glass for public areas. The metal became more slender in profile, away from the heavier industrial gauge of earlier years, but otherwise did not change much. Other details or materials slowly lost or gained currency, such as wood replacing metal for exterior trim during and after World War II.

The system not only included materials and techniques. He designed his office practice as well. Perfected details could simply be whipped out of an office drawer on 8½" x 11" pieces of paper and included in the contractor's "bible" of specs and details: "Systematics to many seems pedantry. The freely creating artist in the architect is often conditioned to yearn for the liberty of tackling every task 'from scratch'... The fact that for transference of a design idea into realization he will have to engage many and diverse elements of human cooperation, up to the owner's acceptance, is often felt as a nuisance as a cluster of extraneous chores. But an architect cannot be an amateur." This approach freed Neutra in several ways: drafting time was reduced; construction costs were lowered because there were predictable ways of doing things; and tried-and-true solutions meant that Neutra could now focus on the site and on user needs.

User needs not only meant the distribution of living spaces, they also meant how to deal with the accumulations of the middle class. In Neutra's hands the storage of things was not mere domestic trivia, but elevated to an art form and folded into the design itself. Built-in furniture ensured order as well as flowing spaces. Neutra didn't so much ask people to get rid of stuff as to account for it. Some clients did perceive Neutra's implicit lifestyle as a welcome opportunity to reduce possessions; others attended no such imperative.

Apart from work for the exceptional client, kitchens and bathroom finishes were humble and generic: linoleum or asphalt tiles for floors, plastic laminate or tile for countertops, painted white or natural wood finish for cabinetry. One classic Neutra detail, which he might well have learned from Schindler, were drawers with a convenient handhold made from an undercut groove in the

Perkins House, Pasadena, California, 1955.
The living room overlooks the garage roof.

wood. It maintained a clean line aesthetically that was also easy to maintain. Upper kitchen cabinets were equally generic, often clean planes or waxed, rubbed Masonite. The overall sensibility is that kitchens and bathrooms are not meant to be sumptuous backdrop scenes but well-designed tools to be used.

There is luxury, it is just that Neutra redefines it. Luxury is in how seamlessly one can accomplish a task or in being in constant relationship with the outdoors. Luxury is in seeing the wood grain of Japanese ash cabinetry maintain the same direction when it shifts from the flat top to the drawer face, so that the grain of the wood flows over the edge and down the face like water. Luxury is in solid construction and in thoughtful "acoustic coloring," not fancy finishes. Neutra's philosophy "began with a house that would last for ever," said John Clark. He and his wife moved into their Neutra house in 1957.

Early Houses

In a way, Neutra's houses of the 1930s were his own private "Case Study Program." However similar or different the houses are, they all show the same inquisitive intention of finding a robust "kit of parts."

Neutra was acutely aware of the power of language in marketing his ideas. To link his work to the idea of technical innovation and behavioral research, he often didactically named houses not after their clients but as "prototypes." For example, the Lovell Health House was the

Demonstration Health House; the Mosk House was titled Study for Steep Hillside Development; the Miller House was named the Mensendieck House, after a "functional" exercise system. Neutra's own house was titled the Van der Leeuw Research House. This drew attention to the commercial or experimental materials that manufacturers donated for the publicity, as well as to the study of maximizing the feeling of spaciousness given an extremely limited site. The name also honored his Dutch sponsor. Even Neutra's most famous client, Edgar Kaufmann, was not exempt: the Desert House was Neutra's title for what he called, rather disingenuously, "in many ways a typical research project."

Neutra's most obvious allegiance to the conventions of the International Style shows up in the long ribbons of steel casement windows separated by load-bearing 4x4 posts. These windows set up a vertical rhythm that alternates with strong horizontal bands of typically white stucco but sometimes tongue-and-groove wood as well. As he began incorporating larger pieces of fixed glass in specific areas, as in the Gill House, he maintained the spacing defined by the narrower casement windows, thus creating two rhythms while maintaining the same tempo defined by the posts.

In general, 1930s houses, such as the Mosk House, the McIntosh House in Los Angeles, or the Scioberetti House in Berkeley, are more likely to be a series of interlocking volumes rather than a series of planes and lines sliding past each other in three-dimensional De Stijl collages, as they were later. Instead many of these early houses, often clad in redwood, are controlled, beautifully detailed and minimal boxes. The roof acts as a lid which does not engage the sky but confronts it as a crisply closed container. Roof overhangs, where they occur, do not extend much beyond the footprint of the house, and they rarely act as the independent, articulated horizontal elements reaching out to the landscape that Neutra used later. One of the best examples of his application of a European Modernism to the hills of Los Angeles is the compact Koblick House (1937). With its strong sense of tight mass, this little building most recalls Neutra's ties to Adolf Loos. It does not unfurl horizontally and parallel to the hill. Rather, Neutra addresses the site by stepping each floor back so that each discrete ground plane springs from the hill. In contrast, the T-shaped Scioberetti House (1939) is placed almost at the top of a hill, the leg of the T jutting out. The change of position creates the sensation of a building not at all wedded to the hill but rather like a young bird struggling to escape it.

Some houses act as pointers to the future: in the two-story Kraigher House, the Davey House and in the Ward-Berger House the sides of the volumes begin to read as independent planes, with roof parapets of different heights not only to hide pitched roofs but also to emphasize their independence from each other, as he had done at the Lovell Health House so emphatically. Neutra had used this technique even earlier on the garage behind the Zehlendorf housing complex in Berlin, which he designed while working for Erich Mendelsohn. In the Mosk and VDL houses, portions of the wall fly free of the building envelope to abstractly capture and define outdoor space, tasks that the spider leg (an extension of a spandrel beam ending with a supporting column well beyond the building envelope) would often assume in the future.

Other exterior elements also became Neutra's own trademark in the 1930s. For night, he placed

Perkins House, Pasadena, California, 1955.
The glass wall divides the indoor-outdoor pool.

strips of lighting covered by translucent glass in the underside of the roof soffit a few feet away from glazed areas. (He used incandescent bulbs until the first practical fluorescent lamps were marketed in 1938.) This quickly became a hard-working detail. It maintained the quality of spaciousness; it softened the transition from interior lighting to the darkness outside; by illuminating the landscape, it acknowledged the biorealistic needs for contact with nature and for being alert to potential danger. Since the light created exterior reflections on the glass and confusing layers of images, Neutra liked to call it an "optical curtain." According to Dion Neutra, his father also believed that by creating light outside the glass line, occupants would not be disturbed by night flying insects. Therefore Neutra sometimes could convince his clients that screens, which he detested, were unnecessary, and on a deeper level prevent any barrier to the immediate experience between the user and the outdoors.

Much of Neutra's work, especially his later suburban work, is closed to the street, apart from a high strip of windows, and open to the garden in the rear, essentially echoing his thinking behind school architecture with its high clerestories on one side of a classroom and full-height openings out to patios on the other. From the street, the Kun House (1936) appears to be a sleek, closed one-story structure, but the valley façade reveals a three-story building open to the views beyond. However, other houses, especially in cities, such as the first VDL House or the Schiff House, do not close their façades to the street. These houses rely on drapes for privacy. An anti-urban stance is not built in.

There was one house that breaks all of Neutra's rules about an openness to nature, and this was the von Sternberg House, completed in 1935 for the Hollywood director Josef von Sternberg, and demolished in 1971. Where often a Neutra site itself offers a house privacy, tucked into a hill or using transitions of planes, Sternberg built himself an all-steel industrial castle, complete with high walls and moat, on flat land that he called barren, forlorn and empty. All the plantings in the aluminum-coated steel, walled patio couldn't create access to nature. Rather the long ellipse, placed at right angles to the bridge leading to the garage roof, creates a sense of two directions straining against each other yet interconnected, like the teeth between two gears. The effect of this beautiful yet strange silver house must have been startling. The building feels like a race-car and the huge sweeping curves around it recall the test track on the roof of the Fiat Factory in Turin (1923). Neutra even creates lanes on his "track" by alternating strips of grass and concrete.

The interiors of Neutra's best 1930s houses reveal his skill in delicately layering spatial transitions. Here the interiors are less aligned with the conventions of the International Style and more with the elusive qualities of the light, thin Japanese tea house architecture that he experienced at Katsura. Nowhere is this influence more present than in the exquisitely detailed Miller Mensendieck House, which successfully combines a pueblo dwelling burrowed into the desert with a disciplined, ethereal Modernism. The house became one of his most lauded achievements. It won the first prize in the 1937 *House Beautiful* competition, a distinction that Neutra cherished because it indicated acceptance of his ideas by the public. The northeast corner of the Miller House is its "pueblo" side, its white stuccoed sides stepping back like traditional native architecture. The southeast corner steps back too, but here is rendered in clear glass, sliding out of its protective pueblo shell in a series of calibrated steps to reveal a reflecting pool under the roof next to a screened porch.

The "pueblo side," however, is not opaque. Except for a horizontal strip of plaster at its base, the north living room wall is almost floor-to-ceiling translucent glass, with clerestories at the top for cross-ventilation. Neutra had determined that the north side of the house should have no openings because of the direction of the harsh sand-carrying wind, knowledge he later applied to the Kaufmann Desert House. Mirrors at right angles to this wall effectively "doubled" Miller's teaching space. High built-in cabinetry, partially shielding her bed, separated this area from the rest of the house; a curtain could be drawn across the room to give her complete visual privacy.

Neutra's datum lines are similar to those used in Japanese residential interiors in their spare but rigorous use. He maintains one such high horizontal line, above which is either clerestory window or solid white plaster. This thin upper plane unifies the room: the *roof* plane, which now "folds down" to form the high upper wall and delicately provides a sense of enclosure. Neutra did this in commercial work, as can be observed in the Norwalk Service Station (1947). Neutra usually does not "fold" an opaque *wall* plane in a similar fashion to create a protective corner, unlike Wright or sometimes Schindler. Other horizontal lines define the low built-in shelves and the top of the fireplace and built-in sofa.

Just as Neutra layered spatial transitions, he also layered functions. As he once said, more hopefully than realistically, "In our house rooms have no names such as living room, dining room, bedroom ... Rooms are portions of our great living space and pragmatically elastic." This "great living space" sounds very much like the Japanese concept of the *zashiki*, or flexible principal room, used for living, sleeping and entertaining. Miller required a "live-work" space that could on occasion accommodate eating, teaching, living, or guest overnight stays. In the Miller House every detail alertly responds to a specific client and acknowledges her chosen lifestyle precisely. For example, near her "day or night couch," where she desired an unimpeded view of the reflecting pond and to the horizon beyond, Neutra pushed the casement windows up to the ceiling, so no vertical mullion line could impede her glance. Next to her closet, Neutra designed an alcove, tiny but flooded with sunlight, for her morning toilette. Here her makeup sat on a floating plane of veined white onyx. The wardrobe is a portrait of Miller: it is her own personal machine for living. Its full-height cabinetry contains seven separate drawers, each a slightly different depth for each category of apparel. "How many sweaters do you own? How many hats?" Neutra wanted to know, as well as the ergonomically correct height for her kitchen countertops.

The Miller House was Neutra's first house in the desert, and tiny at only 1,164 square feet. Grace Lewis Miller said she "didn't want a Rubens, she wanted a Picasso." Her tastes rivaled those of that elitist Modernist Van der Leeuw: she considered hiring Wright, a personal friend, and Mies van der Rohe, whose Barcelona Pavilion impressed her. It was Neutra who arrived in a Packard hitched to a trailer resplendent with pivoting drawing board and awning. (The pivot was to allow him to study sun and wind angles.) He would sketch on site while his wife Dione played cello. Neutra was fascinated by the strangeness of the desert, which he often compared to the moon. The Vienna native seemed to regard it as terrain far more foreign than America itself. The last photograph of his book *Wie baut Amerika?*, published in 1927, is not the expected frenetic steel construction or a bustling metropolis. Rather it shows an image of an empty, wind-whipped desert captioned "the primitive wasteland [near] Palm Springs." Ten years later the Kaufmann Desert House was built not far away from where he took that photograph, and despite its beauty, the house remains a foreigner in the desert.

While Miller considered hiring Frank Lloyd Wright, industrial magnate Edgar Kaufmann did. Falling Water (1934–37) was the epic result, now the best-known American house of the 20th century. Neutra's Desert House, as he named it, expresses his utterly different attitude: made, not grown. It is only a five-minute drive from the Miller House, but the house also represents the other end of the spectrum in Neutra's own work in its very formal planning and detailing. The budget was over $300,000 for the 3,800-square-foot house. Miller's house cost $7,500. Here Neutra is no longer a fellow traveler in step with the International Style, though the Kaufmann Desert House retains the taut, crisp quality of his earlier work. Instead the Kaufmann Desert House distills space into silver horizontal planes sliding above transparent glass. The only pronounced vertical is the chimney flanking the "gloriette," as Neutra called it. This is the sensual rooftop space that crowns the house, a man-made mountain peak. Movable vertical aluminum louvers, acting as a unified but open wall plane, protect the gloriette. Without them, or if they were one solid plane, the house would have a far more stolid presence. Similar antecedents can be see in the von Sternberg House, the Davey House, and the Katsura Imperial Palace in Tokyo.

The sense of strong contrasts in one coherent composition begins with the drawing of the pinwheel floor plan for this house. The landscaping is drawn on the diagonal, percolating through the right angles of the pinwheel. In the Kaufmann plan, even the notated orientation for the "high winds and sand storms" is drawn on the diagonal, this time at right angles to the landscaping. This move animates the drawing, but it also reflects reality: the winds from the northwest are fierce and unforgiving, blasting whatever they can carry into the house. Neutra shielded the house from the dust with solid walls or louvers and exploited the wind's cooling potential by subtle openings in the attics, using the wind to drive out hot air.

The pinwheel also throws the private living areas to the ends of the plan's arms, with the living room at the hub of the wheel. Like the south-facing living room, open to the heat of the sun, this footprint might seem an odd choice for the desert, the very opposite of a multi-family pueblo dwelling massed to conserve energy, but the dictates of the plan speak to other values: since one's vantage point is always changing, every elevation is different, each view unique. The extremes in plan emphasize extremes in social privacy: master and mistress, servants, children and guests could not be farther apart. Shaded walkways, corridors and the outdoor patios connect the private quarters. Idle movement is transmuted into a procession through different zones.

There is a running dialogue between reflecting and non-reflecting surfaces. Glass, water, silver-painted metal, high-gloss Douglas fir planks in the gloriette contrast with the concrete floor (a blend of fine silica sand with white Portland cement) and meticulously laid, dryset stonework. The white stucco, infused with mica flakes, is brilliant in the sun, while the "Neutra brown," very warm and dark, is painted on those planes he wished to recede. Here the painted stucco and the stonework are applied as planes, with none of the monolithic quality of the materials at Falling Water. Neutra used muted, desert-bleached

Neutra and Alexander, Child Guidance Clinic, USC Annenberg Center, Los Angeles, 1963

colors in the bathrooms and some bedrooms, such as salmon, army green, and yellow. Cork is used in the bathrooms (including shower enclosures) and kitchen (including the countertop). Despite its warm look, cork under these conditions requires high maintenance, and seems a perverse choice and untypical of Neutra. Falling Water uses cork in similar locations. One potentially lively detail occurs at the southern gutters. At their eastern end, the metal rain gutters suddenly narrow just before they terminate, allowing any overflow rainwater to flow east beyond the building before it falls on rocks below, a gesture seen in both Japanese gardens and medieval cathedrals. Thus, little regarded and seldom used gutters become Modernist gargoyles adept at romance. This was one of these "honeymoon moments in life" that Neutra believed architecture needed to accommodate as much as any day-to-day chore.

As usual, the boundary between indoors and out is extinguished, but here in the Kaufmann Desert House this is accomplished in very refined ways. The stonework threads throughout the project, running along the garage wall, penetrating the house, jumping to the fireplace; finally it connects the far-flung utility room to the master bedroom area along a long wall. Heating and cooling extends to the pool area, and Neutra even places it in the low seating wall linking the house and the pool, a wry, socially magnanimous gesture that ensures the party continues for shivering wet bathers or formally dressed partygoers on a chilly winter's night. The entire corner of the living room opens to the pool when the two glass walls slide away. The detailing of the steel doors containing the glass and the tracks embedded in the floors could be delicately rendered because they are hung from the steel beam embedded in the ceiling. Neutra preserves the open corner structurally by extending that beam and placing its supporting column out beyond the building envelope. In the Kaufmann Desert House, this beam was hidden behind the metal fascia, but later Neutra exposed the beam so it is one exuberant line running well beyond the roof overhang before meeting a column. This "outrigger" detail became his best-known trademark, the spider leg, the umbilical cord linking two aspects of nature, landscape and the building, a kind of constructed landscape. Extending the beam also relieved him of having to "turn the corner" with the same treatment or material, and thus gave him the opportunity to emphasize differences among elevations. Despite all the moves Neutra makes to insist on the irrevocable integration of indoors and out, the real outdoors is out of reach, just beyond the carpet of bright green grass on which the house rides, out there in the desert.

In contrast, the Tremaine House in Santa Barbara is meshed with its site, sloping and shaded by massive oak trees. Architectural critic Esther McCoy wrote that the house, designed at the same time as the Kaufmann Desert House, "completed Neutra's search for the pavilion." Where the Kaufmann House is a complicated composition, the Tremaine House sounds one very clear note. Its pinwheel floor plan is very similar to that of the Kaufmann House, but here the lengths of the arms are almost mannered in their exaggeration. The structural system for this costly single-family house was based on the system he worked out for rural schools and clinics in Puerto Rico: cheap and quickly built using unskilled labor. The structure is sparse, clear, and unambiguous: reinforced-concrete piers support a girder or spandrel beam, which in turn supports thin concrete joists with an attenuated roof line. The palette of materials is severely restricted to concrete, dryset stone and glass, except for the handsome revolving redwood louvers on the west side of the living room, leading to the terrace. These look almost fragile compared with the concrete joists above them. Terrazzo is the only flooring material indoors and out, and warmed by radiant floor heating throughout, down to the end of the terrace, the longest arm of the pinwheel.

The Miller, Kaufmann and Tremaine houses varied widely in client, site, and budget, expressing points along a journey toward Neutra's systematic architecture. With the Nesbitt House, he dealt with new materials with a different scale, such as brick and redwood, and in new ways, such as mortar oozing out between the bricks and board-and-batten for the wood. In contrast to his early period, with ribbons of windows alternating with white stucco bands, these materials are far more difficult to render as crisp, formal compositions. After this house, Neutra shook off his earlier adherence to the overtness of the International Style, now subsumed by slower, stronger tempos of post, beam and glass.

The early 1950s ushered in for Neutra a golden age of sophisticated, relaxed houses, a depth met and matched by an equally mature Shulman, whose images of this time are particularly striking. In the Moore, Chuey, Perkins, Brown poolhouse, Oyler, and Singleton houses, elements such as reflecting pools, the spider leg, overhangs and remarkable sites are used to great effect in Shulman's hands. He photographs along the line of a beam, pulling us to infinity, or shoots well away from the site, through a glass corner and out again, so the buildings feel almost incidental. Neutra's three-dimensional De Stijl tension of asymmetric sliding planes and lines grows more daring and aggressive, yet is utterly controlled. Sometimes the spider leg flings itself out to a nature barren and exotic, as in the Oyler House; other times, as at the Cole or Moore houses, it rests in a tranquil pool of water.

One of the most beloved houses of this period is the "Perkins house on Poppy Peak in Pasadena, as we used to call it," recalled John Blanton, one of Neutra's chief associates. Constance Perkins had listened to Neutra confidently lecturing about his skill in designing on a budget. After his lecture, she walked to the podium, and threw down the gauntlet: Could he do it for her, a single professional? The Perkins House is a wonderful summation of Neutra's system, and clearly manifests everything he believed. Like a proof in mathematics, it proves his multivalent thesis on space, nature, perception, and the way to attend to humans as generic members of the species and as unique beings. The project was his favorite kind of challenge: a tight budget; an ambitious, intelligent client; a small, awkward site on an urban hillside. He used his full palette of techniques to present a $17,000 house as an exercise in miniature urban planning. Exterior soffit lighting expands evening space, and continuous ceilings become deep overhangs, so that the house feels simultaneously open yet protected and cave-like. The spider leg elongates living space, and links house and site. The 1,310-square-foot house uncoils down the hill in a series of De Stijl planes and lines, ending in the roof terrace above the carport.

Like Grace Miller, Perkins required a functional, flexible space, but her emphasis was not on teaching students but on entertaining them. The small kitchen has an open pass-through so she could talk to guests while cooking. The L-shaped living area, remarkable for its subtle but acute response to her needs, also contains her bed and study desk. Her bed faces the living room, and looks out over the roof garden to the mountains beyond. She insisted on access to nature "for I will not work when I am closed in." Perkins had an architect's understanding for the implications of making (apparently) very small moves. She often reworked his office's drawings with sketches of her own. It was she who suggested the now-famous corner pool at one end of the living room: "I would like the definition of indoors and outdoors almost obliterated with a pool ... that will meander in and out of my living area ... and continuous planting areas establishing the dominant background feeling." The intimate scale of the plantings also complements the distant horizon.

Neutra combined thoroughbred detailing with construction-grade plywood for the built-in furniture. The horizontal edges of the bookcase taper so the line looks narrower than it really is. White plaster contrasts with the Douglas fir of the structural members and redwood decking. Colors like primrose yellow and persimmon (a color taken from a persimmon tree on the site) leap selectively from kitchen countertop, to an exterior door, to outdoor steps. Rubbed Masonite is used on some exterior and interior walls and for kitchen cabinets. Perkins easily matched her architect's intelligence, tenaciousness, willfulness and sense of integrity. She sounds like Neutra when she concluded her seven-page, single-spaced autobiography at his request, "It is necessary to me to feel that I serve a purpose in my life of a broader nature than routine materialistic living provides."

ARCHITECTURE OF SOCIAL CONCERN

Addition to Corona Elementary School, Los Angeles, 1935

Neutra is best known for his houses, but he designed many noteworthy large-scale projects all over the world, more often public rather than private commissions. Often these commissions were treated just as exhaustively as any dwelling, from urban planning down to furniture details. These projects were handled in different ways: in his own practice, in partnership with Robert Alexander and later with his son Dion, or in collaboration with architects typically based close to the project, especially for international commissions or those away from Los Angeles.

With their clear forms, careful siting, and interiors that reflect his obsession with user needs, many of these projects are forthright examples of Neutra design. Certainly the Eagle Rock Park Clubhouse and the Mariners Medical Center are two such outstanding projects. However, at other times the architecture of these larger projects falters, such as that of the U.S. Embassy in Karachi, Pakistan, or the Riviera Methodist Church in Redondo Beach. They lack the self-confidence marking so much of his later work, resulting in tentative buildings with an unresolved quality in their massing and detail. Schools and housing, however, were two arenas in which Neutra suffered no such lack of confidence. In his schools he was a radical. Here his architecture became the vehicle for a new social agenda that not only challenged what school buildings should look like but also how learning should occur. In housing Neutra was a master. It gave him the opportunity to prove that his system of repeating elements could be applied just as successfully to housing as to houses.

The wellspring for much of Neutra's ideas on housing and schools was an urban project for which he himself was the hypothetical client, and a demanding one at that. This was Rush City Reformed, an ongoing personal think tank he designed throughout the 1920s and early 1930s, which reflects his attempt to wed realism and idealism. Between his first book, *Wie baut Amerika?* (1927) and his second, *Amerika: Die Stilbildung des neuen Bauens in den Vereinigten Staaten* (1930), his views on his American building and urban planning shifted. While he still believed American building and urban planning had fantastic potential, he no longer was the uncritical cheerleader bringing news of the promised land to his European audience. While he still exhaustively reported on all kinds of new building technologies, he became increasingly uneasy about the point of all that activity. In *Amerika* he observed that housing was the "most irrational industry ... Before even a spade is turned, obsolescence has taken place ... because of the limitations in the statement of the problem in its original conception." He also observed, ironically, that as cities spread out more, traffic problems only worsened, leading to "irrational commuting," wasting resources and destroying community.

Neutra of course was not alone in creating utopias: Ville Radieuse by Le Corbusier or Broadacre City by Frank Lloyd Wright are obvious examples. But Neutra argued that his solution was based on real conditions, "not an abstract and theoretically rigid scheme." The result was mixed: his prisons are humanized with glass ceilings, skylights, a swimming pool and recreation areas, while his apartment high-rises are chilling in their relentlessly totalitarian appearance, one banal rectangular block marching along after another. His superb office building reconciles an articulated vertical structure with floors of alternating glass and mass. Its lack of cornice allows the building to scrape the sky; its boldly stepped base recalls Neutra's own handling of planes in his houses, albeit on a domestic scale.

Appearance aside, a closer reading of the project shows its appeal as a prototype. Addressing the needs of both adults and children, he carefully analyzed how to allocate space for different people, some in high-rises but many more in one-story houses, using labels such as "Night-Spending Persons" (presumably those working the night shift) or "Space-Taking Groups" (presumably families). While these labels are amusingly eccentric, they were also effective. They revealed the scope of Neutra's re-evaluation, a reconsideration that included any language he deemed "not of its age." For example, he rejected "terminal" as a label for his air and rail stations, arguing that in a modern world people are much more likely to *transfer* to a different kind of transportation than to "terminate" a journey. So: Rush City Transfer.

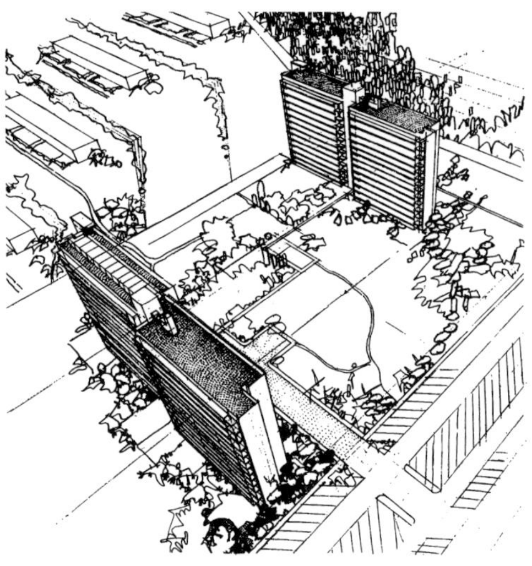

Neutra and Alexander, Elysian Park Heights, Los Angeles, early 1950s. Unbuilt high-and-low-rise project superseded by the Dodger Stadium.

Elysian Park Heights

Neutra and Alexander applied a similar method to allocate space for the unbuilt Elysian Park Heights in Los Angeles. Part of the urgent American housing effort after World War II, this huge project of 3,500 dwellings for 17,000 people was to have been a major step in relieving the city's housing shortage and in eliminating slums which had neither toilets nor baths. Conveniently but successfully renounced as "red" socialist housing at the height of the hysteria of the McCarthy era, it was abruptly canceled in 1953 after two years of intense work by the partners. Sited adjacent to the downtown on hills surrounding a ravine, the project would have dramatically changed the city's character, though Alexander came to believe later that it might have been an urban disaster, displacing a settled community that enjoyed its semi-rural setting. In any case the project attracted formidable talent, such as Garrett Eckbo (the Berkeley-based pioneer of modern landscape design, who had trained under Walter Gropius and Marcel Breuer at Harvard), who drew the preliminary design for the gardens and grounds.

Echoing Rush City Reformed, Elysian Park mixed 13-story towers (with lower floors for small families and the upper floors for couples and single people) and one- and two-story units reserved for larger families. The high-rises, placed on the hilltops since the valley soil was too unstable, were spaced far apart so privacy and daylight were conserved. Because the high-rises were necessary to make the project viable financially, Neutra did all he could to subvert government regulations intended to keep public housing as undesirable as possible, such as including the "luxury" of more elevators so that constant use did not mean chronically broken transport. He placed open-air playgrounds and laundries in the buildings so that mothers could keep an eye on their children, and insisted on ground-level toilets for children out on the playground. Los Angeles housing official Frank Wilkinson said: "Neutra would spend night after night studying the problem or talking with tenants from other projects, even showing them how to build their own furniture out of cheap materials, like a chair from a nail keg, a pillow, and fabric. Or since doors for cupboards and closets were not allowed by regulations, Neutra would show people how to use fabric instead. He wanted to know when people went to work, how they got there, how they did their laundry. He was more interested in what people really did than in what they said they wanted."

Neutra already had experience with low-cost housing, related to two earlier projects in Los Angeles but more significantly to a new policy in World War II defense housing. On April 5, 1941, the U.S. boldly decided to change its policy of using only civil service architects for such housing and to hire languishing private firms, who were to inject new thinking into the huge task. Architects were also allowed to set aside a certain number of units for experimental design and construction out of the total of 30,000 privately contracted dwelling units, as long as the experiments took no longer to design or to implement than more conventional structures. For Modernists it was a once-in-a-lifetime opportunity to show how standardization and good design could engage any challenge, including one in which the budget was rock-bottom, materials were restricted, and the deadline immediate. In less than six months, architects such as Marcel Breuer, Walter Gropius, Louis Kahn, Antonin Raymond, Eliel and Eero Saarinen, Hugh Stubbins and William Wurster had completed wood-frame projects.

Neutra designed Avion Village, a 600-unit community in Grand Heights Prairie, Texas, with collaborating architects Roscoe P. Dewitt and David R. Williams. Their designs, like those of their famous colleagues, were unpretentiously minimal. The two-story brick-clad boxes, with appendages of Texas-style double-height porches of light wood studs look like humble cousins of the articulated façade Walter Gropius designed for the Fagus Factory, while the one-story plywood units look much more like Neutra's work in the 1930s. Even at a low cost of $2,562.50 per unit, with an estimated time of an unbelievable 57 minutes to assemble prefabricated components on site, they managed to include enlivening details such as exposing the wood roofing members in ceilings to unify the interior, or changing the orientation of the exterior plywood panels to emphasize different planes. Large sliding doors dissolved a bedroom corner, enlarging the living room (an interior gesture here that Neutra used on the Kaufmann Desert House exterior five years later). The urban planning of the project is arguably more sophisticated than that of comparable war projects by other Modernists. A huge green park at the center of the project is the primary landscaped area, and is supplemented by secondary elements called "fingerparks," which were long stretches of landscaped greenery that also served as pedestrian accessways between rows of houses, while rear alleys were reserved for cars. Both became familiar Neutra strategies, and were probably first seen at Baldwin Hills Village.

Channel Heights

Channel Heights, a 600-unit project built in 1942 for the wartime shipyard workers at Port San Pedro, was one of the last permanent war housing schemes built. Overlooking the Pacific Ocean and the harbor, sharp canyons cut the rugged 165-acre site, which changed 240 feet in elevation from one end to the other. It was a most breathtaking location for any kind of housing, let alone a low-cost government project. With its larger budget and longer lifespan, its architecture was far less technically innovative; here the experimental quality had to do with spatial requirements and manipulating simple elements and materials. Neutra enlisted the *genius loci* of the site in allowing the hilly topography of the canyons to separate each of three clusters of dwellings of one- and two-story houses of two or four units, thus engendering a subtle sense of identity for each cluster. To minimize risk to children at play, Neutra used extended cul-de-sacs so cars could not pick up speed; to capture both ocean and harbor views units were angled diagonally.

Because materials such as aluminum and steel were scarce, Neutra turned to stucco and to redwood, which was used for window trim, railings, and some horizontal siding. With the thin roof lines, shallow overhangs and crisp stucco planes, the effect of the housing was woodsy and comfortable, but also reminiscent of Japanese architecture in its simplicity, sharp contrasts, and restraint. Interiors were to radiate "studied economy, sturdy simplicity and cheerful color," and echoed the exterior with exposed beams and white plaster walls. Neutra designed most of the simple furniture for the project, including the "Boomerang Chair." Now a rare collector's item, it was published in the layperson's magazine *Popular Mechanics*, so that tenants and others could build the cheap chair themselves. The project's many community buildings were clad only in redwood. The supermarket in particular stands out for its strong design and high-spirited interior. Inside, huge laminated wood roof beams are partially revealed when they slide beyond a truncated plywood ceiling and plunge into a plywood wall lit by clerestory windows above and large glass orbs below. (Neutra used these globes in many applications, aligning them in rows to delineate space.) In its sense of acceleration, the market's sweeping horizontal façade is reminiscent of commercial work by Neutra's former employer Erich Mendelsohn, with its sharply angled exterior soffit, long plate glass windows and spread custom designed letters announcing "Channel Heights Market."

Despite his passion for low-cost mass housing based on European ideals, Neutra increasingly understood that most Americans would overwhelmingly prefer their collective ideal of the freestanding single-family home. He astutely decided to prove the credibility of his approach, American-style. Perhaps because of his essentially European background, he simply did not understand why using a family of predictable architectural methods, flexible enough to be creatively manipulated, could be construed as "boring." Rather, it conferred coherence and identity, he argued, as could be seen in Swiss chalets or in the organic quality of Italian hill towns, achieved by using similar materials and forms over a long time. In contrast, in Neutra's eyes American suburbs were flawed because their makers shrilly insisted on "skin-deep" differences: "Nobody ever seems to have lamented the monotony or uniformity of a tree, but our neighborhoods are found needing to be ... 'relieved of monotony'. Artificial relief [is] sought in the diversity of the elements rather than in the comprehensive framework, and so each house in new suburbs [gets] its own particular skin-deep style."

To prove his point, in the late 1940s Neutra persuaded a family friend, Holger Fog of Denmark, to buy lots a few doors away from the VDL Research House. Neutra sold them on Fog's behalf, and those who bought the lots were contractually obligated to hire Neutra. According to Dione Neutra, "race" laws were still in effect that prevented certain groups of people from buying land in some neighborhoods, laws Neutra blithely flouted when he sold lots to clients of Asian descent.

Neutra called the nine houses, built incrementally between 1948 and 1961 and known as the Silver Lake Colony, a "'postured grouping', meaning the grouping of a team in cooperative action, where each individual posture complements the others and no soulless, mere side-by-side, prevails." They are built with conventional building materials such as glass, stucco, redwood, birch cabinetry, cork tile, clear Douglas fir and pebble-dash concrete. Most range from 1,600 to 1,800 square feet, a compressed footprint

Channel Heights Housing, San Pedro, California, 1943. Intended as temporary wartime housing for shipyard workers of the Port of Los Angeles, the project housed 600 families in one- and two-story units on rolling hills. Demolished.

compared with most American homes, whose average square footage was 2,150 in 1997 and continues to increase. How much space does it take to lead the good life? Not as much as you think, replied Neutra's buildings.

Some (the Inadomi, Kambara, Sokol, Treweek and Yew houses) front the lake directly. Others (the Dion Neutra/Reunion, the Flavin, Ohara and Akai houses) are sited higher, on Earl Street and then-Argent Place (now Neutra Place), a short block on a hill that overlooks the lake and the houses below. "The relationships among the houses were worked out with care to preserve views as much as possible and to minimize unwanted intrusion on privacy by windows," noted Dion Neutra. The result is a community with a sense of sensual, animated tranquility, of accomplished sophistication rendered simply by mature hands. Each house is unique. The Dion Neutra/Reunion House is a simple long rectangle in plan, which when built became a shelter in a dense green forest, a pool of cool dark water beyond the glass living room wall. Others explode in light and transparency, as does the Ohara House with its living room flanked by glass walls. The quiet, reserved Flavin House is U-shaped, with an open courtyard leading to trees farther up the site.

In the Strathmore Apartments (1937) Neutra took full advantage of the short, steep hillside to create split-level spaces and changing ceiling heights. In the Colony, he also used the swift rise between the flat lake and Neutra Place. These dwellings unfold volumetrically, and are much more three-dimensionally complex than many other Neutra houses. The careful insertion of outdoor rooms connected to nature makes the homes feel spacious and unconfining.

In the early 1960s Neutra realized his most refined and comprehensive housing scheme, this time in Germany for a developer, Bewobau Ltd. "The developers were very brave, bright and determined in that they wanted to see a Neutra scheme built and to see the houses sell well to a relatively conservative consumer," said John Blanton, architect and one of Neutra's chief designers. The scheme is outstanding for its elegant though compact composition, its relationship to nature, and its solid craftsmanship. A local newspaper article prophesied in 1963 that the Neutra project would become "an object of pilgrimage for all European architects. How the architecture is composed into the landscape has probably not a more convincing example in the whole world." There were three Bewobau locations, one in Quickborn near Hamburg, a second, Walldorf near Frankfurt/Main, and an unbuilt third planned for Hohenbuchau. All were sited in heavily forested areas. Hohenbuchau in particular had an unusual site on stately estate grounds high in the mountains, where Neutra wanted to have 20-story high-rises "brushing the treetops" amidst lofty views.

As with Rush City Reformed, Bewobau offered a range of alternatives but this time was geared exclusively for middle-class consumers: multiplexes or single units with nine different one- and two-story models at the first two sites. Sizes and prices ranged from 97 to 160 square meters and from 159,000 DM for a four-room house plus a cellar and a garage (which "sold like hotcakes" according to one owner) to 259,000 DM for a two-story house with six bedrooms. Hohenbuchau offered five models, from three-bedroom units to studios of 67 or 79 square meters.

In a typical suburban Neutra house in California, its free plan traverses a generous site with an easy-going elegance so that many sides of the house can open up to the landscape. At

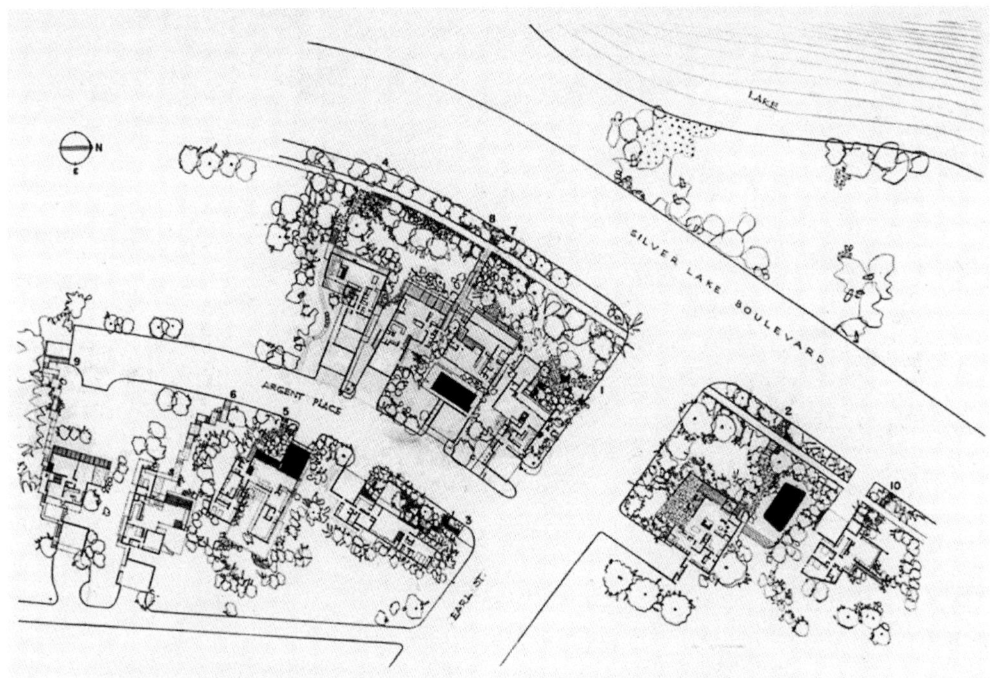

Neutra's famed Silver Lake Colony of ten homes overlooking the Silver Lake Reservoir in Los Angeles, designed between 1948 and 1961.

Bewobau, every move is compact and scaled down but still provides a sense of flowing space. The glass walls linking garden and house are used judiciously rather than with abandon, acknowledging the climate and alert to the implications of being a next-door dwelling. The ubiquitous spider leg is here, used sparingly but also as an indispensable element in its role of expressing the profound umbilical connection between human habitat and earth. With the spider leg composed of a wood beam attached to a steel column, Neutra clearly calls out that these are two different materials by his articulated connection, an articulation he does not voice when the connection is wood-to-wood. Bewobau's language is classic Neutra at its most sophisticated. He sustained the plane and material of the interior wood ceiling to the outdoors to pull the site into the house and extend the house into the site. As with many other housing schemes, he stepped each connected unit back so each unit is expressed individually but its privacy and views enhanced. As with the Mosk House 30 years earlier, a wood fascia hugging the building wall breaks free and continues in space to delineate a sheltered outdoor room.

Schools

Neutra's schools also show a clear link to Rush City Reformed. The "Ring Plan School," so named because the school is laid out in a circle, breaks the old model of a school as a three- or four-story masonry box with double-loaded corridors, each classroom isolated. Neutra's relaxed one-story ring gave each classroom ground-floor access: to the outdoors on both

"New-Idea Class Rooms," sketch, Emerson Junior High School, Los Angeles, 1937

sides of the room and to a protected space in the middle. As a footprint the circle minimized land use.

Schools were one area in which scientific research confirmed his intuitions about the relationship between lighting and learning (or productivity in the work environment). When Neutra designed the Ring School, he introduced clerestories to balance lighting. He suggested that if every detail in the classroom were analyzed, including "minor" details "such as the variation in reflectivity of tiltable desk surfaces, learning would improve." Neutra eliminated fixed desks, so that each child could move his or her desk to hear or see better. He objected to the sole use of vertical blackboards, arguing that children learned more easily close to the ground, as the earliest *Homo sapiens* did. His intuitive rethinking of school architecture was later confirmed by educational studies, but it also made him only more determined to see research applied to architecture. Neutra believed strongly that children benefited from "nature near." When an exasperated school board threatened to cut down some trees at Kester Avenue School because birds nesting there left droppings on faculty cars, he threatened suicide accompanied with plenty of publicity. He got his way, gleefully reporting that "It worked – the trees are still there, and the birds in them, too." Each classroom had an outdoor area, separated only by a wall of upfolding (which later became sliding) glass doors, so that children and teachers had immediate visual and physical access to trees and sky; deep overhangs ensured play could continue despite rain. In publicity photographs, Neutra always arranged chairs in a circle that straddled indoors and out, emphasizing the change from fixed desks in rigid rows as well as the new integration with outdoor space. The teaching role changed too, becoming less exclusively focused on the front of the room and more physically active.

Neutra was not the first or only architect to reconsider school architecture. In England, Maxwell Fry and Walter Gropius designed Impington Village College (1937–39) just outside Cambridge. The school's design also placed classrooms at ground level, both creating new potential for community, and providing each room with bilateral daylight.

The Ring Plan School proved to be a robust prototype for many of the schools Neutra designed, beginning with an addition to the Corona Avenue School (1935) and the Emerson Junior High School (1937), and carrying over into work by Neutra and Alexander, such as Palos Verdes High School (1961) and the Richard J. Neutra School at the Lemoore Naval Air Base (1961), where the Ring Plan School became reality. Whether with his own firm or with his partners, Neutra designed over 25 school and university projects, primarily in California but also in Bangladesh, Pennsylvania, New York, Guam, and Puerto Rico.

Puerto Rico: A Blend of Concerns

Puerto Rico was an important time and place in Neutra's career. In February 1944 he was hired to lead a group of architects in a huge renewal project for what was a U.S. territory. Their brief was staggering: 2,500 rural classrooms in 150 locations, community centers for skills training, health-care centers, and an airport. The semitropical setting he fell in love with during his two-year assignment was idyllic in its geographical beauty but a sharp contrast to the desperate illiteracy, disease and malnutrition he encountered. Neutra was surprised by the existing building fabric. He expected to find a wise vernacular style that had long ago adapted to the humid climate. Instead he found closed masonry "boxes" which he believed were excellent breeding grounds for airborne disease but fit for little else.

The brief was an ideal challenge for Neutra. Here a systems approach to building was not a luxury but a necessity. Structures had to be put up rapidly, on a very lean budget, and still be able to withstand hurricanes and wind storms. Referring once more to Loos' ideal of "lastingness," he argued that reinforced concrete would mean the hospitals in Puerto Rico would compare with any in the world for longevity. For flexibility, he ran electrical services outside the concrete so they could be changed as needed in the future. Neutra had a long-standing interest in health-care settings, and now he needed to design several hospitals, ranging from 300 to 600 beds each.

To exploit breezes, he eliminated any double-loaded corridors in favor of single corridors with covered passages on one side, not only to eliminate static air but also for psychological reasons. "I thought the restlessness of patients in poorly ventilated wards adds more to the nursing load than anything else, and truly overburdens the nerves of the attendants also ..." he wrote in *Architecture of Social Concern in Regions of Mild Climate*. He earnestly suggested that since "coffee and rum were usually served for recuperation after bleeding, blood banks could be pleasantly connected to a general refreshment pavilion." This was also part of Neutra's effort to know and use local practices to engender

Eagle Rock Park Clubhouse,
Los Angeles, 1953

positive associations with health care so that people would be more willing to be inoculated. This was the pragmatic "realism" in biorealism.

For the Puerto Rico schools, he designed a system of modules: simple, minimal classrooms that could stand alone or in connected rows, built with unskilled labor. As with Channel Heights, he provided scenarios for conventional construction using timber and concrete block (with no formwork required) or for using prefabricated concrete beams (functionally superior, and form lumber could be recycled). The rooms consisted of two solid side walls, a rear wall with a large, glassless clerestory opening with louvered metal "earthquake shutters," and a front wall that could open entirely by pivoting up from supporting columns. In this one design move, Neutra accomplished many things: the wall in its alternate horizontal position now shaded the side of the classroom closest to the opening. The opening *per se* provided ventilation, and the sense of shelter by the "porch" evoked local buildings with their deep porches. Finally, the instant porch opened up to a patio, which Neutra counted as part of classroom square footage, thus justifying smaller floor dimensions for the rooms themselves. Neutra used a long concrete "spandrel" beam on the long sides of the classrooms, which in turn supported the roof beams, and left the spaces between the roof beams open to the breezes that would flow out through the rear opening, a technique he used in the Tremaine House in Santa Barbara, where the roof appears to float above the glass walls.

For his community centers he followed the social custom of the "Village Fountain," grouping buildings around it. The town size would be determined, he suggested, by "the maximum walking distance we shall choose to tolerate from the house to the fountain!" He advised teaching schoolchildren to wash plates right after eating, and for the schools to install electric fans near their kitchen doors to discourage flies. Thus what Puerto Ricans received was not only flexible kit-of-parts designs for many building types but also whole sets of instructions on how to improve their lives, which was to Neutra the architect's heroic but fundamental job description.

The Eagle Rock Playground Clubhouse

This minimalist pavilion in a large public park, winner of a national AIA award, is both intellectually rewarding as architecture and a superb community facility. Since its completion in 1953 it has been used non-stop for proms and plays, as a meeting hall, and as the focal point for several athletic organizations in the neighborhood. It is also a finely proportioned composition in asymmetry, whose broad horizontal planes and overhangs contrast with the precise rhythm of thin steel columns that sometimes function as spider legs. The deep overhangs are also an expression of generosity for children playing underneath them in rain or hot sun.

The structure consists of a light steel frame clad in stucco and brick. Three sides open at will, which fosters its enduring flexibility for different uses. The main hall has wide lift-up doors on the east and west, which encourages activities to flow between indoors and out, and emphasizes the idea of a light, transparent shelter with minimal intrusion from structure. To support the large overhang on the east, Neutra employed the same strategy as he did for the balconies of the Lovell Health House by suspending the overhang's roof beams with slender steel hangers from the cantilevered beams of the tall main hall. Dion Neutra pointed out that the columns "supporting" the deep porch were placed there later by park officials who, believing the cantilever would fail, inserted the clumsily detailed steel columns thus re-introducing the collision hazard for children, which the original design avoided. On the north side, a stage opens up either to the main hall, a small "club and crafts" room on the east, or to an outdoor amphitheater set into the base of the hills rising to the north. The stage is separated from the amphitheater by a pool and landscaping designed by Garrett Eckbo. The amphitheater has a sense of permeable enclosure created by lengths of walls that are set wider apart as they process up the hillside, tying the composition and the low mountains together. The clubhouse manifests Neutra's gift, as Dione Neutra often said, for creating architecture not as an arbiter of human behavior but as a neutral canvas charged and primed for human endeavor.

PROJECTS 1928–1968

JARDINETTE APARTMENTS

with Rudolph Schindler
5128 West Marathon Street
Los Angeles, California, 1928

According to an unbylined front-page-center article in the *Journal of Commerce* dated September 24, 1927, it was the Architectural Group of Industry and Commerce, Neutra's deliciously awkward title for his sometime early partnership with Rudolph Schindler, which prepared the drawings for three "towering" apartment blocks with "many startling departures from the more conventional architectural designs ..." Only one was built, the Jardinette Apartments. A number of features excited journalists: a new elan for Hollywood, the projecting balconies which "would yield the fragrance of many flowers," the "ultra-violet plate glass"; the reinforced-concrete framing which allowed ribboned windows to run the entire perimeter of the H-shaped, four-story building; the rooftop terrace. Or so it appeared: Neutra was publicly scolded in the exhibition catalog for the Museum of Modern Art's 1932 show on modern architecture, because he had painted the horizontal bands between the windows black, a gesture curator Henry-Russell Hitchcock interpreted as willfully deceptive because it visually indicated the windows were uninterrupted. (However, Neutra used paint to introduce strong contrasts for other reasons than structural deceptions for his entire career.) By summer 1928, the *Christian Science Monitor* and the *Los Angeles Examiner* were citing only Richard Neutra as the author of the Jardinette Apartments. The windows proved to be problematic with bankers: it was difficult to find loans for a structure whose "windows on each floor went round the corners instead of being broken by corner posts in the style of precantilever masonry" wrote the *Monitor* reporter. That area of Hollywood never achieved that promise of grandeur, nor did Los Angeles become an urban city of "cliff dwellers" as the media and Neutra himself had forecast. But the building still serves a role as vital housing stock for a multiethnic community.

The lobby's concrete floor was stained a brilliant "Cherokee" red, the same red that Frank Lloyd Wright introduced to many Modernists, including Neutra. The lobby featured a beautiful, large skylight that spanned the entire four-story height, from the roof to the lobby.

After almost a century, the drama of the black-and-white exterior has returned, as part of the rehabilitation of the entire building. It is striking that the Lovell Health House and the Jardinette Apartments, polar opposites in many ways, share 2025 as their year of rebirth. View facing southeast.

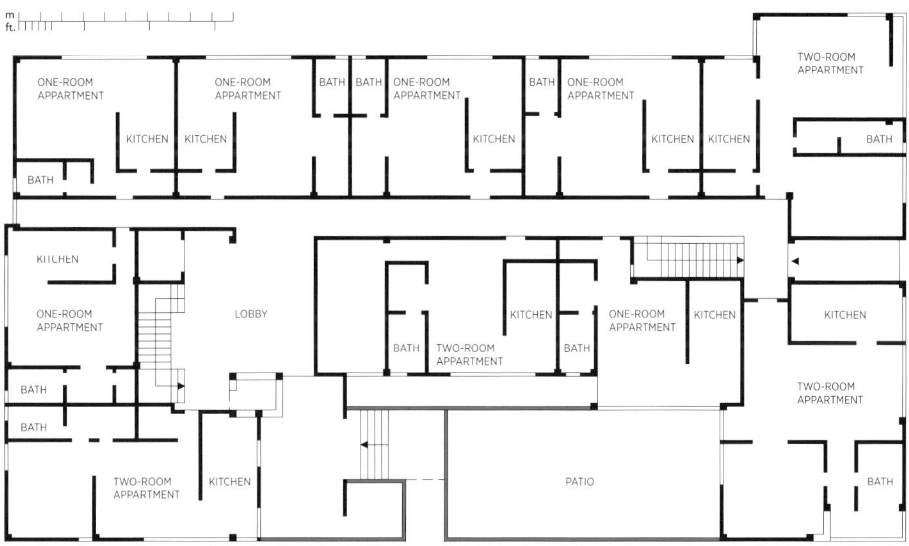

LOVELL HEALTH HOUSE

4616 Dundee Lane
Los Angeles, California, 1929

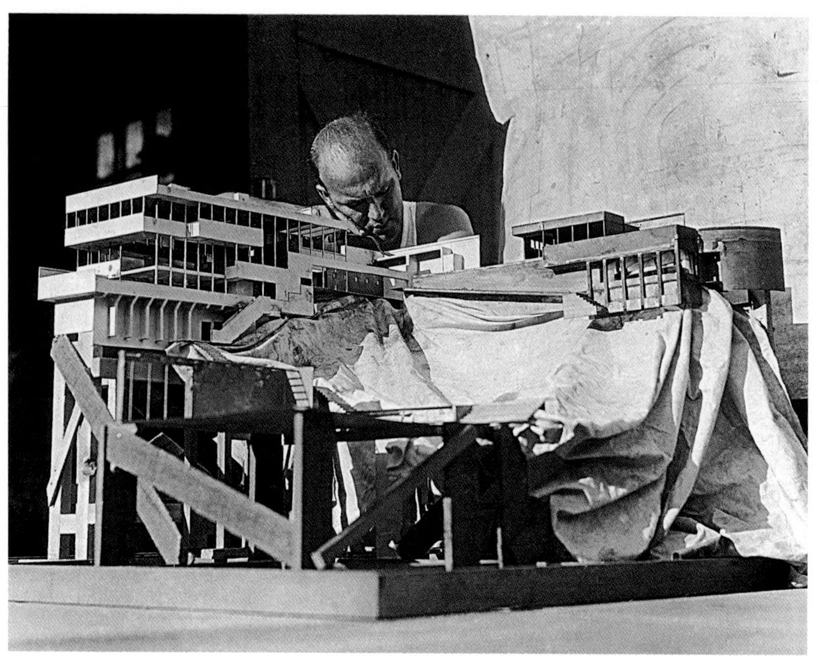

Previous: So daring that no contractor would touch it, forcing Neutra to take on the role, the glass, steel, and lightweight concrete house cantilevers above the steep canyon below.

Above: The elaborate, beautifully crafted model was featured in the legendary 1932 exhibition on the International Style at the Museum of Modern Art, New York.

Opposite top: Upper level floor plan. Neutra insisted on labeling the three bedrooms "living rooms."

Opposite bottom: The long monumental walk to the entrance feels like a walk across the valley below.

In 1962, 33 years after it had been completed, Neutra was invited by Bethlehem Steel to photograph the Health House. He hadn't visited the house in so long he was startled by the lushness of the landscaping. "The steel building has been described in all its details in many publications around the globe, where it has been paralleled with the automobile, especially the Studebaker, President's Straight 8 of 1928, designed in 1927," he wrote in August that year. (The advertisement purred, "Richly appointed, strikingly modish body lines – as handsome a car as ever skimmed the boulevards.") "It is queer and ridiculous," he continued, "to see this car pictured side by side with the Health House, which has not aged at all in its spirit ... Ideally speaking, if [man] would be properly housed, if all the knowledge and insight based on current research was worked into a health house, it is hard to see why it would have to change every spring and fall like ladies' hats. It should inconspicuously support all its organic processes that underlie human life and all steel framing, all shot concrete, all plate glass are not a matter of fashion but an instrument of supporting vitality." Neutra was delighted that the car was "long, long ago on the rubbish pile" while the building's stylistic resilience pleased him not only as "an artist, but as an investment counselor," which he believed was also the architect's role.

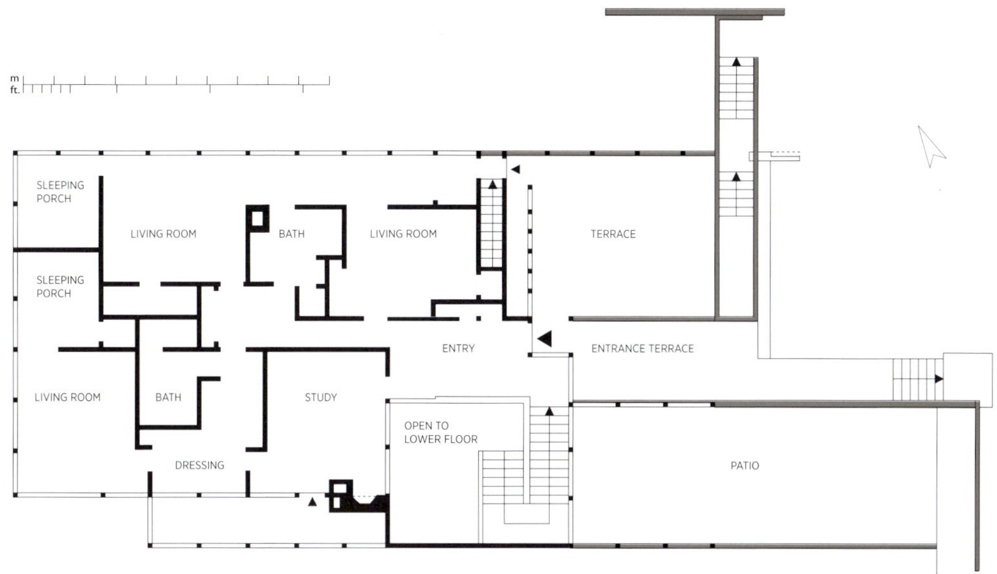

m
ft.
SLEEPING PORCH
LIVING ROOM
BATH
LIVING ROOM
TERRACE
SLEEPING PORCH
ENTRY
ENTRANCE TERRACE
LIVING ROOM
BATH
STUDY
OPEN TO LOWER FLOOR
DRESSING
PATIO

4616

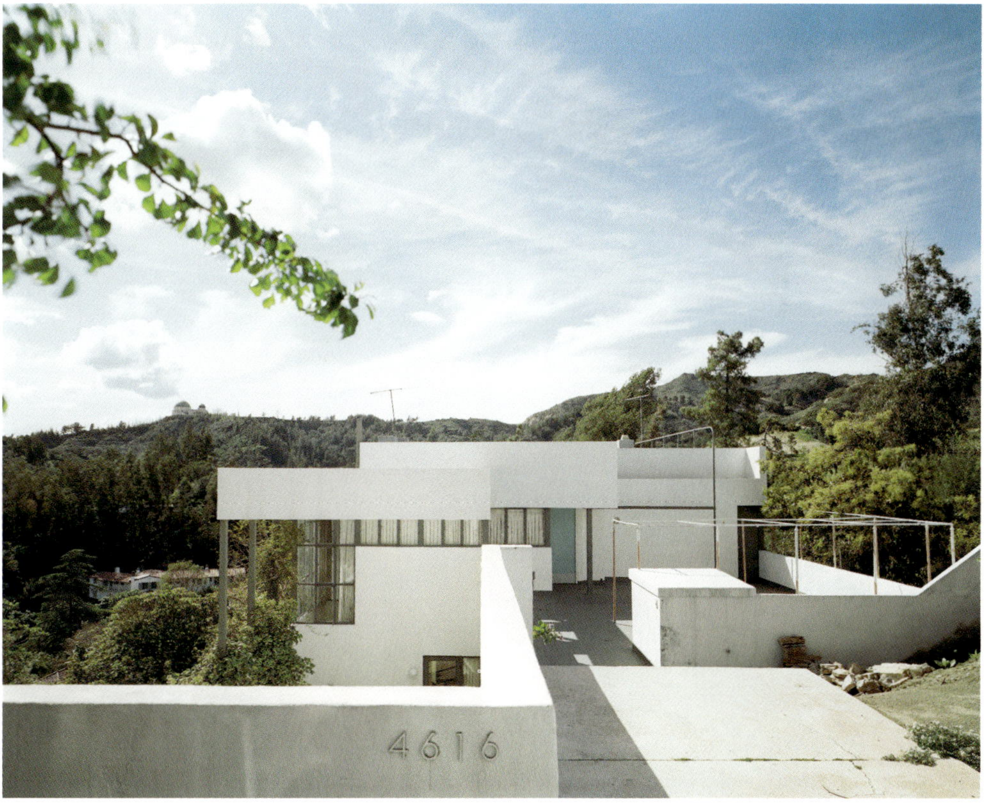

What emerges from early construction photographs is of course the gradual appearance of an avant-garde building, years ahead of its time, whose final clarity belies its complicated frame. Surely one of the most exciting images is one of naked steel in which the steel casement windows, attached to impossibly thin vertical metal stays, float amidst the larger steel columns, the I-beams of four-, eight- and ten-inch depths "electrically welded" to open web steel trusses that supported corrugated metal underneath insulating decks. What is equally clear, however, is that with such a radical new paradigm Neutra would have to design the process of construction as well. For Neutra that meant becoming a general contractor to reduce costs, inspire the workforce of 70 odd men, and apply the commercial methods he learned in Chicago and while writing *Wie baut Amerika?*. Even the scale of the scaffolding was amazing for a residential building: to handle the concrete being mixed at the top of the hill, he designed a long wooden shoot – looking something like a log flume ride – both steep enough to keep the concrete flowing and long enough to go out from the hilltop 200 feet, to where the building would one day look as though it were barely tethered to the hill. Neutra created a "measuring fence" on which numerals and letters designating the coordinates of his unit system were painted. Lines of thread were stretched, intersecting points for the grid of four-inch H-section columns were plumbed

Below: Neutra's shifting planes of solid and void emphasize the composition's strong horizontality.

Opposite: Neutra flips the Renaissance concept of the *piano nobile* by designing a monumental staircase leading down, not up, to the public spaces.

Note the window framing: when relaxing in one of the Neutra-designed lounge chairs, one's eye-level view into nature is uninterrupted. Operable casement windows are above the view windows.

Below: Floor plan, LR level. Originally open, the porch was first intended as a dance floor before it was enclosed to become the dining room.

Bottom: Floor plan, pool level. The lowest level includes the nursery play area, originally open, later enclosed, and now restored.

Opposite: A magical swim can be had in the pool, back and forth: into the light of the canyon and back into the dark underbelly of the house.

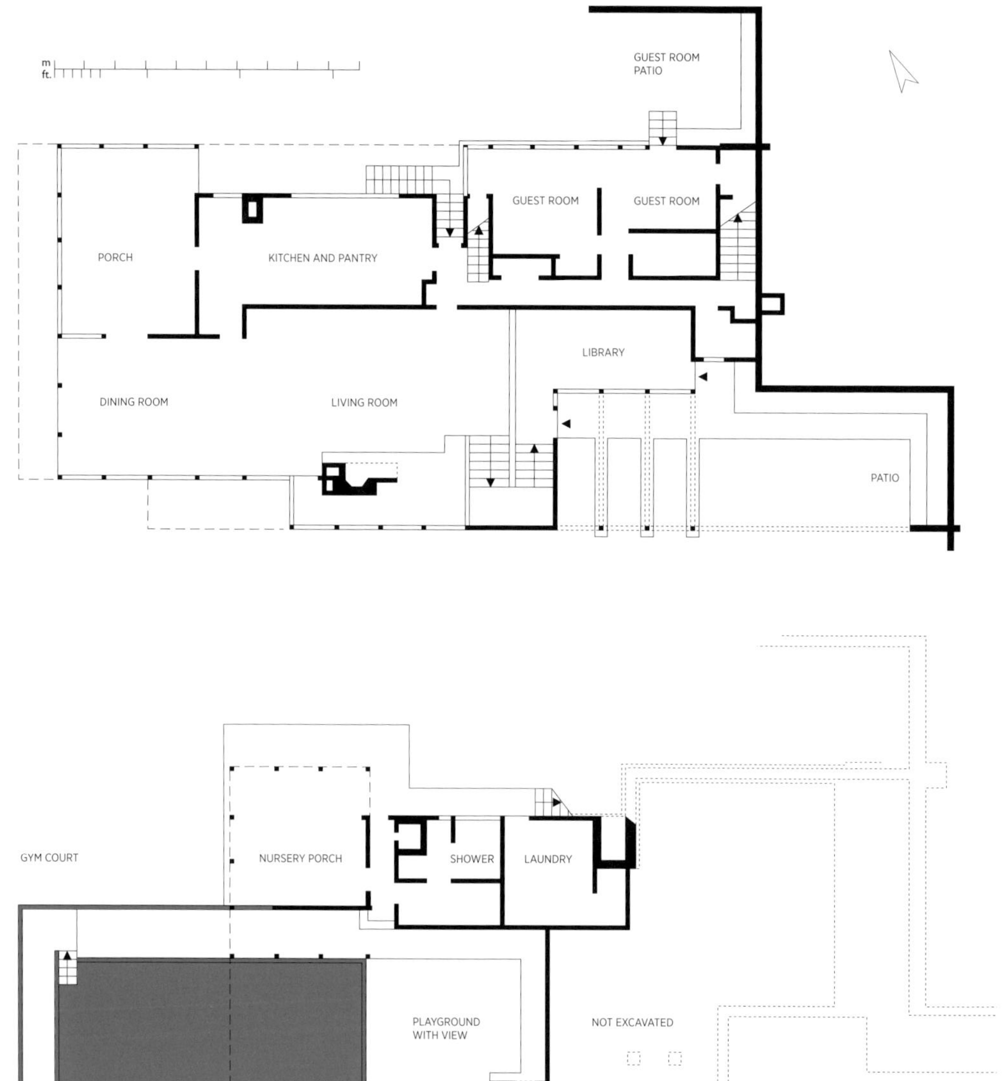

down to the ground and the trench excavation started. The foundation also supported the pool in a steel and concrete cradle that minimized the number of individual foundations for the transmission of load to the rugged landscape. It was highly custom work, and expensive. Just before leaving for his round-the-world tour, on May 15, 1930, Neutra calculated the total bill for the Lovell Health House at $58,672.32. His fee was $5,450; the balance due him from Philip Lovell was $413. He was anxious to see the now famous building properly maintained, and left the Lovells instructions: "I now wish to remind you that in order to keep a cement topping over a composition roof waterproof it is desirable that the surface be sealed once a year by means of a waterproofing liquid like Sealex in two coats ...," adding that he was off to "bring the gospel of new architecture to the heathens in the Far East." Of course, he shortly learned that Japan had far more to give than receive, as his writings show.

VDL RESEARCH HOUSE

Van der Leeuw Research House
2300 Silver Lake Boulevard
Los Angeles, California, 1932

Neutra intended that his new family complex be an experiment both technologically and spatially. It was a case study house in materials and an urban live-work prototype, a laboratory that feels much more spacious than 2,300 square feet. Neutra chose a site strikingly similar to that of his patron, the young Dutch industrialist Kees van der Leeuw, whose Rotterdam house overlooks the Kralingse Plaslaan. The Neutra home occupied a slightly sloping 60′ x 70′ plot of land a few hundred feet from Silver Lake, the name referring to both a beautiful reservoir and a hilly residential neighborhood not far from downtown Los Angeles, now widely known for its dense thicket of brilliant small houses by Neutra, J. R. Davidson, John Lautner, Rudolph Schindler and by Gregory Ain, H. H. Harris, and Raphael Soriano. These last three architects all worked for Neutra on the ground-floor drafting room of the first VDL in the 1930s. The asymmetric H-shaped complex elegantly resolved a very demanding program. Like a sophisticated kit-of-parts, it elastically responded to a number of different occupancies, from draftsman's apprentice to music groups to family member. To coin Neutra's words, that program included a "minimum family

Previous: View north toward the San Gabriel Mountains. Overlooking the Silver Lake Reservoir to the west, the tiny rooftop structure in 1932 was rebuilt in 1966 with an elevator and glass walls after the fire in 1963.

Above: Facing Edgewater Terrace, the 1966 elevation includes the 1939 guesthouse, left, and the 1966 garage, right.

dwelling with kitchenette and studio in the rear; a bachelor's dwelling; living quarters with dining room, kitchen, lake porch and separate bedroom wing ... a workroom basement ... children's playground, two roof terraces, two garden courts." Like the second VDL, there are two doors at the entry of the two-story main structure, one to the north leading to Neutra's office and studio, the other leading to the family wing upstairs, where a roofed outdoor patio with its low black leather seating separated the living and sleeping quarters. The "web" leg of the H joining west and east wings contained a maid's room (where a small open terrace is located now); a miniscule bedroom, assigned to a variety of small boys over the years, starting with Raymond Neutra; a laundry/bathroom, and a dressing area that doubled as indoor play area. The H-shaped footprint of the compound's connected volumes pushed its ends out to the two streets it faced front and rear. The strategy permitted Neutra to fill in the remaining spaces with outdoor rooms, thus assuring each room access to nature on two or more sides. Just as he had cleverly interpreted the newly established building and zoning codes to allow him to build out almost to the sidewalk

Facing the Silver Lake Reservoir, the 1932 building accommodated a busy office below, living space above. Note the extension of the terrace, above, to shelter the entrance: a nod to what would become the spider leg.

for the main 1932 building, Neutra presented the guesthouse to the building department as a garage to qualify him again to build out to the setback. An integral piece of the design, the 1,333-square-foot guesthouse was completed in time for Christmas 1939. It contained a living/dining room measuring 16′ x 23′ and a kitchen, and cost $4,300 to build, Neutra wrote. One of its main features was the set of three glass-and-steel sliding doors which opened almost the entire west end of the living room to the garden whose paving was insulated. Exterior soffit lighting recessed into the overhang joined interior and exterior at night, further linked with similar lighting to the larger dwelling. (In exhibition photographs it was labeled "Dione Neutra's Guesthouse." In those same images, giant palm branches appear to crane their necks deep into the guest living room, so unnaturally long and horizontal that it appears someone just beyond camera range must have been holding them, as though determined to press home the idea of seamless outdoor/indoor integration.) In contrast to other projects, designed and executed as individual projects, this house and site were reconfigured throughout the Neutras' lives. Lighting, furniture, wall surfaces changed, appropriate to an architect-inhabited experiment that was meant to respond to changing conditions over time. The post-and-beam wood structure burned down on March 21, 1963, while Richard and Dione were traveling in Europe. The guesthouse was spared. The maid's life was saved because though her door to the patio was already burning, she could flee through the other door leading to the outdoors. Dion Neutra must be credited for doggedly retrieving many of the water-sodden office files and materials from the destroyed home. With his father's aid and oversight, it was he who designed the second VDL (the Neutra VDL Studio and Residences), rebuilt on the same footprint.

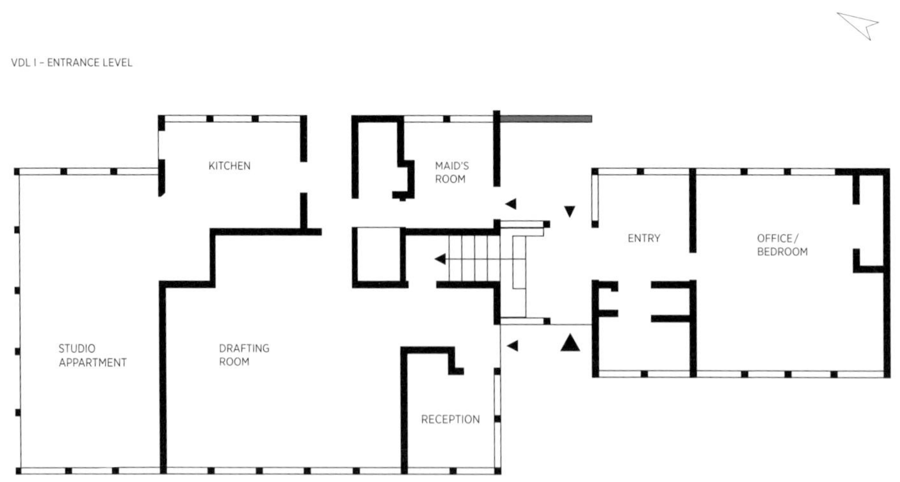

m
ft.

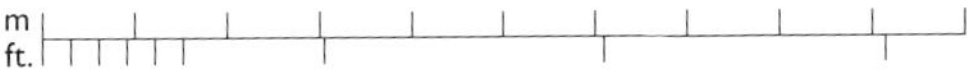

VDL I – GARDEN LEVEL

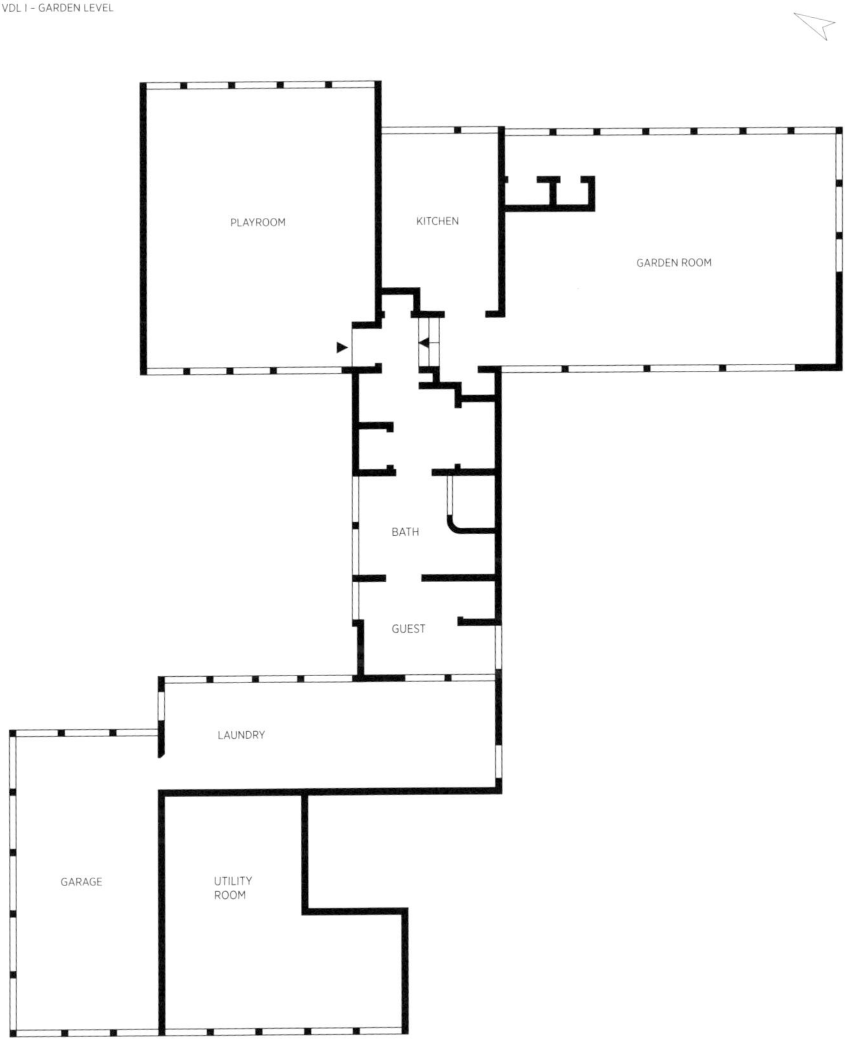
PLAYROOM
KITCHEN
GARDEN ROOM
BATH
GUEST
LAUNDRY
GARAGE
UTILITY
ROOM

Above: The sensual living room with the Neutra-designed "Cantilever Chair" had folding doors that opened onto a patio with low, built-in black leather sofa. View facing south.

Right: Adding to the sensual feeling of the outdoor patio, the wainscoting was clad in midnight-blue-baked enamel-steel panels, never seen before in a residence. Neutra had persuaded a manufacturer to develop the product. View facing west.

The living room of the 1939 guest-house was an ergonomic delight: communications, power, storage, music, heating, all immediately to hand from the inviting day bed.

ERNEST AND BERTHA MOSK HOUSE

Study for Steep Hillside Development
2742 Hollyridge Drive
Hollywood, California, 1933

Anticipating his "spider leg," Neutra stretched the band of silver wood siding beyond the house ... and well beyond the property line. Neutra adored the Mosks. Older than he, the Hungarians gave him his first job after work slumped following the triumph of the Lovell Health House. They put their trust in the young radical and he delivered. Ernest died a year after the house was completed; Neutra designed his only tombstone for the family.

The once gorgeous, now sad, Mosk House is indeed a seminal work of architecture. First, Neutra still employed the horizontal banding rhythms of the International Style, but instead of white stucco, he now spoke with an American accent: shiplap siding, seen again in the far grander 1938 John Nicholas Brown House. Second, Neutra intended the Mosk House to be the first unit of a hillside community that anticipated his built Silver Lake Colony two decades later. All demonstrated his three-part requisite of common vocabulary, individual character, and unique site response, in the freestanding American house. (Only the Mosk House was completed, and Neutra named the house not after its owner, as publication convention dictates, but as a prototype, a "Study for Steep Hillside Development.") Third, instead of steel as at the Lovell Health House, he used the cheaper VDL strategy that transformed American wood framing know-how. Here a prefabricated concrete joist foundation supports wood posts with diagonally braced wood trusses above and below the window bands. Neutra's "normalized wood chassis," includes 4x4 posts whose locations were based on the two-leaf commercial steel casement windows, whose hinges "precisely fit into the rebates of the posts, windows thus forming an integral part of the skeleton." The lower wood skeleton was clad in "waterproofed insulating slabs of 'Puzzolan'," steam-pressed slabs of wood shavings and Portland cement, while interior walls were clad with Masonite or Celotex. Floors and built-in furniture tops were covered with darkish red battleship linoleum.

The house glimmered with two silvers, with aluminum paint for the shiplap and a darker tone below the windows that anchored the exuberant design to the earth. The two-story living/dining volume breaks the one-story envelope on both the west street side and sharp drop-off on the east. Like many 1930s houses, the "public" ceiling was tall, measuring nine feet, and casements were placed above fixed glass for cross-ventilation. However, it shared an unfortunate early feature with its more glamorous siblings, the Lovell Health and Brown Houses: a southwest glass bedroom wing unencumbered by overhangs.

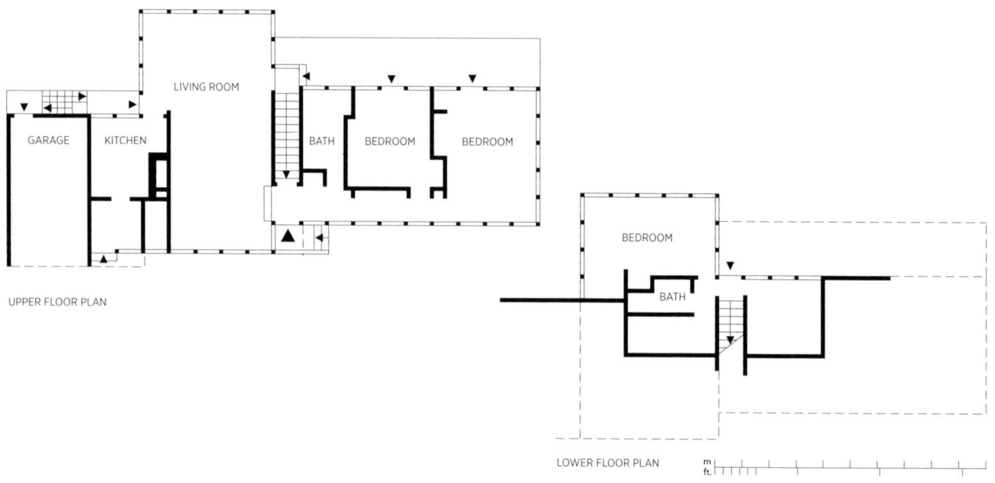

Top: Sited on a steep hillside in Hollywood, the rear elevation offered magnificent views and a deck.

Bottom: Neutra used the same strategy for the Mosk windows as he had done at the Lovell Health House: the lower windows had no partitions to compromise the view when seated.

WILLIAM AND MELBA BEARD HOUSE

with Gregory Ain
1981 Meadowbrook Road
Altadena, California, 1935

In a file named "Early Steel Constructions" Neutra wrote that "the organic structural pattern of the inner skeleton, as with amphibians, reptiles and mammals, brought [me] to get interested also in the contrary successes of nature, the exoskeleton of the beetle." This was a biological metaphor for the Lovell Health House (the mammal) and the Beard House (the beetle). Despite his daring in using the Chicago skyscraper-style steel frame and then spraying it with its Gunite skin, the Lovell approach was costly. It was also conventional in the old equation of frame + cladding = wall. The system he used at the Beard House promised much more: cladding, load-bearing, air-conditioning all in one hard shell that was a pretty low-brow package. This off-the-shelf, kit-of-parts system was devised not by world-famous architects like Adler and Sullivan but by a local man, Los Angeles-based architect/contractor Vincent Palmer, who welded steel panels to corrugated steel roof decking made by the H. H. Robertson Co. In the Beard House, Neutra's load-bearing walls cantilevered from concrete footings, embedded 16 inches, so essentially the walls *were* the foundation, the foundation *was* the wall, "designed to take the lateral stresses such as wind attacks or earth shocks." By then welding the walls to

The all-steel Beard House survived the Eaton Fire in Altadena of 2025, which started in the San Gabriel Mountains rising up behind the house. View facing northwest.

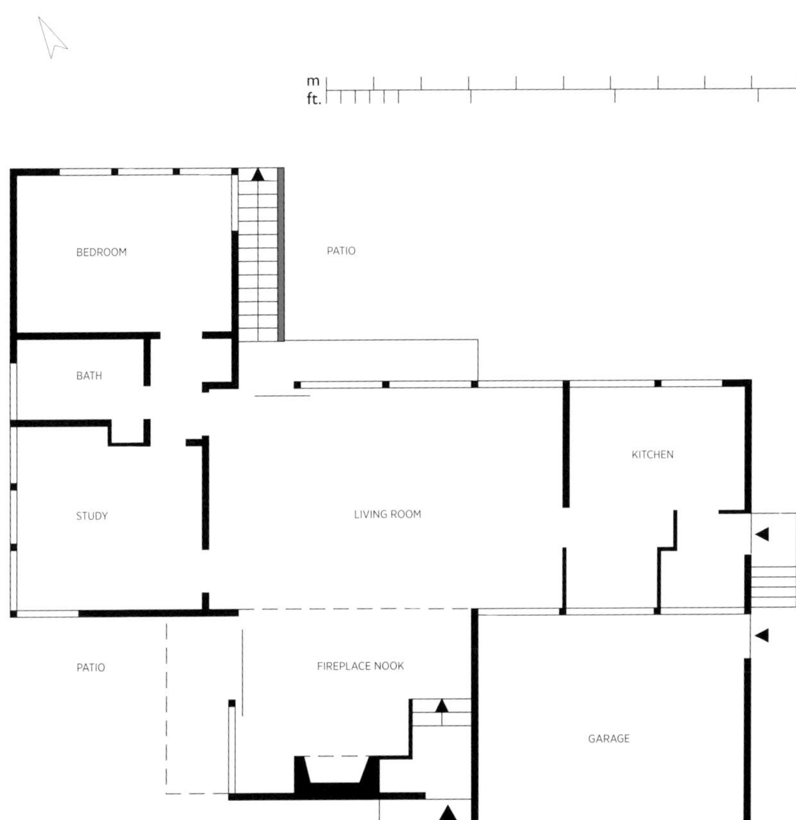

the roof decking and steel bar joists, the system made it very difficult indeed for the building to be ripped off its foundations. The hollow corrugations, Neutra believed erroneously, could also be harnessed to "inhale" cool air from the base of the wall and "exhale" it at the top by inserting small vents. (The vents let rain in, too.) Sited in an area of Southern California notorious for sudden, swift-moving fires roaring down the hills in the autumn, the all-steel house was fire- and termite-resistant. The house was experimental in many other ways. Special glass reduced solar gain. It was also here Neutra introduced what may have been the first domestic U.S. application of commercial ball-bearing sliding glass-and-steel doors (which of course is now an American residential default). The entire structure was originally painted with bright aluminum paint to reflect heat (to the chagrin of Melba and William's neighbors, who complained that it looked like a water tower, an odd comment since such a tower is typically round and tall; in any case the Beards later painted the house a softer gray.) In some ways, the house is a gawky adolescent spatially, as though the passion for the promise of new technology dominated the architectural exercise. It follows the slope of the hill, with the rather cramped entry a few steps below the living room, putting the visitor in an immediately subordinate position to the occupant. The interior of the bathroom can be seen (if one notices) as one mounts the steps. That said, there is something peculiarly alluring and satisfying about the proportions of the little house with its nine-foot-tall ceilings, so that it is often lauded as "eminently livable." In any case, it is the beauty of the intimate landscaping and soaring mountain through the huge expanse of glass beyond that the visitor first sees. (Perhaps intuitively following Neutra's dicta on Gestalt theories of perception, the current owner disabused the bathroom of its original white interior and painted it a dulled brown gray so the eye doesn't stumble on it.) Because the house is now back to its aluminum color, its relationship with light makes the house almost alive, always changing in color depending on the weather and time of day, e.g., a rosy glow at dawn, a rich pewter during rain. As usual, Neutra placed tall windows on the north sink wall of the kitchen with a "full mountain view for the benefit of the housewife" and ran 12 feet of white rubber as a countertop/drainboard, an innovation he rarely repeated because it was too difficult to maintain. The radiantly heated floor, with its air plenum sandwiched between a 12-foot-deep double-shell of diatomaceous earth construction, was to act like one monolithic heat panel, like an updated "ancient Roman bath," Neutra wrote. He also planned ahead for a

second-story study for William Beard, or a roof garden in the same place. (Hence the handsome staircase was placed immediately beyond the 5′ 8″ wide glass and steel door.) He also planned a separate building as a master bedroom addition to the 1,200 square foot house in 1947, but when the Beards insisted on attaching it to the house instead (they did not want to be physically separated from their small children), forcing the occupant to walk through a bedroom, he abandoned the project while they proceeded, paying him $ 500 for his extra labor.

Above: The steel-clad walls, designed by architect Vincent Palmer for industrialist Harold Hansard (H. H.) Robertson in the early 1920s, are hollow, which Neutra believed could facilitate air flow within the walls. Rear elevation, view facing southeast.

Opposite: While indisputably based on industrial components and paradigms, the sliding door (opposite the stairs to the rooftop terrace) is highly custom, as is all the window hardware. View facing west.

CALIFORNIA MILITARY ACADEMY

5300 Angeles Vista Boulevard
Baldwin Hills, California, 1935

This quietly handsome one-story building was built at the same time as the Beard House, and Neutra employed the same H. H. Robertson steel paneling system devised by Vincent Palmer. Since he was on a strict budget, the detailing is more crude than that of the Beard House, and he used exposed Robertson panels as a primary design element applied as classroom dividers, exterior walls and even for stair rails. One porch entry is particularly effective, with horizontal panels employed as a roof overhang – elongated just enough to seem Mannerist – that floats between the clerestory above and window below. Sliding glass and steel doors, very similar to those employed at the Beard House but not as idiosyncratically customized in size, open the classrooms to the outdoors. Skylights illuminate double-loaded corridors. Neutra also used tilting windows in the middle of larger fields of classroom glazing.

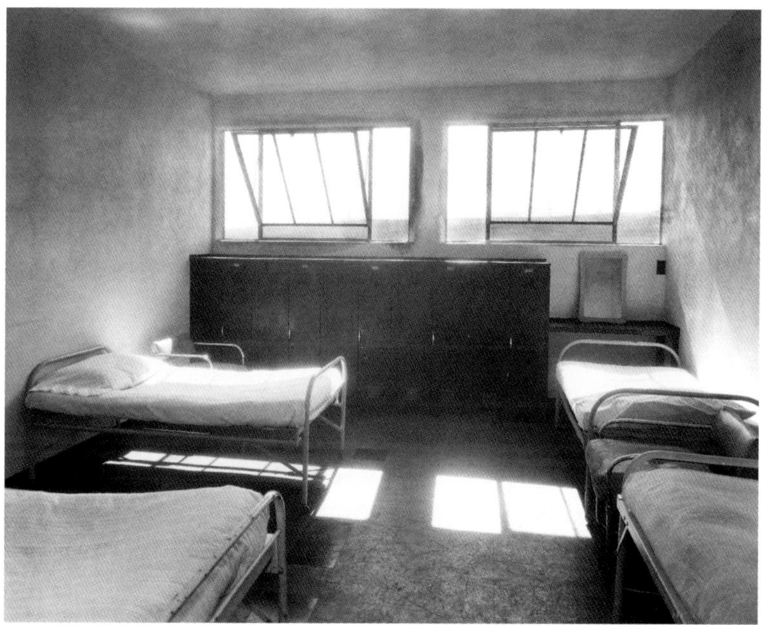

Opposite: Neutra used the same all-steel Robertson system for the austere Academy, perhaps a more predictable building type for such a material than a house. Demolished.

Top: Note the unclad steel decking serving as the overhang, sheltering the huge sliding glass door and walls of glass. The sheer amount of glass demonstrates Neutra's ardent belief in connecting to Nature, even in a strict military environment.

Bottom: The window grouping for the no-nonsense dormitories acts as a "hopper," meaning opening into the room. Unusual in being hinged at the bottom and with their slender, delicate frames, these would definitely not be permitted today.

JOSEF VON STERNBERG HOUSE

All-Steel Residence
10000 Tampa Avenue
Northridge, California, 1935

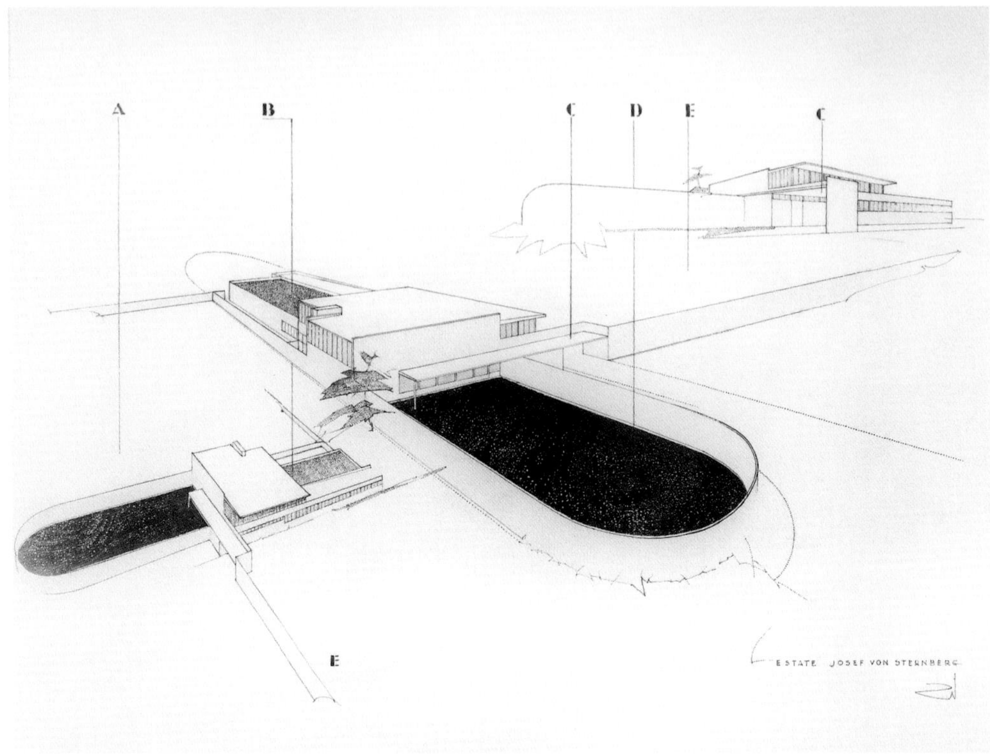

"Were it not for the fact that I dislike creating anything permanent in this part of the world I should have asked you long ago to build something for me," wrote the famous Hollywood director Josef von Sternberg to Neutra on February 18, 1932, on the Paramount Pictures letterhead. Ironically, Neutra built him a house whose building technology ensured a very long life.

Unfortunately this enigmatic house was demolished in 1971, unfortunate because it would have shown an atypical approach for Neutra. It was a grand construct whose hard reflectivity and high curved walls with a 12-foot moat amidst a 20-acre plot all kept the hoi polloi at bay and untidy nature at a distance. "Elaborate illumination and full electric equipment of 100,000 watts, an all-steel wall, steel joist construction with steel sash and exterior plate-glass doors determine the character and appearance of the building," wrote Neutra, referring to the same load-bearing steel Palmer/H. H. Robertson system he used for the Beard House and the California Military Academy.

Above: The rendering shows the three-car garage on the left of the driveway. One space was taller and longer to house von Sternberg's Model J Duesenberg or perhaps his gift to Marlene Dietrich, a Rolls-Royce Phantom 1.

Opposite top: The all-steel villa breaks all of Neutra's rules but obeys all of von Sternberg's. The high steel walls forbid any connection to nature. The moat can be seen as a rejection of humanity.

Opposite bottom: The baroque extremity of the ellipse ennobled a languid procession into the garage.

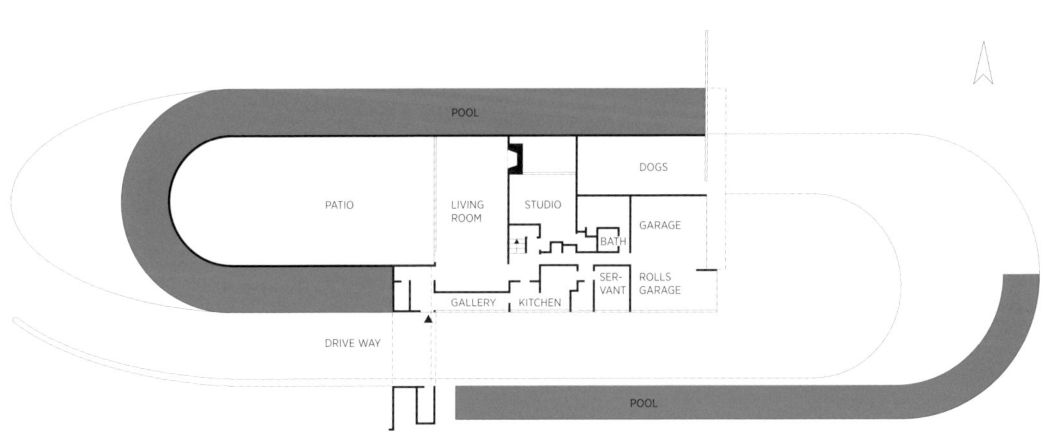
POOL
DOGS
PATIO
LIVING ROOM
STUDIO
GARAGE
BATH
SER-VANT
ROLLS GARAGE
GALLERY
KITCHEN
DRIVE WAY
POOL

The access to the silver-painted building was to the south, whose approach drive was lined by a row of eucalyptus trees, and a second moat to the far south. The driveway led under a *porte cochère* illuminated at night by a ribbon of recessed flush soffit lights; the "elaborate illumination" to which Neutra referred also included light strips used at the tops of interior railings, sandwiching a series of incandescent bulbs between the layers of a typical plaster wall and just below a strip of opal flash glass. (This was a type of glass that Neutra favored because it diffused light well and disguised any single source of light.) One can easily imagine the building at night with its glowing layers of lighting amplified by silver paint, hard surfaces and mirrors.

Paved with black terrazzo, the living room was two stories tall, and on the west end opened to a 68′ x 37′ "*hypaethral* room," also paved with black terrazzo. Neutra's use of the word *hypaethral* (from the Greek, "open to the sky, having no roof") is telling. Well educated, he had both a deep and fluid command of the Classical world. He was so intimate with Greek philosophers and architects as to treat them as intellectual equals well worthy of serious engagement and easy, familiar sparring, thus the use of the word *hypaethral* was not pretentious but the word which succinctly fit the use.

By using single or doubled lengths of the steel decking and extending them as long columns to the roof joists, Neutra was able to achieve a wider six-foot module for the windows and glass slider opening out to the curved outdoor room. This was surrounded by an opaque eight-foot wall, making any vital connection with the immediate landscape quite impossible and contradicting every Neutra dictum about linking the greater context of the site with a building. Like a movie set, the room was to be cooled by artificial rain, which, Neutra wrote, "will descend into a glittering curve cylindering into the patio ..." (probably quite handy given the potential solar gain on a west-oriented patio paved with black terrazzo).

The second story, comprised of the upper balconies of the living areas and the master bedroom suite, had continuous window exposures toward the south, east and north, overlooking the entire estate, replete with a large roof pool for tropical fish. On ground floor, there was only one bedroom in addition to a studio, two rooms for servants, a long narrow gallery to the south, and a two-car garage to supplement the separate, larger garage for the Rolls-Royce.

The second owner was Ayn Rand. There is a great story about her that Neutra contractor Fordyce "Red" Marsh tells. Once when Neutra took a group of people to see the house, she spotted the tall, handsome Red for the first time. She brushed past Neutra and grabbed the unsuspecting builder by the shoulders. "You are the physical embodiment of Howard Roark," she exclaimed. Red knew nothing of the hero architect of Rand's famous novel *The Fountainhead* and was bewildered at her actions. Neutra, feeling excluded, gathered up his group and left.

Opposite: In reinforcing the ellipse, even the driveway was essential to the design. Three, not the typical two, strips of concrete alternate with meticulously manicured strips of grass.

Right: Writer Ayn Rand and her husband, Frank O'Connor, owned the house from the 1940s until 1963.

Opposite: A walkway overlooks the living area and leads to the villa's sole ground-floor bedroom (apart from servants' quarters) and the infamous mirrored bathroom with no locks, tempering outbursts by suicidal starlets.

Above: Von Sternberg insisted that the living room's shiny black terrazzo extended to the terrace (and the blazing Valley sun). The sensual aluminum Deeco chairs were first designed as pilot seats for World War II bombers. After the war, Deeco pivoted to patio furniture: no wonder Neutra loved them.

DOUGLAS FIR PLYWOOD MODEL DEMONSTRATION HOUSE (BRICE HOUSE)

427 South Beloit Avenue
Brentwood Glen, California, 1936

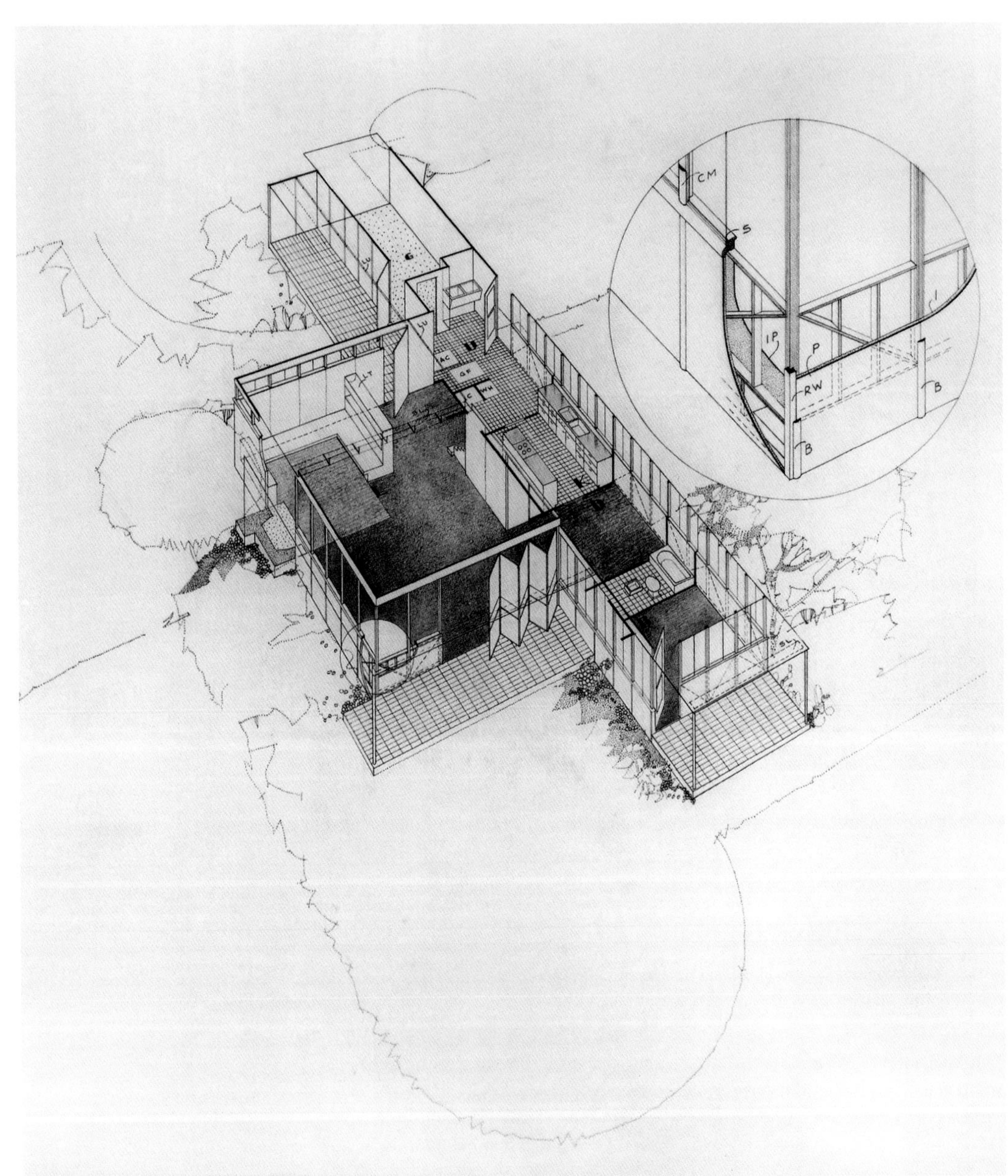

This 1,618-square-foot house was included in an exhibit sponsored by the Los Angeles Building Center of homes using new building materials and methods. Exterior plywood, which Neutra used, had just been formulated with new glues to enhance water resistance. The exhibit itself showed no new architectural impulses, in spirit like a miniature version of the Columbia Exposition of 1893 in that it hearkened back to period styles ... except for Neutra's. He stacked the master suite above the kitchen to create a smaller second story with a generous roof deck. The exterior, with its white-stained plywood panels held in place with metal strips, creates a similar rhythm on the façade as the Robertson panels he used for his all-steel buildings. Neutra's drawings show a careful analysis of the opportunities to cross-ventilate the house in every room, aided by the T-shaped footprint opening rooms to the outdoors. As usual, he adroitly addressed the need to have both a public entrance, steering the visitor through the living room to the view beyond, and a family entrance to the kitchen near the utility room. Like the rest of the model homes, it was raffled off in a free drawing with the stipulation that it be moved. With its light steel frame and demountable panels it was readily reassembled at its new site in Westwood.

Opposite: Neutra's gorgeous axonometric pencil rendering of the ground floor includes the cutaway sketch of the section with plywood skin and wood stud frame.

Above: The gated entrance to this private yard is actually to the left, out of the picture. The primary façade looks northwest across the grounds and past an artist's studio.

Above: Beyond the well-illuminated terrace, you can just make out the original reading nook, with its plywood walls and top-lighted bookcase that acted to both frame the nook and, when entering, to slow visual access to the living room.

Opposite: With the low walls below the rhythm of the large windows, Neutra provided a feeling of security while the folding doors (similar to the VDL's), opening to the terrace, invited liberation.

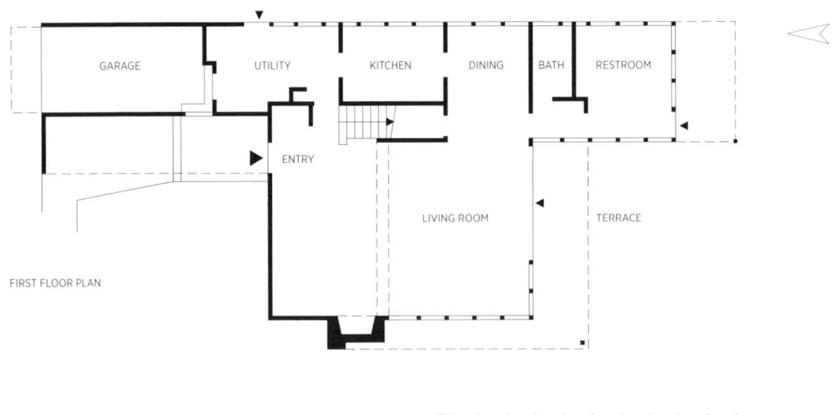

FIRST FLOOR PLAN

SECOND FLOOR PLAN

JOSEF AND GERTRUD KUN HOUSE #1

All-Electric House
with Gregory Ain
7960 Fareholm Drive
Los Angeles, California, 1936

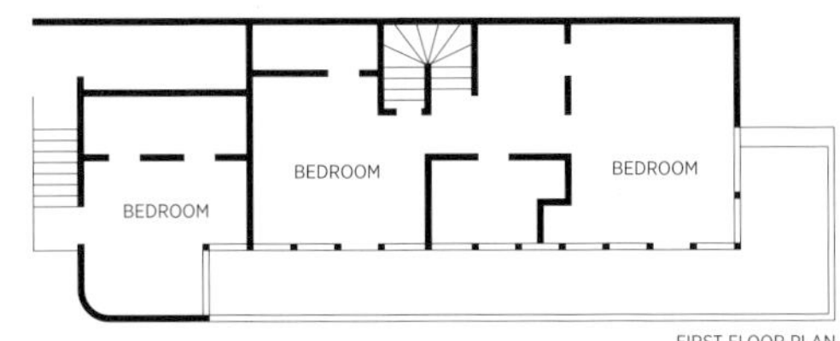

FIRST FLOOR PLAN

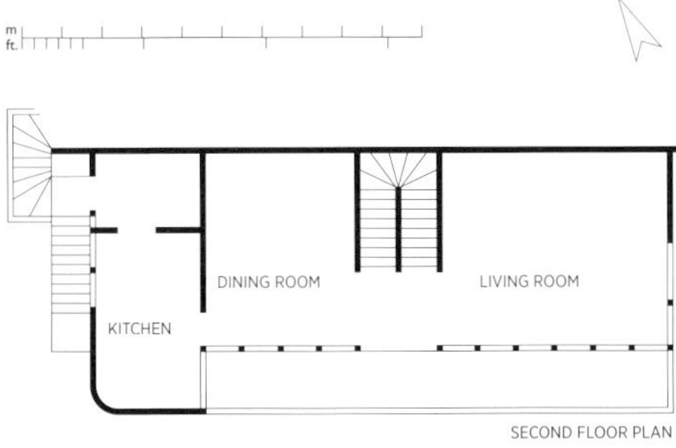

SECOND FLOOR PLAN

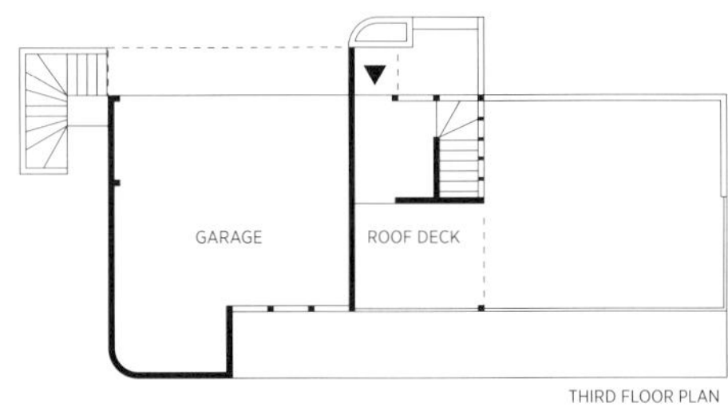

THIRD FLOOR PLAN

This house of "unit-type wood chassis with continuous truss bracing ... follows largely the system developed for the VDL House," Neutra wrote. It was the first house Julius Shulman photographed as an amateur fascinated by what he saw. His work so impressed Neutra that the architect hired the young man for the bulk of his work and helped launch one of the most famous careers in architectural photography. The third-floor entrance and garage were level with the curving Hollywood Hills street; the two floors below each had almost 40-foot-long balconies with a southern exposure over the very steep hillside lot. One unusual feature of the compact kitchen, rendered in tones of "light silver grays to almost white" included a structural glass drainboard and tabletop. Shiny "Indian red" ceilings offset cream-colored walls in a lower bedroom.

Previous: The careful balance of asymmetry – the long, solid wall of white stucco against the silver-and-glass voids of entry and garage – makes Kun #1's façade especially arresting.

Left: The low sweep of an apparently one-story home on Fareholm Drive doesn't prepare one for the breathtaking rear elevation, which hugs the steep slope even as it plunges downward. Recently structurally reinforced, now anchored to the hill, it may be just the place to be during a seismic event.

LANDFAIR APARTMENTS

with Peter Pfisterer
10940–10954 Ophir Drive
Westwood, California, 1937

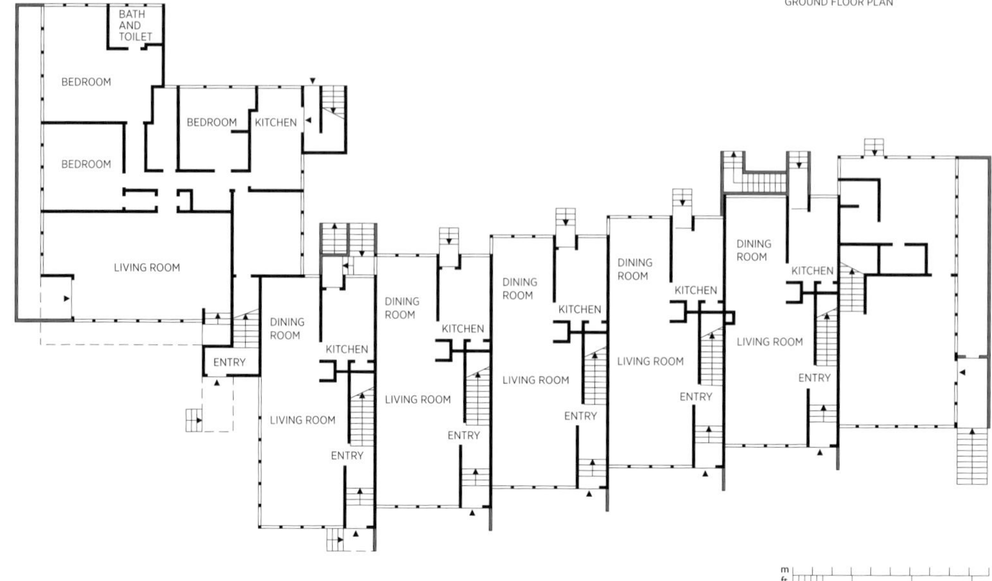

Below: Neutra tempered the rhythmic façade, alternating solid and void, by staggering the units. View facing southeast.

Opposite: The staircase anchors the hinge of the L-shaped building. View facing south.

Neutra anticipated Westwood, the area around the University of California, Los Angeles, would one day be a densely populated neighborhood. But he also recognized that housing such as the two-story Landfair would be a strange sight to most Southern Californians, both in its appearance and as a building type. In its aesthetic of the *Neue Sachlichkeit* – the "New Objectivity" – it looked like a displaced fragment of the flat-roofed designs of the European *Siedlungen* (municipal housing projects). But while multi-residential row housing had centuries of historical precedent in Europe, the Landfair was a foreigner in Los Angeles. A staggered row of six flats with four rooms is sited on the west. On the east, two units with five rooms pivot away from the rest of the composition, their porches facing away from the L-shaped composition for privacy. Each of the row units had a balcony and a staircase leading to a little rooftop penthouse; lower units had internal clerestories to drive daylight deep into the interiors. The sharply contrasting bands of windows and stucco below a fascia of shiny crimped metal, along with the penthouses joined to each other with wooden trellis, established a crisp, uncluttered rhythm on the exterior. Along with the nearby Strathmore Apartments, completed the same year, it was a pioneering, elegant example of the International Style in Los Angeles. It has been UCLA student housing since 1941.

DAVID MALCOLMSON GUEST HOUSE

Mother's House
with Peter Pfisterer
491 Mesa Road
Los Angeles, California, 1937

Opposite: The original rear entrance featured a humble façade enlivened by the elegant Streamline Moderne rooftop ladder "for economy," as Neutra said, and a cantilevered canopy whose length ensured protection even for those not so able-bodied. View facing northeast.

Below: From the street, the original 523-square-foot dwelling "on stilts" presents a series of stepped opaque panels with no hint of the curved, light-filled studio. Nestled amidst the woodland, it was nicknamed the "Baby Grand" because of its shape in plan. Cost: $3,500. View facing west. The bathroom walls were clad in blue Bakelite with aluminum trim.

Neutra called this the "Mother's House," built as a "minimum-house for an old lady as a pied-à-terre." David Malcolmson's mother must have been in good shape: the "ocean view terrace" for this little house is only accessible by a curved brushed aluminum ladder. The main feature for the one-story structure is the curved living room cantilevered out over the hill and pushing out from a higher volume behind it. The façade is comprised of a deeper-than-usual metal fascia, stucco, and a band of deep casement windows around two sides of the living area.

GRACE LEWIS MILLER HOUSE

Mensendieck House
with Peter Pfisterer
2311 North Indian Avenue
Palm Springs, California, 1937

Though now corraled by a busy and built-up Palm Springs, this brilliant little Modernist pueblo started off surrounded only by scrubby windswept brush. It was treasured by its owner, a highly astute and courageous woman who transported a European "Mensendieck" exercise technique to the desert and then taught it to high-end clients in this house/studio when the city was new and raw. One elegant glass corner of the structure emerges from its stucco shell to be embraced by a sheltered reflecting pool; on the other studio side, large translucent lights of glass, not quite floor-to-ceiling, serve to illuminate the moving body while conferring privacy upon it. Over recent years it has been badly treated, winding up as a down-at-the-heels rental, and is slowly being restored by its new owner. But the house still retains many original features and details that speak volumes to a profoundly rich collaboration between architect and sophisticated client, not least a quality of taut serenity about the place. It was she who insisted the ceiling be raised six inches for a feeling of lightness; it was he who knew the reflecting pool would cast dancing light on the white ceiling, who designed bedroom cabinetry calibrated precisely to house specific hats and sweaters. Nearby, an onyx makeup table bathed in northern light through the translucent panes.

Above: The studio's translucent windows granted privacy to Miller's clients. They were also functional, reducing cleaning by obscuring the impact of the dust blowing from the northwest.

Opposite: Neutra's jagged stones mark the boundary between the desert and domesticity.

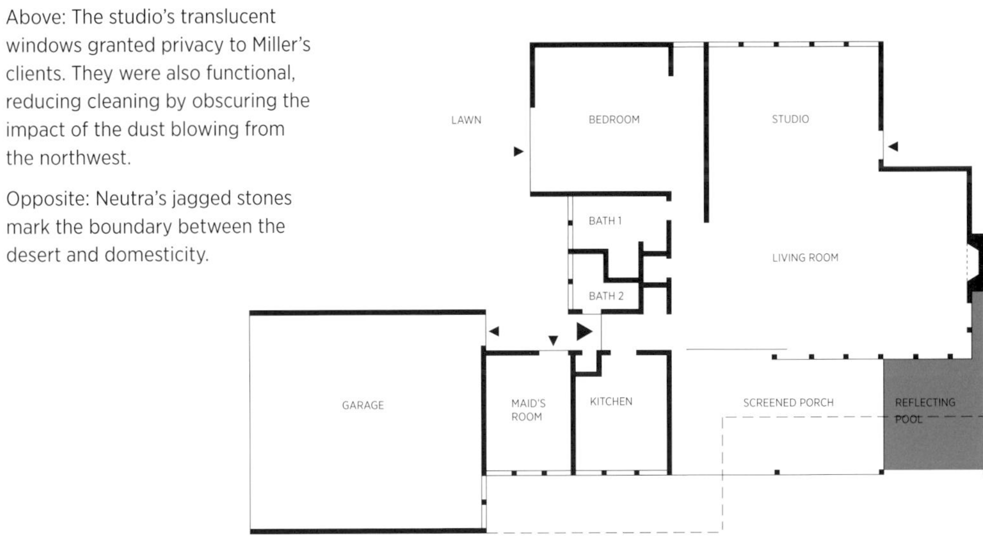

LIFE

Mrs. Miller reading on the screened porch in the late afternoon, the desert heat tempered by the reflecting pool.

STRATHMORE APARTMENTS

with Peter Pfisterer
11005 West Strathmore Drive
Westwood, California, 1937

The last photographs in *Wie baut Amerika?* (1927) are of Lloyd Wright's guesthouse under construction in Palm Springs. The project deeply impressed Neutra, who also admired the pueblo dwellings he saw in Albuquerque and in Taos with their stacked dwellings and rooftop terraces. That approach is apparent in the Strathmore, in which Neutra had a 50 percent interest. Though it was completed in the same year as the Landfair Apartments, and uses the same vocabulary of ribboned steel casement windows and white stucco, it is altogether different in design strategy. While the elegant Landfair looks to contemporary European precedents of repetitive units connected in single-depth rows, the Strathmore comprises four buildings, six larger, two-bedroom, two-bath apartments and two one-bedroom flats. The sloping site, with four different levels and abundant landscaping, ensures not only privacy but individuality for each unit, none exactly alike in section or plan. Though the composition tightly interlocks volumes that are stacked on top of one another, with some changing ceiling heights inside, the effect affords relaxed, easygoing living. In organization, two smaller buildings with rectangular footprints are situated on the upper part of the sloping site. The two lower, slightly larger

Opposite: Neutra loved the challenge of hillsides. The monumental staircase is flanked by the garages – white stucco with aluminum-silver doors – that anchor the composition as it rises up the slope. View facing south.

Above: Each entrance is different, some near the staircase, some set back, always oriented to ensure privacy when coming or going. View facing north.

buildings relax and spread out over the site as broken U-shaped volumes facing each other. A spine of central stairs connects all the flats, which may also be reached more privately through two lengths of stairs at the north and south ends of the lot. The Strathmore has always enjoyed social cachet and boasted a number of famous residents such as Orson Welles. The playwright Clifford Odets and the film star Luise Rainer lived there; earlier, as friends of the Neutras they stayed at the VDL guesthouse; Dione reported that she and Richard tried to be good listeners when the famous younger couple argued. On February 16, 1938, Luise wrote to Neutra saying she "bit by bit went closer to such modern places [as the apartments] just like one comes to examine a wild animal, with jitters and a certain curiosity ..."

Above: The bookcase (at the top of the drawing) prevented an unobstructed view of the brilliant daylight beyond.

Below: Ground-floor site plan. The seventh and eighth flats form the two westernmost apartments (top of the plan).

KITCHEN
LIVING ROOM
BATH
BEDROOM
BEDROOM
LIVING ROOM
KITCHEN
BATH
BEDROOM
BEDROOM
BATH
BEDROOM
KITCHEN
LIVING ROOM
BEDROOM
BATH
KITCHEN
LIVING ROOM
KITCHEN
LIVING ROOM
BATH
BEDROOM
BEDROOM
GARAGE ON THE GROUND FLOOR
LIVING ROOM
KITCHEN
BATH
BEDROOM
BEDROOM
GARAGE ON THE GROUND FLOOR

m
ft.

Above: The bookcase/closet at the entrance was top lit, light bouncing off the ceiling, and painted a high-gloss finish.

Below: On February 16, 1938, Luise Rainer wrote to her friend: "The clearness, the long lines of windows which allow ... the eye to rove out far, far ... There is nothing disturbing to the eye, nothing disconcerting to your mind. I have never felt as happy as I feel now living in your building. I thought you might be happy too, to know about this! Most cordially yours ..."

JOHN NICHOLAS AND ANNE BROWN HOUSE

with Peter Pfisterer
Fishers Island, New York, 1938

This celebrated, long-demolished house haunts many Neutra lovers because it is so maddeningly real in two dimensions: the documentation on this huge, 14,510-square-foot house is formidable. The house was really the witness of the combined ambitions of a powerful, unyielding, socially prominent client, John Nicholas Brown, and a young, brilliant architect in forging an exceptional house. It blended the sensibilities of that old East Coast tradition in America of the enlightened Puritan with the European-born Neutra's equally spiritual calling to a new architecture. (Brown even sometimes spoke in the language of Nathaniel Hawthorne's early 19th-century New England when he wrote Neutra to say he was "glad you raised the stud of the main portion ...") The result was a severe, elegant house which defined luxury as efficiency, permanence, and unimpeded access to the Atlantic Ocean, to sailing, to the sea. Certainly some of Neutra's specifications were blithely democratic, such as Marlite, a shiny, Formica-like surface he

Opposite: The multi-vehicle garage introduced the severe palette and rectilinear organization of the composition.

Above: The Brown family named their beloved summer home, painted with three coats of aluminum paint, "Windshield." The corner closest to view was the Music Room, the most important room of the house for this family of music lovers.

used in scores of bathrooms regardless of the client's socioeconomic status. Buckminster Fuller's two prefabricated units forecasted new bathrooms for all. But this was also a house whose kitchen included a remote control gramophone radio, dimmers and weather instruments. Tellingly, the clocks were to have "plain and simple hands." It took money and persistence to track the right clock manufacturers down to find such Shakeresque hands.

The ground floor, reserved for a play and cinema room, garage and servants' quarters, is dug into the hillside at the north. The top floor of the long three-story house stepped back so it was wrapped in terraces and overhangs; Neutra seized and reestablished the ground plane on the two upper floors so that each has its own layered series of transitions and independent relationship to the outdoors. Like the Mosk House of 1933, this house is sheathed in horizontal shiplap; like the Kun House of 1936, a strong vertical volume anchored the horizontal bands allowed to run freely to the south, held in check by the discipline of the rhythm of the windows. The heart of this house was a music room, but what a music room! It could be thrown open to the ocean in two directions by means of three massive aluminum-framed glass doors. It was also art gallery and family gathering place. The devotion to it was so fierce that its voice became the standard for making every architectural decision in the house, such as the size of the

sections for the windows. (Neutra and his collaborator Peter Pfisterer kept hammering at window manufacturers to devise less bulkly modules.) Some of the materials used in the house were extraordinary, sometimes reminiscent of the "original" VDL House in Rotterdam in their ethereal qualities. In the dining room, blue rubber floors contrasted with white velvet drapes, silvery gray woodwork and steel gray "grass" cloth. The 9 x 9 walnut block flooring in the music room lined up with the window divisions precisely. Even the ribbons for the aluminum venetian blinds were heraldic: in the dens they were lacquered; in the guest rooms they were salmon-colored. Neutra not only handed out six-page exams to prospective contractors querying their work ethics and understanding of local building habits; he also supervised the landscaping. "All rigid regularity should be avoided," he wrote September 18, 1937. The planting should "densely portion off certain outdoor rooms ... In general the landscaping should emphasize, underline, support, accentuate the natural circumstances of the site and should work against them as little as possible. The building on the other hand is by necessity a geometrical construction and an interesting contrast to the organic exfoliating informality of the landscaping surrounding it." The wood-framed house suffered heavy damage in a hurricane in 1938; was restored and structurally improved, and burned down in 1975.

Opposite: The Browns' fierce embrace of modernity and technology didn't exclude color but celebrated it; the luxe bathroom.

Below: After two tries, Neutra designed the table and the white leather chairs to the Browns' delight. The tabletop was alcohol-proof lacquer, while the base supports were U-shaped laminated plywood supports with a chromium base and longitudinal center tube. The adjacent built-in buffets were clad in white linoleum.

In 1937, Neutra and Brown selected aluminum rather than steel for the long expanses of windows. While novel, Neutra's quest for ever-leaner frame dimensions along with the softer material contributed to the building's hurricane damage just a year later. View of the second-floor gallery.

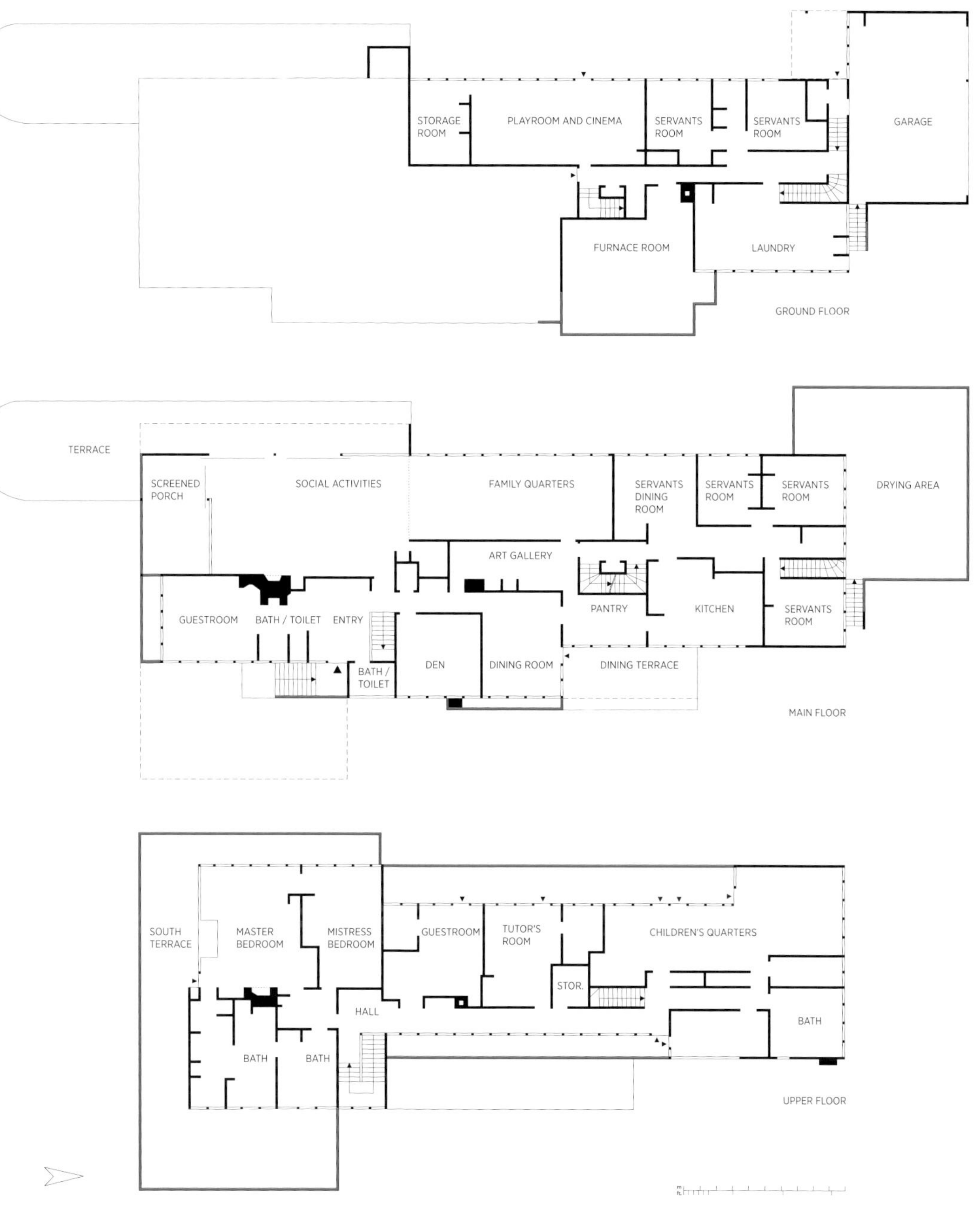
STORAGE ROOM
PLAYROOM AND CINEMA
SERVANTS ROOM
SERVANTS ROOM
GARAGE
FURNACE ROOM
LAUNDRY
GROUND FLOOR
TERRACE
SCREENED PORCH
SOCIAL ACTIVITIES
FAMILY QUARTERS
SERVANTS DINING ROOM
SERVANTS ROOM
SERVANTS ROOM
DRYING AREA
ART GALLERY
PANTRY
KITCHEN
SERVANTS ROOM
GUESTROOM
BATH / TOILET
ENTRY
BATH / TOILET
DEN
DINING ROOM
DINING TERRACE
MAIN FLOOR
SOUTH TERRACE
MASTER BEDROOM
MISTRESS BEDROOM
GUESTROOM
TUTOR'S ROOM
CHILDREN'S QUARTERS
STOR.
HALL
BATH
BATH
BATH
UPPER FLOOR

ALBERT AND MILDRED LEWIN HOUSE

with Peter Pfisterer
514 Palisades Beach Road
Santa Monica, California, 1938

Built for the powerful and highly cultured movie mogul Albert Lewin, this 6,727 square-foot house with a four-car garage and separate wing for the cook, maid and chauffeur cost a princely $65,000 in 1938. In plan the original design is much like a ship cutting through the waves. Because the lot was so narrow (the building measured 35′ x 110′) the living room was curved with panels of glass to create a 180-degree view, like the Sten-Frenke House. There were two separate master bedrooms on the upper floor and two dressing rooms for ocean bathers on the ground floor. Though built for a wealthy man, the original interior materials were humble and standard Neutra repertoire: silver gray carpet blended with battleship linoleum. The terraces were integrally colored concrete and the kitchen built-ins were aluminum-trimmed linoleum. Neutra instructed that all exposed metal and steel window frames be painted a dark blue. The interior specifications for paint are incidentally interesting: to achieve a semi-gloss finish, four coats of paint were needed, starting from flat paint, with the third coat 50 percent enamel. The last coat, 100 percent enamel, was to be rubbed down with pumice. In the 1970s restoration was done by Charles Gwathmey and in 1998 Steven Ehrlich Architects made an addition to the house.

Opposite: The original south elevation, a play of solids and voids. View facing west to the ocean.

Below: The rounded ellipse of the all-glass sitting room offered a 180-degree sea view.

Bottom: View facing east towards America's fabled "Riviera Row," home to movie moguls whose equally famous architects included Julia Morgan, Wallace Neff, and Paul Williams.

Above: Recalling the opulent von Sternberg bathroom, the master bath was a study in mirrors amidst polished aluminum, Moderne lighting, and chrome.

Opposite bottom: The extended overhang provided a protected walk to the garage.

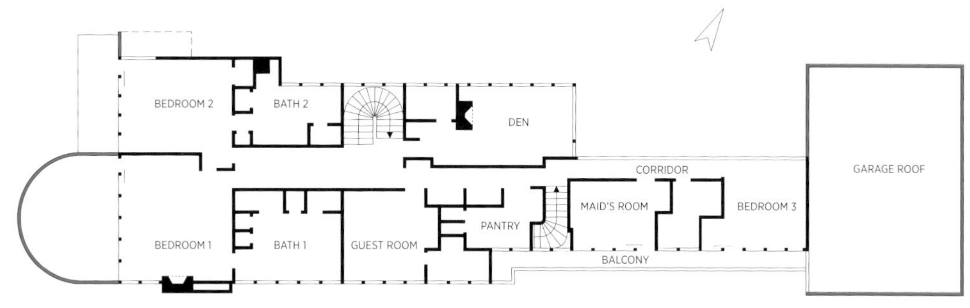
BEDROOM 2
BATH 2
DEN
CORRIDOR
GARAGE ROOF
MAID'S ROOM
BEDROOM 3
PANTRY
BEDROOM 1
BATH 1
GUEST ROOM
BALCONY

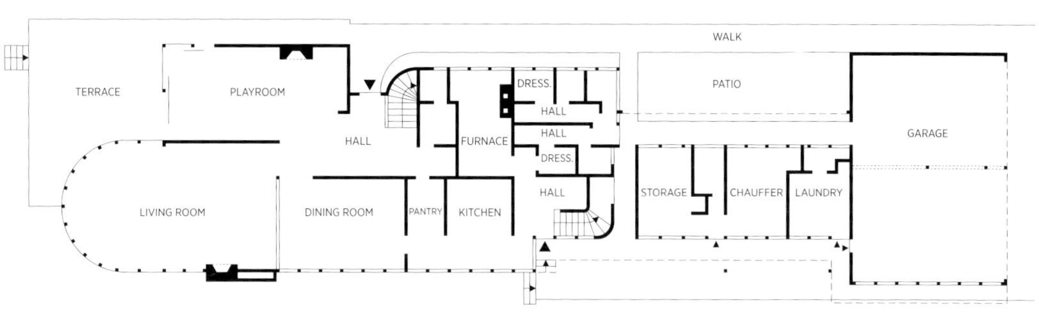
WALK
TERRACE
PLAYROOM
DRESS.
PATIO
HALL
HALL
FURNACE
HALL
GARAGE
DRESS.
HALL
STORAGE
CHAUFFER
LAUNDRY
LIVING ROOM
DINING ROOM
PANTRY
KITCHEN
m
ft.

HARRISON AND JESUSITA ("HESS") MCINTOSH HOUSE

1317 Maltman Avenue
Los Angeles, California, 1939

This spare, lean house steps back from its quiet Silver Lake street in a series of low, compact volumes wrapped in horizontal redwood siding. The disparity between private and public agendas is extreme: the house is irrevocably closed to the public and exuberantly open on the view side. Even though the house only cost $3,800, it has very special details such as its unique casement windows. Here is the first indication of a move away from the ubiquitous steel casement windows towards a larger module, and thus to a slower "tempo." Neutra described the windows as "frameless, exactly fitting into the milled and rebated members of the standard unit-type timber chassis. The special crank handles are reached through the structural 4x4 posts." In plan the house is three cubes; in section the house is broken into two levels, with kitchen and living quarters opened to the south and west with glass, where a terrace wraps the house. Even in this little house, Neutra provided four separate entrances, ensuring easy use no matter the agenda.

The McIntoshes' son, Harrison Edward, suggested Neutra as the architect to design the family home. The precocious son, who assisted Neutra with the design, went on to fame as a ceramic artist. View facing west.

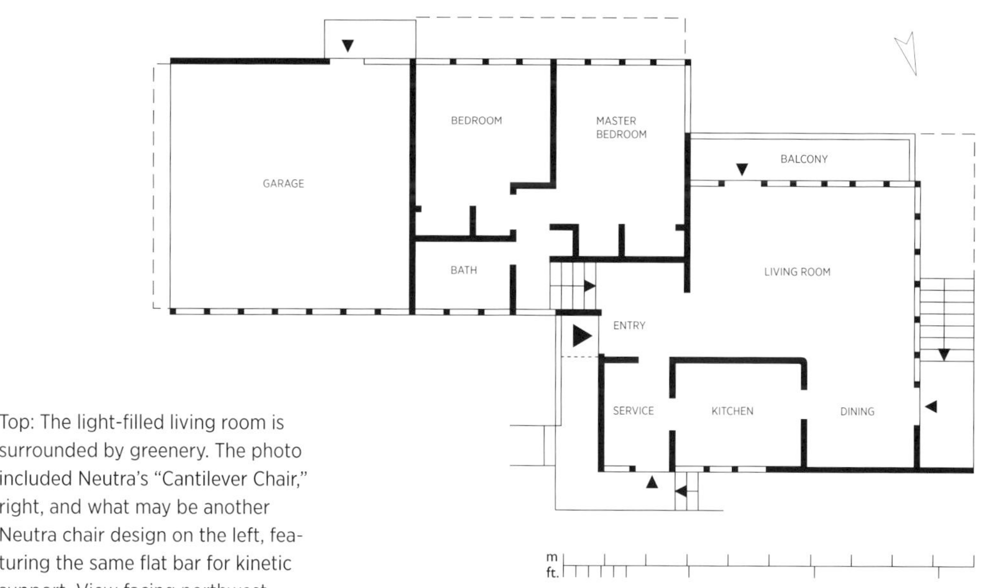

Top: The light-filled living room is surrounded by greenery. The photo included Neutra's "Cantilever Chair," right, and what may be another Neutra chair design on the left, featuring the same flat bar for kinetic support. View facing northwest.

PACIFIC RESTAURANT COCKTAIL BAR FOR LEIGHTON INDUSTRIES

with Peter Pfisterer
417 South Hill Street
Los Angeles, California, 1939

A very elegant and sophisticated setting with aluminum light troughs running down the length of the bar, and concealed downlighting in the wall above the curved booths. Material choices included terrazzo floors, birch, chrome and glass.

WARD–BERGER HOUSE

3156 Lake Hollywood Drive
Los Angeles, California, 1939

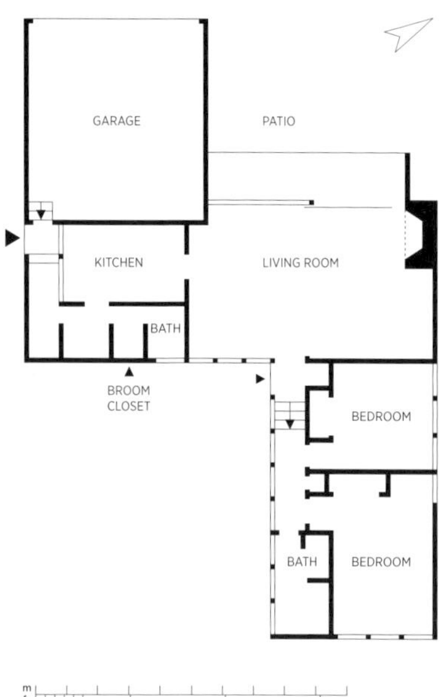

The fireplace and the tall trees beyond are the first things the visitor sees from the public entrance located at the crotch of this small, L-shaped split-level Hollywood house, and it is exemplary in showing how Neutra employed brick on different planes for different purposes. Long, smooth, crisply edged Roman fire brick, which resists higher temperatures, was used for the walls of the fire box. The fireplace walls of rougher, white-painted common brick contrast sharply with the dark-painted wall parallel to and slightly behind it, bringing the fireplace forward while the wall recedes. A mere double depth of the exposed flat brick used for the hearth runs outdoors, where it terminated the northeast end of the patio and serves to integrate indoors and out. Perpendicular to the wide

sliding glass-and-steel doors, the fireplace itself was located so that the hearth addressed both living room and patio simultaneously.

The longer garage wall serves to give the patio a protected quality. Overlooking the San Fernando Valley in the Hollywood Hills, the house was built for a working couple for about $5,000. It was packed with low-maintenance built-ins which also prevented any "feeling of restriction" in the little building, Neutra wrote.

In contrast to the openness of the living-room area with its glass wall, a high bank of clerestory windows is punched into the southern (entry) wall of the private bedroom wing, giving it an International Style feeling. It is also reminiscent of the north sides of the Dunsmuir Apartments completed two years earlier by Neutra's former employee, Gregory Ain, which shares the same contrasting flavor between opposing north/south faces of a building.

Opposite top: The small house is one of the most intact of all Neutra projects with an astonishing repertoire of original colors and features, down to an unusual steel countertop device for disposing kitchen scraps through two metal flaps (sealing off odors) leading down to a tiny waste bin accessed by a small exterior aluminum-painted door, for easy disposal from the street.

Above: The dwelling marks a significant change in Neutra's approach to single-family homes, more relaxed, evidenced by the gigantic opening out to the terrace, a total of 19′ 7″, to integrate indoors and out.

EVANS PLYWOOD BUILDING

Lebanon, Oregon, 1940

This building was designed not long after plywood was beginning to be widely distributed, and was intended as an advertisement for its versatility. It housed the offices for the plywood mill located close by, with apartments on the second floor for overnight visitors to this rugged rural area. The principal façade contrasts ribbons of light (plywood) and dark (glass). The long clerestoried wing to the right is the garage. Neutra introduced a curve into the balcony wall of the outdoor sheltered deck, and then pulled the parapet of the balcony away so that the ribbon seems to float freely, disengaged from the building, thus clearly stating plywood's ability as a pliable skin. On the ground floor, 32 feet of glass block for privacy run the length of the façade to the door. In contrast to the bone white of the sheathing plywood, the undersides of the plywood decking glisten, stained a rich gold and finished with high-gloss spar varnish. Indoors, light stained plywood wall panels are laid horizontally. Neutra created a very subtle banding effect by changing the depths of the panels towards the tops of the walls from two feet to one foot and then down to about six inches where they meet the bottoms of ceiling vents. A 14-foot section of the living room walls slides back as an opening onto the porch.

Opposite: Charles and Ray Eames probably introduced Neutra to Evans Plywood, which produced the famous leg splint that they invented when living in Neutra's Strathmore Apartments.

Right: In 1940, Lebanon became known as "Evansville" because Evans built the biggest plywood mill in the world there. The view out from corporate headquarters was protected by a curvaceous overhang.

Below: The kitchen was designed to serve executives in the plywood industry.

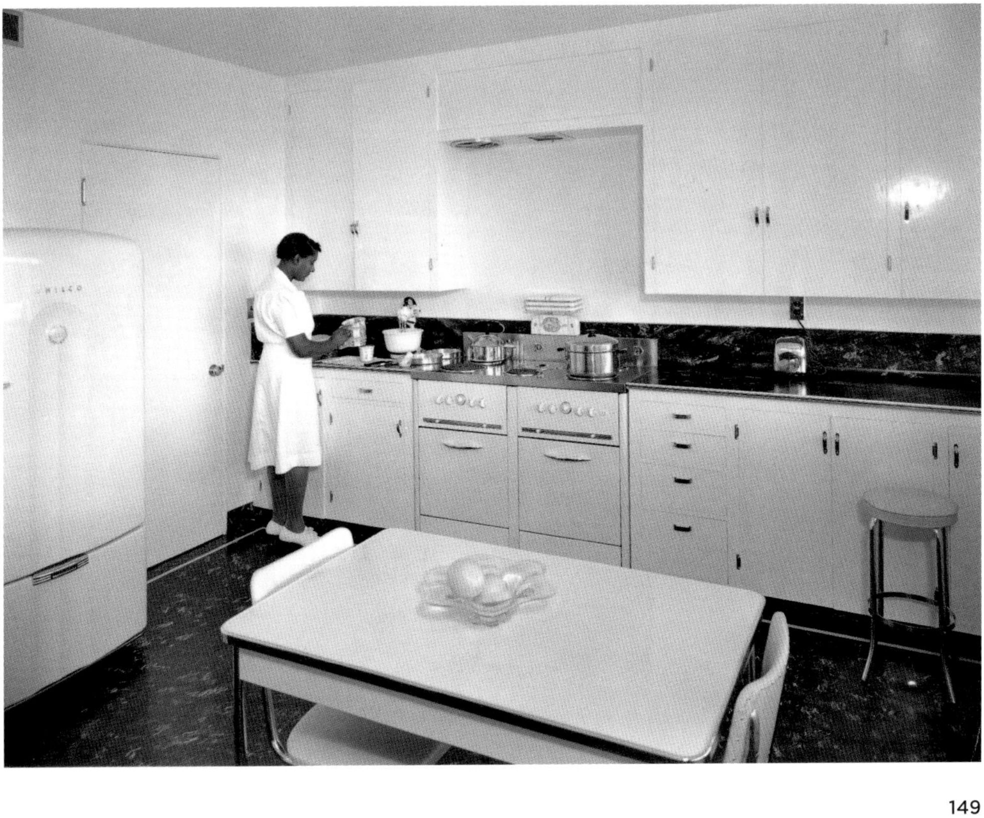

SIDNEY AND JULE KAHN HOUSE

66 Calhoun Terrace
San Francisco, California, 1940

Previous: Balconies on every floor ensured one of the most exclusive views of the Golden Gate Bridge in San Francisco. View looking east across the San Francisco Bay.

Right: A solid west-facing plane ensures privacy for the solid-void rhythm of the windows wrapping the house, whose elevator to the living room and wood-paneled bar on the top floor included shelving to transport people ... and their drinks. Kahn got around: a 1934 gossip column in *The San Francisco Examiner* referred to the financier as "one swell guy." View facing south.

The Kahn House looks precariously perched high on a rocky outcrop on Telegraph Hill overlooking the Oakland Bridge. This lavishly appointed urban, vertical house of four stories helped inspire Neutra's "Dual-Use Table" also known as the "Camel Table," which could "elastically" double as coffee or dining table in confined spaces. Mr. Kahn, the stockbroker-owner, also purchased the low, very deep chairs similar to those designed for the Lovell Health House, chairs reminiscent in their subtle perversion of scale of the work of contemporary furniture designer Roy McMakin. The house, framed combining steel and wood, has protected view balconies on the top three floors. It included a library and film projection room. The interior materials included Japanese ash and Philippine mahogany for built-ins and two tones of chartreuse green for the upholstery.

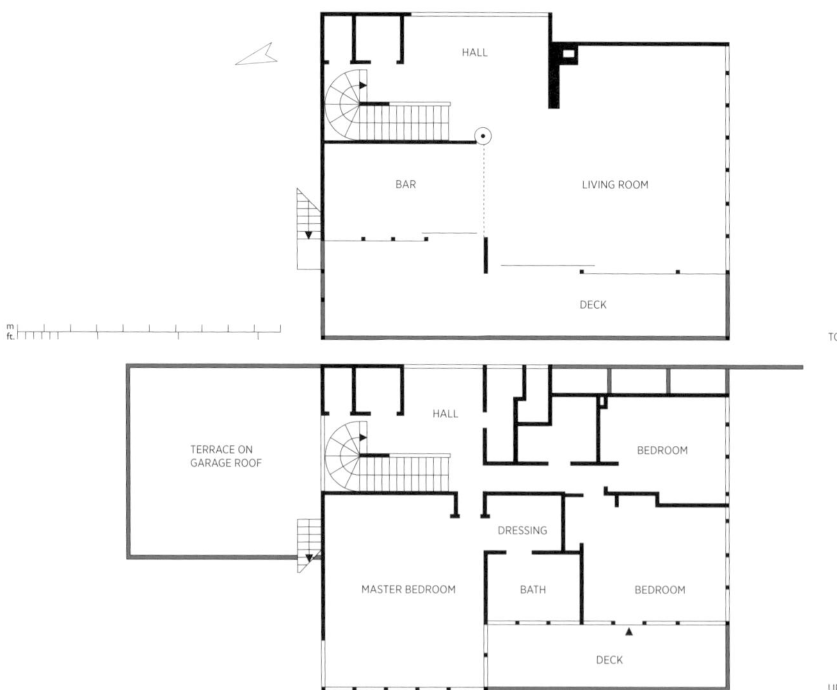

HALL
BAR
LIVING ROOM
DECK
m
ft.
TOP FLOOR PLAN
HALL
TERRACE ON
GARAGE ROOF
BEDROOM
DRESSING
MASTER BEDROOM
BATH
BEDROOM
DECK
UPPER FLOOR PLAN

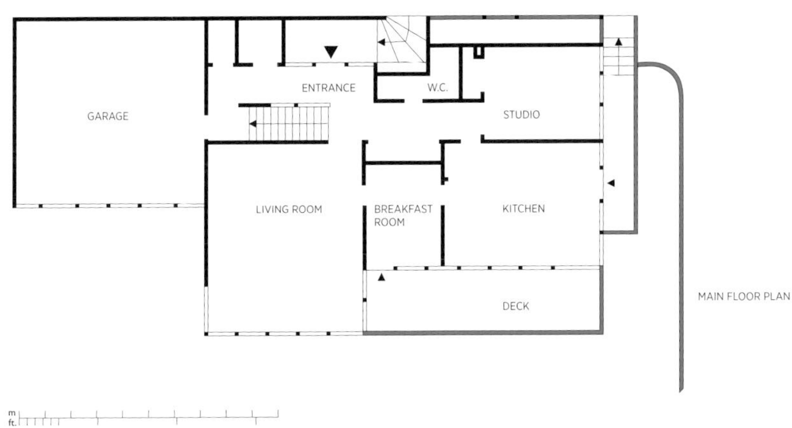

MAIN FLOOR PLAN

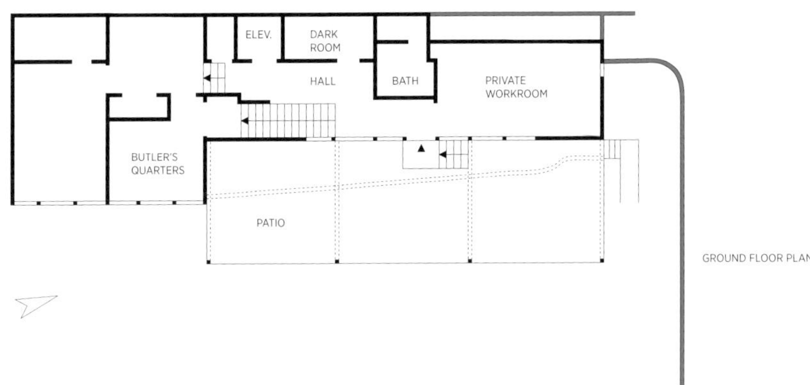

GROUND FLOOR PLAN

Opposite top: Not surprisingly, the Kahn House is often referred to as "San Francisco's Lovell House" for their opulence and also for the sheer audacity of their sites.

Right: One of Neutra's favorite contractors, Fordyce "Red" Marsh, demonstrating the "Camel Table," for which Neutra applied for a patent with furniture maker Paul R. Williams on September 5, 1941; it was granted on September 13, 1943. Red built many variations of the "Camel Table" later in the 1940s.

AVION VILLAGE HOUSING

with David R. Williams and Roscoe P. DeWitt
800 Skyline Road
Grand Prairie, Texas, 1941

This 300-unit complex was completed in August 1941 for $ 992,000 and designed for the young families of the defense workers at the new North American Aviation Plant. Neutra was hired as a consulting architect to work with architects David R. Williams and Roscoe P. DeWitt by Colonel Lawrence Westbrook of the Federal Works Agency. Westbrook oversaw war housing and was a can-do visionary who had the power to implement his cherished idea of "park living," which sought a more harmonious balance with nature in urban residential design. His views meshed nicely with Neutra's own sensibilities, so Avion Village was a model for residential development that included features such as separate car and pedestrian ways; slender but effective "fingerparks" between groups of units, and paths for children that ensured they would not cross "rolling" traffic, an adjective that Neutra often placed before "traffic." The houses ranged from single homes to fourplexes and were made of walls of ⅜-inch plywood panels attached to both sides of wood studs. All details were reduced to utter simplicity; in the painted white ceilings even the humble 2x4 blocking between joists was exposed. Although the houses were so simple to erect that in a contest one house went up in a record 58 minutes, they were sturdy and well adapted to local conditions: Neutra had the windows "cut below bed level so that on stifling Texas nights the sleepers can let the air directly in on themselves." In publicity material he suggested that the "war boom will accustom people to prefabricated homes" – a hope Neutra never really abandoned. The complex of little houses was so successful that when it was sold as private homes for $ 750,000, the federal government got back 81 cents on the dollar. The norm on such a sale was 49 cents.

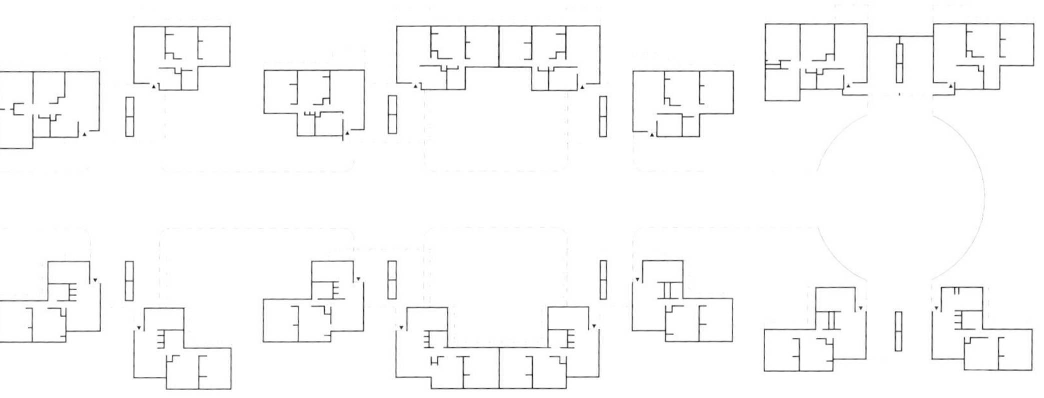

Opposite: Part of the wartime Mutual Housing Ownership Program, one of Neutra's most successful multi-family housing projects is also its most unusual. As an alternative to traditional paradigms of ownership, the cooperative of residents owns the land and the owner has rights to a specific house.

Top: Bare in 1941, today tidy green lawns and an abundance of trees grace the modest but beloved homes.

THEODOR AND LOIS BONNET HOUSE

2256 El Contento Drive
Los Angeles, California, 1942

Below: Like the Hailey House, the original fireplace was indeed painted white. A planter is tucked behind the firebox, carefully located off center, while the fireplace's front plane rises alone to the ceiling. The interesting gesture permitted ease of movement when ascending the stairs.

Opposite: The narrow board redwood volume rests above the white stucco box. View facing northeast.

This 1,800-square-foot house shows how Neutra permits the site to inform a design with strategies apparently eccentric to his repertoire. It is greatly animated in section, following the terrain of a very steep Hollywood hill which is then echoed by the long lines of a sweeping shed roof paralleling the slope. The redwood-sheathed building is pulled into the hill while a stucco cube below, housing the garage and storage room, juts out in front. At the base of the structure a stucco staircase boldly crosses the façade (un-Neutra like) as it ascends to a wide porch leading into the living room, originally clad in dark wood contrasting with white plaster. (Along with the choice of materials, the occasional curved wall enlarging space is reminiscent of the Bald House completed a year earlier.) From the glass wall adjoining the porch, a short soffit of 7′ 6″ rises to 11′ at the far side of the living room where a short flight of steps leads to the bathroom separating two bedrooms, one of which has a floor-to-ceiling six-foot-wide pane of glass, marking a change from the march of narrow steel casement windows of Neutra's earlier work to a larger module. In plan the kitchen angles in (un-Neutra like) from the rest of the rectilinear composition following the setback line on this tight lot.

KELTON APARTMENTS

646–648 Kelton Avenue
Westwood, California, 1942

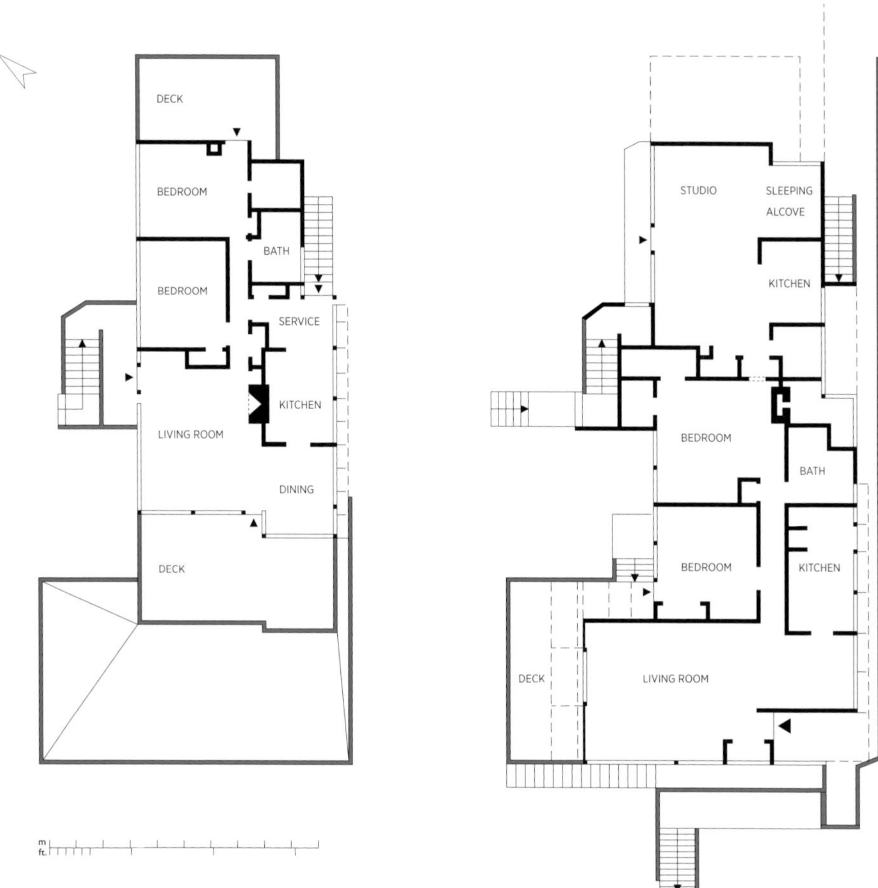

This was the third and smallest apartment project in Westwood and the second in which Neutra invested his own funds as a partner. The triplex cleverly appears to be one large gracious house. On the sloping site, one leg of an L, a cube with a balcony protected by a deep overhang steps down toward the street. A tall stucco spur wall separates the two ground-floor units visually. The volumes on each of the ground-floor units are not monolithic but sometimes step a few feet in and out, creating more variety in engaging the landscape. Meanwhile, the top floor retains its clean rectilinearity which anchors both street and rear façades; this strategy also provides shelter for the more animated ground-floor plan when it steps back from the plane of the upper wall.

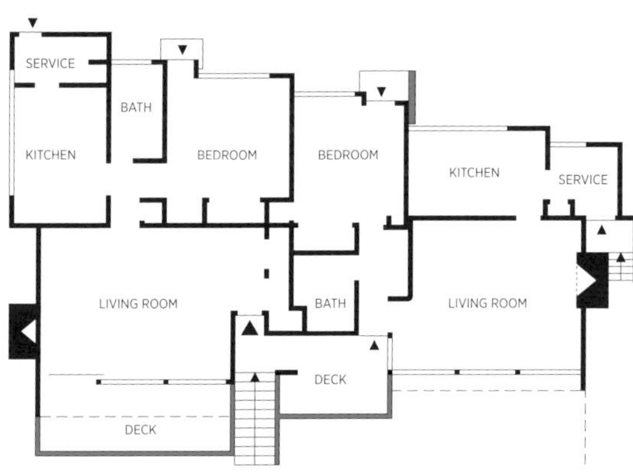

A stained, plywood-clad dining area off the living area provides a sheltered alcove off the kitchen. A shallow balcony with deep overhang protects from the western sun. View facing southwest.

JOHN AND BERNICE NESBITT HOUSE

414 Avondale Avenue
Los Angeles, California, 1942

Recently sensitively remodeled, this house won a first place award from the American Institute of Architects for its juxtaposition of urban sophistication, cultural refinement and rustic simplicity. It was also one of Dione Neutra's most beloved houses because of its rich textures and intimate relationship with the garden. A long pedestrian approach reorients the visitor away from the upscale suburban street into a "controlled paradise." The angle of this brick path serves to deflect attention away from the garage attached to a separate building at the northern end of the lot containing a studio and bedroom, a kitchenette, fireplace and two bathrooms. The path then meets the house and runs alongside it to the front door under a wide overhang that protects the house from the western sun. After the sustained procession past a closed, protected façade, at the entrance suddenly the visitor is welcomed with glass walls on both sides of the living room, and almost shot through the room into the arms of the garden beyond. At the door, a lily pond slips under the glass wall to the interior entry, further tying outdoors and in. The smaller dwelling is connected to the larger house by a covered pergola, but also separated from its social quarters by a long serpentine brick wall. (Neutra intended that the small house could be rented out "in a case of need.") The rustic quality is achieved by using exposed beams, redwood board-and-batten walls, and common brick inside and out. Here the brick

is a hard-working architectural element: as a ground plane, the unmortared brick connects indoors and outdoors. As a vertical plane, it is used with conventional light mortar indoors on the fireplace, while outdoors the mortar is often allowed to ooze out from the face of the brick, a technique Neutra used on other houses such as the Bailey and Taylor homes. The board and batten is also used as a fascia concealing the shed roof, while the huge glass sliding doors of the dining area and living room open the house to gardens and terraces.

Opposite: The Nesbitt House is renowned for its intimate connection to the garden, afforded by the large glass walls, here showing the easy relationship of the two dining areas, one indoors, the other outdoors. World War II restrictions necessitated many changes: away from metal and in finding good carpenters too old for service. View facing south.

Above: Sanctuary after Nesbitt's long day in front of a microphone: the simple clarity of wood, glass, and nature. Nesbitt, a radio entertainer, also was one of Neutra's few clients who understood his architect's objectives of well-being, often challenging him in fierce, affectionate debate.

MAXIME AND ETTA VAN CLEEF HOUSE

651 Warner Avenue
Los Angeles, California, 1942

The lot for this house is highly eccentric: a long, shallow isosceles triangle in plan that rises about 40 feet in the middle. The L-shaped, shed-roof house, designed for a retired couple with a grown daughter who often visited, is 1,350 square feet. The unusual lot led to a complex response. In section it follows the irregular contours of the hill on three different levels; in plan the house also traces the property line setback (the hypotenuse of the triangle) to maximize square footage. A two-car garage is tucked below the northeast terrace, four steps below the bedroom wing. In a rare non-orthogonal move, the shed roof of the redwood and white stucco house is angled out from one stucco wall of the north-facing kitchen, which is itself angled in and runs along the setback. Redwood is used for the walls and gable ends, while stucco is reserved for the balcony walls meeting the ground, creating a visual base for the building. Neutra used his standard post-and-beam system to support the heavy glass-and-steel doors leading to a large patio opening to the northwest, while above fixed clear windows with much thinner mullions follow the pitched slope of the roof.

While the frequent changes in the ground plane create an ever-changing section, the tongue-and-groove redwood ceiling forms a monolithic plane tying the disparate spaces together, further enhanced by the uniform beige carpeting throughout. Metal sash and intermediate wood supports were painted an "Indian" red, the kitchen and breakfast nook in

light green, the end wall in a deep green, and the rear bedroom and bathroom in bright yellow. The floors were covered in Armstrong cork and battleship linoleum.

This house's homey appearance is belied by the many experimental techniques and materials Neutra incorporated, such as prefabricated electrically vibrated Schlueter cement joists, Reynolds heat reflectant aluminum foil-covered felt in the walls and ceiling for insulation, panels of combined diatomaceous earth and terra cotta, an undefined "Resilith" and "heat mirrors" of laminated glass with metal core (presumably used in the bathrooms for reflecting body heat, as Neutra said he used in the powder room on the ground floor of VDL Research House).

Opposite: Using the same motif of redwood siding and gables surmounting a white stucco base as the Bonnet House, a series of perpendicular steps leads up the slope from shady Warner Avenue. View facing south.

Above: The Van Cleef family loved color; in the angled kitchen Neutra plays off white cabinetry and appliances. Elsewhere, colors enriched a palette of wood ceilings, white plaster, and brick.

CHANNEL HEIGHTS HOUSING

Western Avenue and 25th Street
San Pedro, California, 1942

m
ft.

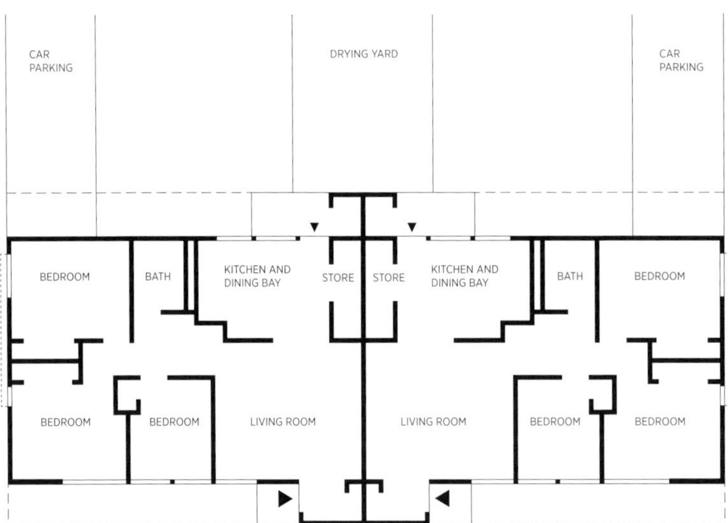
CAR PARKING
DRYING YARD
CAR PARKING
BEDROOM
BATH
KITCHEN AND DINING BAY
STORE
STORE
KITCHEN AND DINING BAY
BATH
BEDROOM
BEDROOM
BEDROOM
LIVING ROOM
LIVING ROOM
BEDROOM
BEDROOM

Superbly sited overlooking the harbor of San Pedro, this was one of Neutra's most accomplished housing projects. While for decades it was a thriving, popular community and known as socially progressive in its inclusion of all races and in its cooperative spirit, by the late 1970s it languished under absentee landlords. This was a federal public housing project for low-cost homes funded by the Federal Works Agency (like Avion Village, with the participation of FWA personnel David R. Williams and Colonel Lawrence Westbrook) and constructed for $2,600 per unit. Almost 600 families were housed in 222 units. The dwellings ranged from one to three bedrooms of four different types in mostly one- and sometimes two-story plexes which were grouped in three major blocks over 165 gently hilly acres occasionally deeply cut by small canyons. Like much of Neutra's work during the years of World War II, when metals were scarce, the exteriors are sheathed in redwood and plaster; interiors were painted soft pastels.

Opposite: Neutra treated the restrictions of war as an opportunity: the spartan palette of wood and stucco, the play of solid and void, and the simple volumes recall Japanese vernacular architecture.

Above: His "Boomerang Chair" made its debut in not an architectural journal but in the April 1947 issue of *Women's Day* magazine.

CHANNEL HEIGHTS STORE AND MARKET BUILDING

San Pedro, California, 1943

Foreshadowing today's supermarkets, this community market building, sited on the west side of the project, was vigorous in the monolithic sweep of its large glass façade topped by a massive angled redwood soffit and bold spread aluminum letters. These strategies served to show what was inside the building and to capture and hold a driver's attention. Huge laminated beams animated the interior as they emerged from a lowered soffit as exposed timbers beneath a tall clerestory at the rear of the store.

Opposite: Long demolished, the Channel Heights Market was a *tour-de-force* of design and the center of the multivalent community.

Above: Every element had work to do: the market's clear signage communicated energy while the redwood overhang protected drivers walking into the store.

470

KAUFMANN DESERT HOUSE

470 West Vista de Chino
Palm Springs, California, 1947

Opposite: The pivoting aluminum louvers tempered the dust from the northwest winds. From left to right, the guest wing (closed panels), the "gloriette" (open panels), and the garage. View facing southeast.

Above: The grass, improbable in such a harsh climate, is adorned by carefully placed boulders, part of the "endowment" of Little Tuscany, renowned for its boulders. View facing west toward San Jacinto.

One of the century's best-known houses, the Kaufmann Desert House is located in what Neutra called the "Badlands of the Cordillera." "Badlands" is a geographical term meaning extremely rough and inhospitable to human habitation, with tortured divides between pinnacles and gullies. *Cordillera* is a Spanish term describing the spines of mountains bracketed by the Sierra Nevada and the Rockies, but the phrase also reflects Neutra's breadth of knowledge, darting from history to geography to science, and his unchecked joy in the expansive power of language which assumed a reader as educated as he was. In any case, most of us know these "badlands" as Palm Springs, the queen of Hollywood getaways, its blue pools and green golf courses improbably wrapping the base of rocky, barren, mighty San Jacinto. The new passion for all things Modern has brought life surging back into the city with its many landmarks by architects such as William Cody, Craig Ellwood, Albert Frey, John Lautner, Don Wexler and E. Stewart Williams. Frey had already begun his own remarkable house in 1940, and Neutra's Miller House was completed in 1937, but the 3,800-square-foot Kaufmann Desert House was the first Modernist grand villa here, an unabashed social extrovert in this "grandiose waste," in Neutra's words. The arms of its pinwheel plan push out into the desert, silver during the day, glowing at night. This house, too, has come back to life after a four-year, multimillion dollar restoration and reconstruction by Marmol and Radziner and clients Beth and Brent Harris.

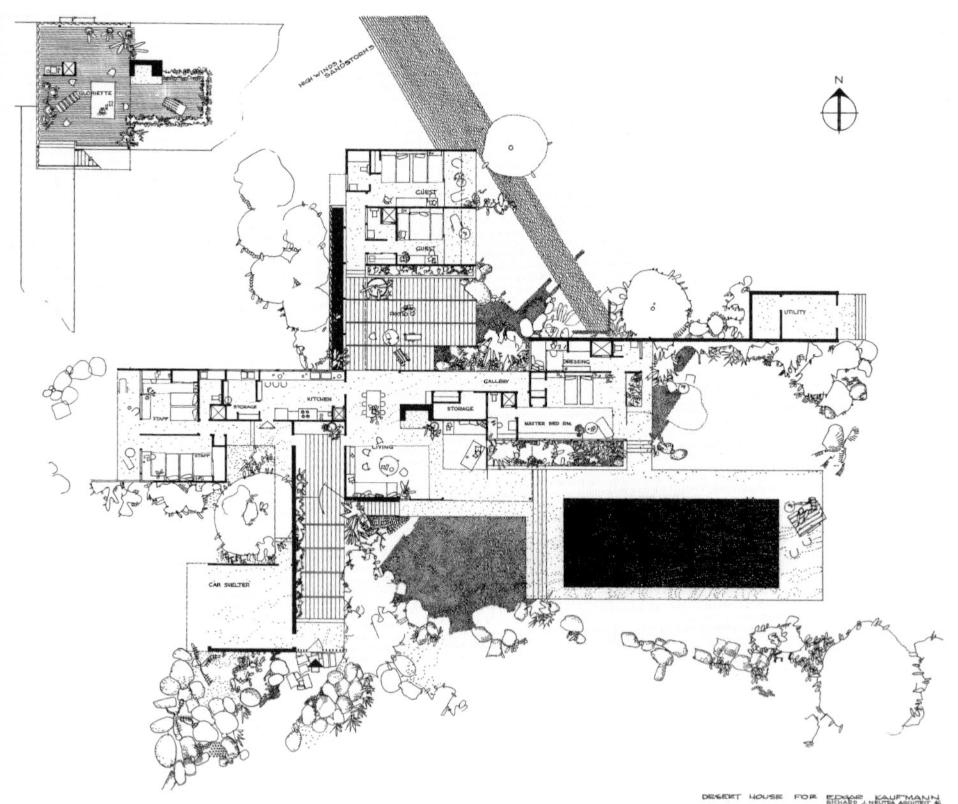

Depending on the season, the pool's concrete patio was either warmed by radiant floor heating or water-chilled. View facing west.

In Neutra's long list of clients, only John Nicholas Brown might be Edgar Kaufmann Sr.'s rival in terms of the formidable collusion of wealth and architectural sophistication, if not in background. A decade earlier, the department store magnate had hired Frank Lloyd Wright to design what is now known as Falling Water, and now Kaufmann wanted a different but equally brilliant voice to beget his West Coast base.

Over and over in his writings on this house Neutra emphasized his architectural distance from Wright: this was a building "inserted" into this harsh backdrop, "set on footings," whose juxtaposition of artifice and artificial climate underscored "the weather, the silver-white moonlight, and the starry sky." The structural system combined wood and steel in a series of delicate connections that reduced the number of requisite vertical supports (which are slender in any case). This is most emphatic in the southeast living room whose glass-and-steel walls slide away to spatially link the house and the pool. The act of negating the corner is driven home because the roof and beam supporting the

Above: The stones lead from the garage to the kitchen wing. View facing northeast.

Opposite: Not many rooms can match the glory of the gloriette at sunset. Neutra adapted the louvers from designs by Julio Villalobos that he saw when visiting Brazil in 1941, although those were in wood.

glass and steel sliders extend toward the pool beyond the room's footprint. To stand there is to be engaged in a physically charged moment. (This stretching of the beam, in future connected to a column located beyond the roof, became Neutra's signature spider leg.) The composition juxtaposes layers of strong horizontal planes with the diaphanous vertical planes of aluminum louvers on the west side of the gloriette and of the patio. The louvers (37 feet of them, Neutra remarked) and the long dark quiet lily pond connect the guest wing to the rest of the house, creating a protected and water-cooled patio. A second strata of contrast is manifest in the materials: the light-colored, dry-set (mortared from behind) "Utah buff" stone Neutra used threads its way through the entire composition and unifies it. Horizontally the stone runs joyfully into the land, vertically the stone presides as the chimney. The texture of the rock creates a vibrato of light and dark chiaroscuro that only enhances the smoothness of the glass, steel, plaster and stucco. However, the stonework is also a precision piece of artifice, both originally – when Neutra trained the masons himself – and in the restoration. Both times, in 1945–46 and half

a century later, each stone was chiseled to fit its own asymmetric place by craftsmen working under arduous conditions, beneath a punishing sun and in temperatures that can easily reach 120 degrees Fahrenheit. In the gloriette, the vertical rhythm of the louvers is enhanced by the horizontal plane of the redwood flooring, strips of 2⅝-inch redwood, a ½-inch thick, meticulously spaced ⅜-inch apart. As always, certain hallmark Neutra details appear, such as the elegantly tapered edges of the horizontal shelves in the built-in bookshelves or the lowered soffit inside the living room that washes the ceiling with light. One change was made in the restoration that was contrived to be easily removed. To get to the bedrooms on the west arm of the pinwheel (formerly the bedrooms of Kaufmann's staff), one had to exit the kitchen and walk west and outside. While this might have been appropriate for adult staff, these are now the bedrooms of the children of the current owners, who did not want to be so physically separated. An interior hallway was seamlessly inserted on the south and can be deconstructed as desired.

Opposite: The living area beyond the dining table. View facing south.

Above: Full-height walls slide away to seamlessly meld indoors and outdoors. View facing southeast.

STUART AND LUCIA BAILEY HOUSE

Case Study House #20
219 Chautaugua Boulevard
Pacific Palisades, California, 1948

This modest, award-winning house combines a number of ideas Neutra had brewing for years, primarily his beloved "Four-Courter House." It is located on the spectacular five-acre meadow-and-woodland tract overlooking the Pacific Ocean that John Entenza, editor of *Arts & Architecture* magazine, bought as a site for three other Case Study Houses including the famous Charles and Ray Eames House of 1949. Stuart Bailey was a 30-year-old dentist who bought a lot from Entenza and then chose Neutra on a friend's advice; part of the appeal of the Case Study House program for the new family man was discounts on building and furnishing materials from the manufacturers. These included furniture, 12′ x 8′ sliding glass and aluminum-coated steel doors which weighed 1,000 pounds and most importantly, a prefabricated utility core called the Ingersoll unit "that still works fine after 51 years," says Dr. Bailey of his centrally massed plumbing and heating equipment. The compact house (1,320 square feet for $19,600) has four articulated wings jutting out into the landscape. Because of their short lengths, these wings gather in space, in a gesture of domesticity, rather than push imperiously out into the landscape, as the larger Kaufmann (built a year earlier) and Tremaine houses (built a year later)

Page 188: Recalling his beloved African acacias, Neutra rendered his trees so that the canopy's drip line was above the roof. The exuberant spray of pointillist blue dots to represent the sky was pure Neutra.

Page 189: The deep overhangs included in-plane lighting at the edge, providing a wider field of vision at night.

Now renovated, the original house radiated serenity and clarity, as ever blurring the boundary between indoors and out.

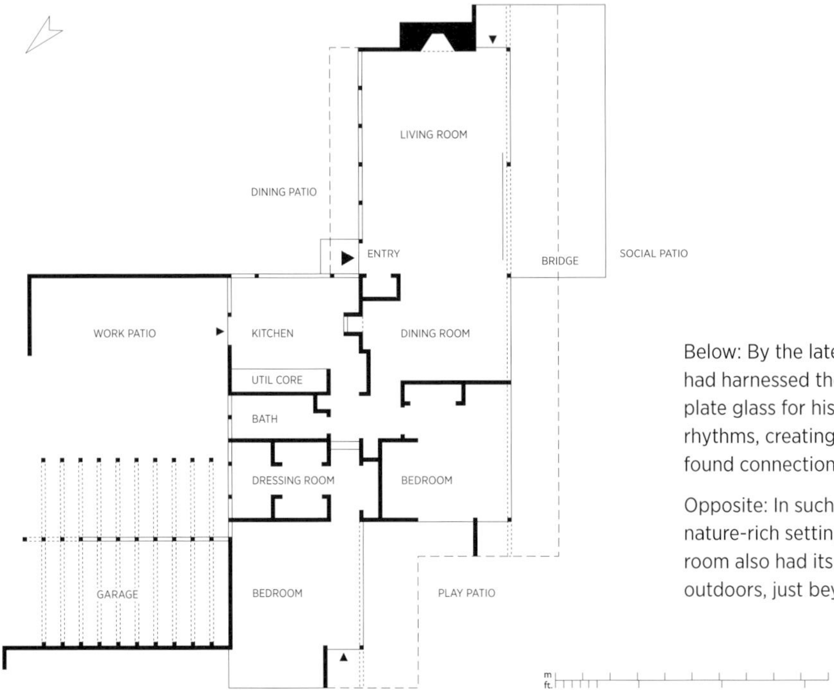

LIVING ROOM
DINING PATIO
ENTRY
BRIDGE
SOCIAL PATIO
WORK PATIO
KITCHEN
DINING ROOM
UTIL CORE
BATH
DRESSING ROOM
BEDROOM
GARAGE
BEDROOM
PLAY PATIO
m
ft.

Below: By the late 1940s, Neutra had harnessed the potential of large plate glass for his post-and-beam rhythms, creating an ever more profound connection to the outdoors.

Opposite: In such a sheltered, nature-rich setting, a child's bedroom also had its own path to the outdoors, just beyond the bunny.

do. The resulting outdoor "four courts" included social quarters, play quarters, dining quarters and work quarters, essentially doubling the size of the house. The contrast in the office letters between Bailey's dry, laconic wit and Neutra's earnestness make for lively reading. "When the lot and your fee are paid I shall be helpless ... I assure you I have no hidden source of wealth which could be drawn on in emergency ... I like cove lights, trough lights, klieg lights, clerestories, lights in closets and cupboards and all manner of decorative lights. Never use a 200-watt bulb where a 300-watt bulb can be squeezed in. You may have no pity on my electric bill.

I also have a 30 lb. dictionary that needs a home ..." In contrast Neutra is "very anxious to continue the spur wall to the southwest of your bedroom so that it will project farther than the roof projection ... I am also very anxious to extend the finished casing of the lintel beam over your bedroom farther than the southwest fascia of the roof overhang ... I am convinced that this will improve the looks greatly," he wrote four years after the house was completed. Bailey tells the story of asking if the closet interiors could be painted white, to see things better, rather than dark. "Mr. Bailey," Neutra said sternly, "the closets must recede. If you paint them white, I will remove my name from the project." Neutra designed two additions for the family, both 700 square feet, one in 1950 and one in 1958. The closets were dark.

HOLIDAY HOUSE APARTMENTS

27400 Pacific Coast Highway
Malibu, California, 1948

This Malibu restaurant-hotel almost touches the ocean below on its sunny, sloping site overlooking the panorama of the ocean and surrounded by olive trees. The hotel is a series of three groups of south-facing wood-framed units, each group tied together as one composition by a continuous fascia running past cantilevering, with tapered cross girders supporting the roof overhang.

On the south, each unit is monastically divided by spur walls ("spur" means a short appendage to a supporting structure) so every occupant can commune privately with the sun, wind and water; climbing vines were immediately planted at the end of each spur wall. Materials included eucalyptus plywood for the spur walls, redwood tongue-and-groove siding, asphalt tile, and Roman brick for fireplaces. Transparent white "Rippolite" plastic was used for fencing, attached to three-inch aluminum pipes sunk in concrete. This use of plastic would become much more popular in later Case Study House projects.

Opposite: The building opened to the west and the ocean, to its crashing waves and the smell of the sea.

Above: The slender wood open frame beyond the overhang signified the edge of a protective tree canopy, defining liminal space.

WARREN AND KATHARINE TREMAINE HOUSE

1642 Moore Road
Montecito, California, 1948

Neutra wrote much about the *genius loci* of this place, most poignantly in *Mystery and Realities of the Site,* and one immediately senses the overwhelming power of the location. From the ocean below, roads to the house twist and turn, until one turns off into a small road completely sheltered by the long embrace of the California oak trees, their trunks grotesque and deeply furrowed. It is silent; only the smell of the sea and the rustle of the oak leaves fill the senses. The site is interrupted by veins of "enormous stone blocks like sculptures by Arp," Neutra wrote.

Like an albatross, the oceanic bird whose legendary powers of flight allow it to descend to land only to breed, the Tremaine House unfolds and spreads its mighty wings, hovering majestically in an ancient oak tree grove above Santa Barbara and the Pacific Ocean. Only a

Above: The driveway up to the carport. Neutra's drawing skills, often in oil crayon, can be seen in the variety of techniques he employed to convey texture.

Opposite: While accomplished, the model doesn't capture the dense woodlands around the house.

Following: "Lyrically expressed, a building of proper design may answer a question that is asked by the setting. It is a response ...," Neutra wrote (*Architectural Forum*, 1949).

row of precise white beam ends are visible, as though they were the now-petrified joints of the bird floating above the glass amidst the dense landscape. That single beckoning gesture is the street "façade," though one's journey toward the house is then defied by the stone walls defining the patio and the guest wing. It is one of many moments of tension and transcendence rendered here in a poised equilibrium, a dialectic on many levels, between floating and anchored, between solid and opaque, between machine-made and nature-wrought.

What makes this house unique in Neutra's oeuvre is the union between architectural expression and structural system. Articulated concrete pillars bear the long frontal girders, which in turn support cantilevered roof beams below an impossibly thin-looking roof slab, all rendered in reinforced concrete, partly in response to the threat of forest fires. Like Neutra's theoretical Diatom IV House of 1923 and his Puerto Rico classrooms of 1944, the system allows for both continual ventilation below the ceilings and ambient daylight; at night, concealed illumination spills over from the interior to express the strong bass notes of the structure.

Where a younger Neutra accepted structural redundancy in a building system (e.g., the Palmer technique of load-bearing walls in the Beard House), the elder Neutra used this concrete system with masterful intention. The columns and beams follow a 16-foot module when needed, asserting a classical rhythm. Where other concerns and the load-bearing capabilities of a column and beam connection coincide (as they do at the northern end of the "social quarters"), he exploited the latent plastic qualities of the grid, and here the spacing increased to 20 feet. At the southeast corner of the room, he used a round stainless-steel-clad column where a concrete

Opposite: The photo captures Neutra's "Cantilever Chair" on the near terrace, while a group of his "Boomerang Chairs" happily gossip on the far terrace.

Right: The house is not so much framed by nature but fitted into it. The legendary landscape architects who contributed to the house include Ralph Tallant Stevens, Lockwood de Forest III, and Isabel Greene.

pillar would be expected, visually ensuring that no one would mistake the column as a room divider or door opening. Instead, the eye flows around it, in good biorealistic fashion, encouraged to connect spaces rather than to separate them.

In contrast to the crisp edges of the white of the beams and the roof slabs, Neutra used a rough native stone for walls for contrasting texture. There is no plaster in the house: all the aluminum glass frames were carefully detailed to connect directly with the concrete pillars. The terrazzo floors continue inside and out and are radiantly heated, even to the end of the extravagantly long 56-foot west terrace, further serving to extinguish the boundaries between indoors and out. On the west side of the "social quarters," Neutra placed detailed, revolving redwood shade louvers at the edge of the overhang.

Like the Kaufmann Desert House, the Tremaine House is a pinwheel in plan. However, even though the east and west arms are far longer here, it is more socially "compact" and centralized than its desert cousin. The Kaufmann Desert House was built as a second home for one couple where the hegemony of adult privacy prevailed, while the Tremaine House was designed for a family with three children. Originally it was meant to be a two-story structure but was later scaled back. Below the house there is an art gallery which opens to a "garden hall." To the north, it in turn leads to an intimate fern and tree-shaded area below the house and, on the south, to a broad oak-studded meadow, somewhat reminiscent of the famous meadow at the Eames House. The master bedroom is particularly impressive because the ground plane comes up almost to the window sill, so that nature is alive and very present in a muted, gentle daylight. At this northern end of the house, Neutra cantilevered the roof eight feet, extending the line of the roof beyond the grid; another plastic move without which the composition would have been flaccid and inert. Inside, spaces flow into each other easily. Huge glass or opaque wood (walnut or birch stained a "very dark purplish black") sliding partitions provide opportunities to elastically redefine uses. The "Camel Dining Table" (as always) lowers to coffee-table

height; portholes to the pantry close, partitions disappear, the sectional ottomans are dispersed and the "rooms" are dramatically reconfigured.

In measured drawings Neutra specified and planned for each and every rug, drape and bedspread in the house, down to knowing exactly how many yards of fabric were to be ordered, and encouraged the use of color for the children's bedrooms, one in chartreuse, another in yellow, the third in salmon. He designed much of the furniture, such as unusual ash and leather side-arm chairs. Many off-the-shelf items were customized: copper porch furniture was specified at a ⅞-inch outside diameter, narrower than the manufacturer's conventions, and its curves at a four-inch radius, the tightest the maker could provide. Neutra even cautioned the Tremaines about how to look at materials, and in what kind of light to judge them: "The swatch of the light natural carpet wool-tufting in the sample makes the carpet look darker than it is, that there will be a dense sprinkling of shadow over it, so take care when holding it against the Terrazzo and [see] how the center section of a swatch has a modified brown." It may come as no surprise that further office correspondence between Neutra and the Tremaines reveals an uneasy and unresolved concern that they consider the house "their" home.

Above: The kitchen looked out to a blend of exotic succulents and Coast Live Oaks. Note the rotary-cut plywood breakfast nook. Quality rotary-cut plywood is rare today ... and often misunderstood as cheap. Opposite: Below grade, with seamless window corners, one feels enveloped by the earth and its cycles.

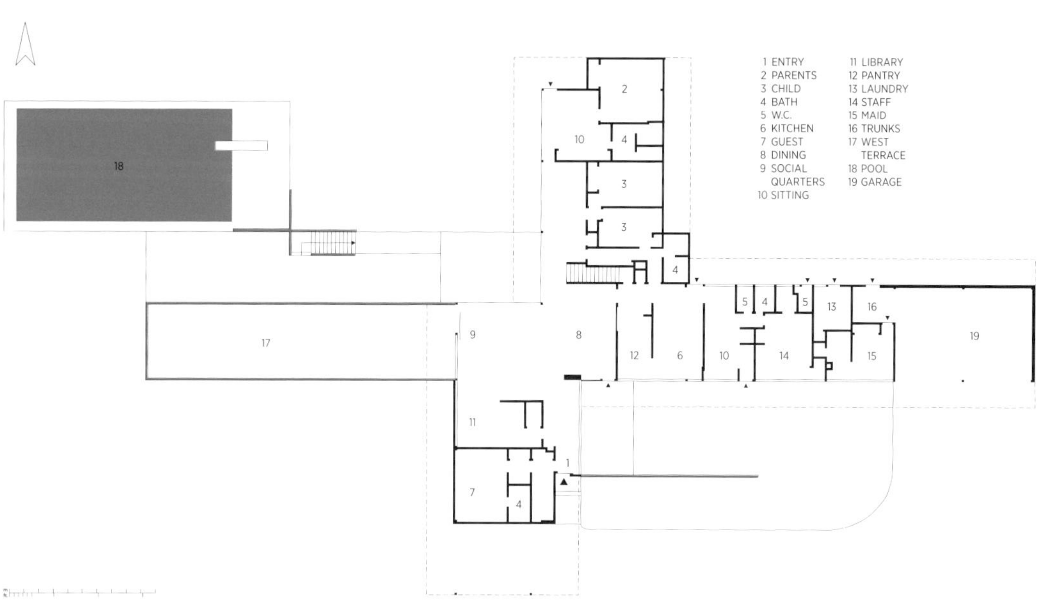
1 ENTRY
2 PARENTS
3 CHILD
4 BATH
5 W.C.
6 KITCHEN
7 GUEST
8 DINING
9 SOCIAL QUARTERS
10 SITTING
11 LIBRARY
12 PANTRY
13 LAUNDRY
14 STAFF
15 MAID
16 TRUNKS
17 WEST TERRACE
18 POOL
19 GARAGE

Inspired by his wartime schools in Puerto Rico, the clerestories above the exquisite rotating wood panels ensured cross-ventilation when the panels were closed.

The majestic *basso profundo* of the concrete and Neutra's clever theater of lighting against the polished terrazzo is one of the reasons the house is a masterpiece.

DAVID AND BERDINE TREWEEK HOUSE

2250 East Silver Lake Boulevard
Los Angeles, California, 1948

Another member of the Silver Lake Colony, this sleek, compact two-story house has a multitude of terraces on the lake side to the west and to the south that act as buffer zones between the house and the boulevard and neighboring houses, respectively. The two bedrooms on the second floor are really independent suites, each running the east-west length of the house and with their own bathrooms and private terraces. The ground floor was specifically designed with the assumption that "all services would be done by the hostess," an office memo stated. That programmatic requirement is reflected in the laundry/kitchen area which opens both into the dining area and to the large patio to the south, a place often used for outdoor dining. A built-in breakfast niche and cabinetry in birch is complemented by soft cork tile floors (easier to stand on) and hardy stainless-steel countertops and backsplashes in the cooking area. Beyond the south patio, Neutra placed a row of eucalyptus trees for further privacy. A freestanding stone

Opposite: Here are the typical Neutra sliding planes and layers of glass, but now rendered in stone and redwood, exploiting the natural orientation of the wood to oppose horizontals and verticals.

Below: Now almost completely obscured by overgrown plants and trees, the hand of the legendary Modern landscape architect Garrett Eckbo can still be seen from the sky, revealing remnants of his angled and curved geometries playing off Neutra's orthogonals.

fireplace separates the dining and living spaces. Though far more refined, the stone is similar in color to the rose and buff tones used for the outside terrace walls, plainly visible through the large sliding glass doors. "The building cost, including furniture: $45,000," noted another office memo. In April 1949, five months after the house was completed, Berdine Treweek wrote to Neutra: "Living in a house whose design and character has been molded by you has things to offer that people can never appreciate until they enjoy the experience of living with it every day. It actually takes the deep breathing of everyday problems to [be able to teach] people there is a better way to live at home and enjoy it. Our living has begun to expand ..."

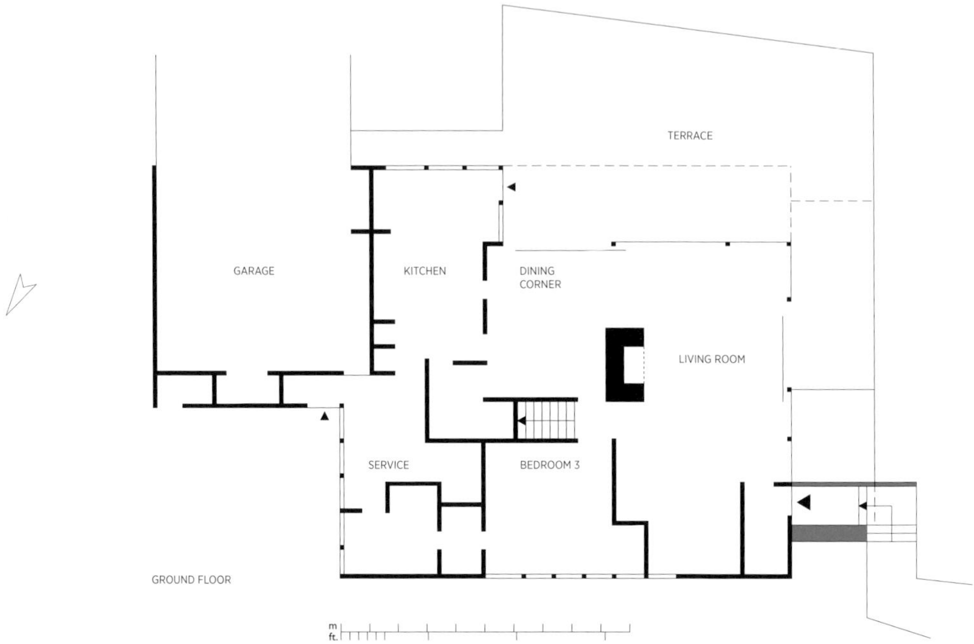

TERRACE

GARAGE

KITCHEN

DINING CORNER

LIVING ROOM

SERVICE

BEDROOM 3

GROUND FLOOR

m
ft.

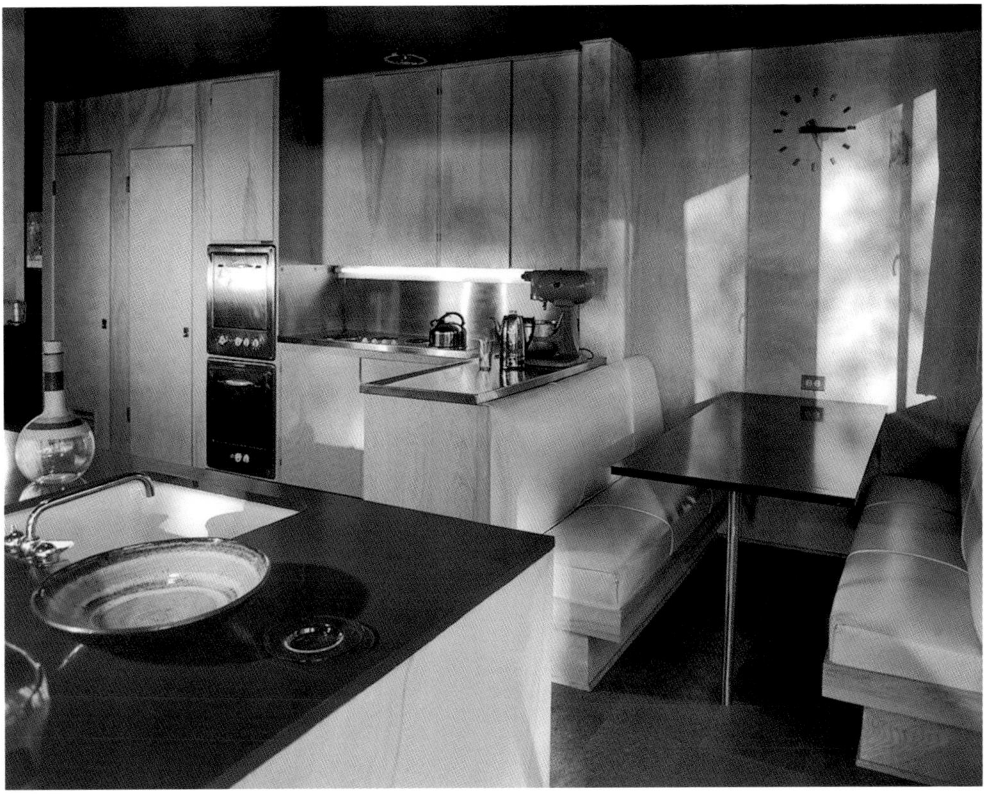

Opposite: A long line of windows offering views of the Silver Lake Reservoir to the west.

Above: Little seen or known today, Shulman's many photographs of 1949 reveal Neutra at his best. The kitchen's warm birch woodwork, the spatial layout, the breakfast nook all invite a family to enjoy spending time together.

SECOND FLOOR

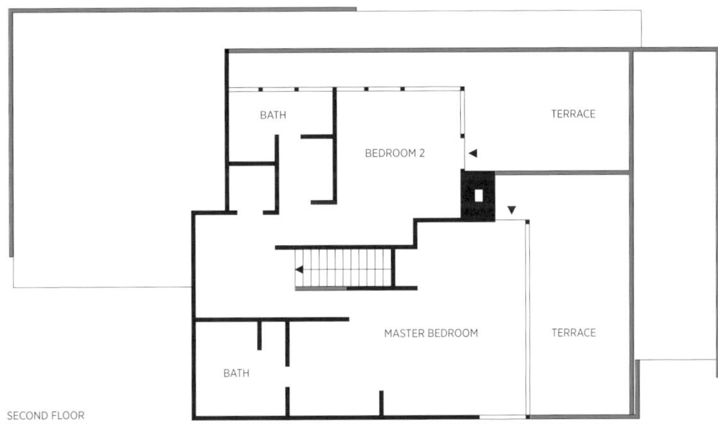

The fireplace's stonework is more refined than that of the exterior walls, but no less warm.

BENEDICT AND NANCY FREEDMAN HOUSE

315 Via De La Paz
Los Angeles, California, 1949

Left: Lost in the Pacific Palisades fires, the beautiful 1950 photographs by Julius Shulman and John Ellis 50 years later become critically important in remembering the home that overlooked the Pacific.

Opposite: Nancy Freedman, who with her mathematician husband wrote nine novels, suffered from poor health. Here she relaxes on a day bed, looking out to the terrace and their son Michael, who grew up to be world-class mathematician. Benedict stands at the back of the pool.

In this small writers' sanctuary, the gradations between interior and exterior are rich and effortless in a house that organically responds to multivalent demands. The clients were a successful, up-and-coming screenwriting couple who wrote movies including *Mrs. Mike*; in addition to needing serious work space they were soon to have a child. The house on a corner lot is sited well away from both streets to provide privacy.

In plan, a large protected patio separates the only bedroom on the west from the rest of the house on the east, pulling the house apart. Here, each side of the house has glass sliding walls to completely open the house on the north and south. Meanwhile, both the pool and the quarry tile paving (running from a garden patio in the front, through the protected patio and out to the pool) are perpendicular in orientation, so that space flows easily in both directions. A generous built-in chaise longue next to the bedroom allows someone writing or lounging to look up and watch their baby. Clerestories run above several bookshelves and originally there was a small built-in organ. The ceilings are high, with a plate line rising from 8′ 10″ to 11′ 5″, increasing the sense of spaciousness and lightness. The master bath can be entered from the bedroom or the pool. "We splash a lot," Nancy wrote to Neutra. "Can't the splash behind the tub be higher?" At the back of the pool, Neutra wove horizontal and vertical strips of redwood to create a series of pergola trusses visually joining the pool to the rest of the board-and-batten house; the trusses, soon to be overgrown with vines, also served to hide the next-door Mediterranean-style houses.

GEORGE AND ELIZABETH ROURKE HOUSE

9228 Hazen Drive
Beverly Hills, California, 1949

Except for one wall, this 1,250-square-foot L-shaped Beverly Hills bungalow is quintessential Neutra on what surely must be a given: a steep slope. Here is the requisite palette of Neutra materials and techniques circa 1950: tongue-and-groove wood ceiling; exterior strip lighting flush with the boxed wood soffit; deep overhangs; extended gutters; spider legs that double as pergolas for climbing vines; sliding glass doors; exteriors of white stucco and wood. His conventions continue indoors: a living room with glass walls (here west and east) to create a sweeping, transparent view; overhangs and outdoor patios; an asymmetrically located firebox within a Roman brick fireplace; adjacent flanking stainless-steel cabinetry of a height that matches that of the firebox; well-built, practical built-in birch cabinetry located where people need storage; a window wall above a high backsplash where the kitchen sink is placed. The one exception occurs in the west bedroom, whose angled footprint departs from the orthogonal, following the setback of the property line and capturing desired views. At the end of the other leg of the L, Neutra designed another bedroom suite with a separate entrance for the Rourkes' grown son.

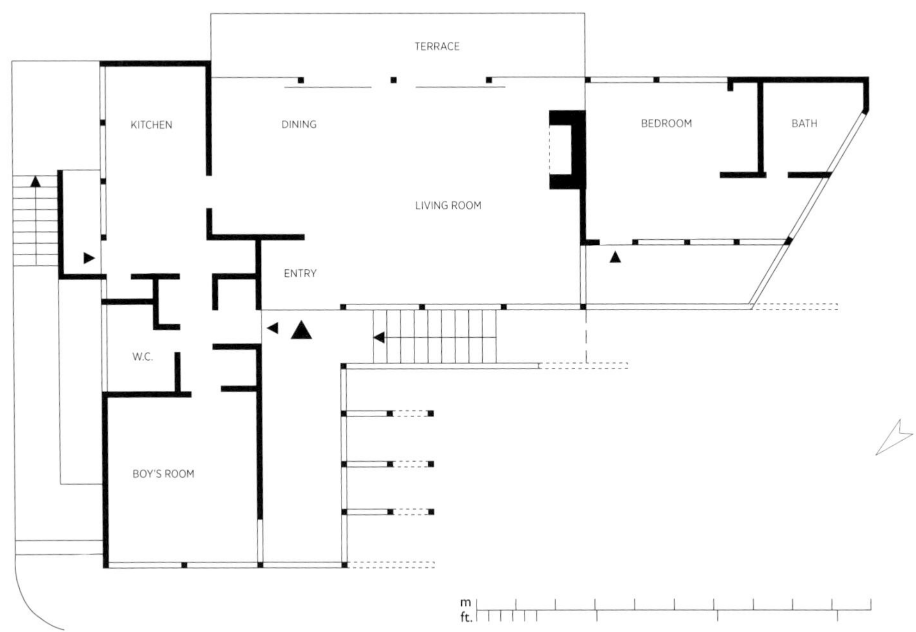

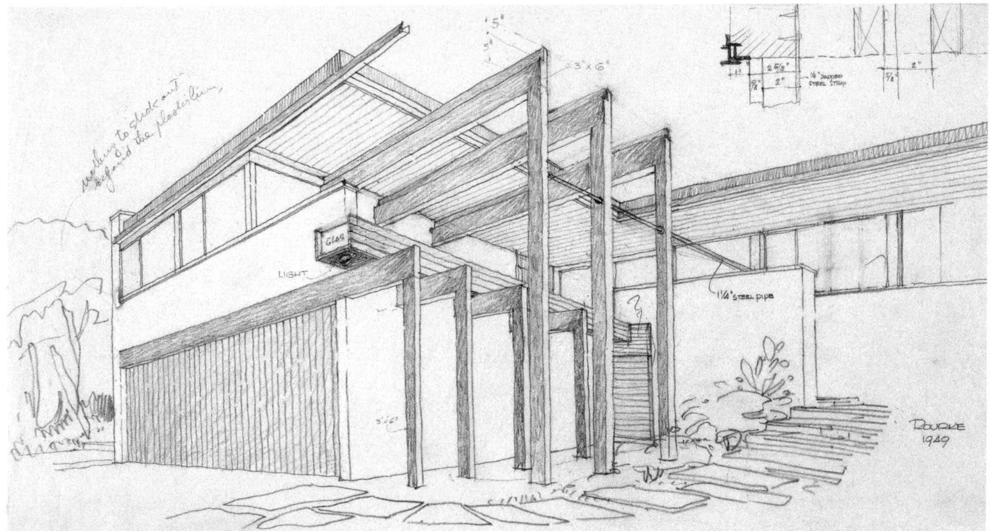

Above: Typically Neutra's spider legs expressed load-bearing that continued beyond the building footprint. In the Rourke House, the three spider legs are functional in extending interior space.

Below: View facing east to the elongated, increasingly private approach to the front door.

The Rourkes' Neutra-designed furniture included a dining set, a coffee table, and chairs.

GORDON AND MARY WILKINS HOUSE

528 Hermosa Street
South Pasadena, California, 1949

In architectural literature it has always been stated that Neutra's Case Study House #6, Omega, and #13, Alpha (featured in the March 1946 issue of *Arts and Architecture*), designed as a pair on adjacent lots, remained unbuilt. Neutra named his hypothetical Mr. and Mrs. Alpha (clients for #13) and Mr. and Mrs. Omega (clients for #6) to show his architecture fit humanity from A to Z, though the couples were white suburban Americans.

It is now likely that Neutra "lifted" the Alpha design and applied it to a real client on a real lot. The drawings for #13, a one-story, L-shaped house, were as complete as for any real client, drawn at full scale. A generous flagstone breezeway at right angles to the entrance path and cutting through the building separates the two arms of the L; the big gesture runs out beyond both sides of the house, creating two separate but linked angled terraces, another variation on Neutra's "Four-Court" idea. The fireplace with its two fireboxes, one indoor, one for outdoor entertaining, acts as the hub of the plan. Mrs. Alpha requested that it be laid in flagstone because "on the occasion of picnic parties, with youngsters about, there would probably be continuous traffic from one open air terrace to the other – root beer to be spilled and greasy sandwiches to drip." Coincidentally, a Mrs. George Wilkins – a real client who with her husband purchased a quiet, wooded double lot in South Pasadena in late 1947 – had the exact same concerns about root beer and greasy sandwiches. And like Mrs. Alpha, it was her "specific wish" that

there be a "psychological connection" between the two terraces. So Neutra designed identical breezeways for both women. In fact, portions of the client descriptions for real or hypothetical client match word for word, just as the plans agree almost line for line. One length of a building wall was 22′ 11″, the other plan called out the same wall at 22′ 9″. The detailing of the house included a little-seen but elegant ventilation strategy in the living room and master bedroom, with screened birch panels placed below a row of casement windows. Hinged at the top, they introduced air inside when curtains were drawn. It also allowed the casements to be without screens, which Neutra avoided where possible because they compromised the outdoor view.

Accessed from a long private driveway, the house is near the lip of the wooded arroyo. The living room looks west and opens to the terrace and the lawns beyond. View facing north.

NEUTRA OFFICE BUILDING

2379 Glendale Boulevard
Los Angeles, California, 1950

The Neutra Institute for Survival Through Design owns the building, which is a designated historic landmark. Here, the painted wood fiber Auditone "Slotted Acoustical Tile" is being installed; it is still there today. View facing west.

The east façade, facing busy Glendale Boulevard, is a straightforward commercial statement in glass and stucco while the rear west façade has the hallmarks of Neutra residential architecture, with a balcony terrace, generous overhang, extruded fascia, exterior soffit lighting and garden access. The two faces reflect the multipurpose character of this long 2,800-square-foot building which incorporates living and working. Following the downward slope of the hill and west of the large open drafting room, the building splits into two levels. The front commercial area, level with the street, was used for offices. The rear has split levels with two one-bedroom apartments. Of special note are the well-detailed, suspended aluminum light troughs in the drafting room. It continued to house the Neutra practice until 1999.

Previous: This is an essay in how a 1950s architectural office operated. Physical, not virtual. Men in white shirts, often short-sleeved to avoid graphite smudges. The famous Dazor Drafting Lamp and the Vemco Drafting Machine which made changing angles effortless, even sexy. Robert E. Alexander, Neutra's partner during the 1950s, sits next to Neutra; according to notes from Neutra, "engineers Parker and Lemos" are in front of them. View facing west.

Right: Planes sliding past one another, a landscaped entry, and glass wrapping a corner creates a quietly handsome building. View facing north.

REUNION AND DION NEUTRA HOUSE

2440 Neutra Place
Los Angeles, California, 1950

This shallow rectangle, a solid spine dug into the slope to the southeast, unfolds and opens into a taut De Stijl essay on point, line and plane, rendered in wood and glass, on its "street" façade. One enters the zigzag path to the entry, thick with trees and plants next to a dark, languid pool. One is deep in a forest in the middle of Los Angeles and a stone's throw from the "rolling traffic" of busy Silver Lake Boulevard.

The Reunion and Dion Neutra House, earlier known as the Earl Street Reunion House, is a pivotal member of the Silver Lake Colony, which Neutra called a "postured grouping, meaning the grouping of a team in cooperative action, where each individual posture complements the others and no soulless, mere side-by-side prevails." It is also the most private, in contrast to its neighbors which are far more engaged with the surrounding cityscape. The building was built "on spec" with a hypothetical client: grandparents whose hospitality fostered all kinds of reunions. One goal was to arrange spaces in such a way as to afford privacy for both primary residents as well as their visitors, so that the master bedroom is at the north end of the house while children and guests are near the kitchen and garage. Another goal was to create ways to keep a relaxed eye on the children, thus, a patio/yard flanks both the dining room and the breakfast nook, confirming the kitchen's role as "command central." Dion Neutra, project architect of the house and long-time owner, remodeled the original 1,620 square feet in 1966 and added a 640-square-foot one-bedroom apartment over the garage two years later. "I remember prices of around $12/15 square feet in the 1950s for the average house; I would guess the budget for our house would be in the $20–22K range."

No element is unimportant to the overall gestalt: even the gutter reaching beyond the fascia plays a critical role in the composition – as well as ensuring water runoff occurs well away from the building envelope. Much of the De Stijl quality here is due to the dual orientation of the "spider-leg outrigging," first employed in houses such as the Nesbitt House (1942), used as tools to extend planes and stretch space into the landscape. In a 1968 letter to Richard and Raymond Neutra, Dion Neutra noted that this was an example of Neutra's "sudden touch of originality or genius which would give rise to the spider leg rather than the old mitered beam [a beam cut at a 40-degree angle to meet another perpendicular beam] that had been used so far."

Opposite: Dion Neutra added the mirror above the bookshelf, elongating the space. The fireplace of golden Roman brick anchors the living room. View facing north.

Below: The unusual ceiling of overlapping Douglas fir planks extends outdoors. One of three such known designs, it may be the last extant example in the Neutra canon. View facing southwest.

Previous: Using client notes, Neutra sketches a layout. The original book-matched cabinet behind him was replaced with an L-shaped unit of desk and drawers wrapping the interior corner. View facing north.

Above: The original lower cabinets featured rotary-cut plywood fronts and Formica countertops trimmed in aluminum. View facing northwest.

Opposite: Dion replaced the "Camel Table" in the breakfast nook with a drafting board so that he could be nearer family activity in the kitchen. View facing southwest.

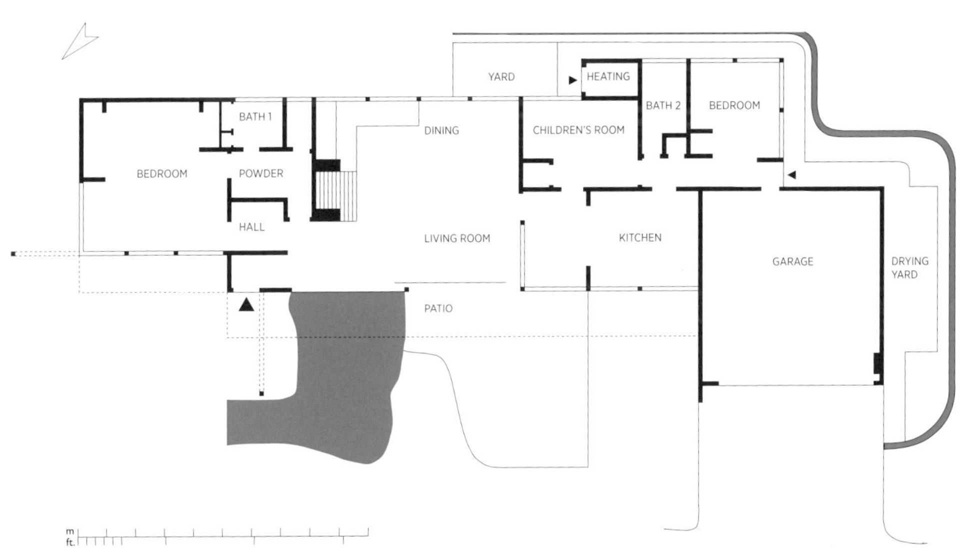
YARD
HEATING
BATH 1
BATH 2
BEDROOM
DINING
CHILDREN'S ROOM
BEDROOM
POWDER
HALL
LIVING ROOM
KITCHEN
GARAGE
DRYING YARD
PATIO
m
ft.

MR. AND MRS. J. C. O'BRIEN HOUSE

4740 Richmond Avenue
Shreveport, Louisana, 1950

The clients gave up a large Southern mansion in favor of a dignified Modernist home whose brief included handling three generations simultaneously. The broad flagstone path is the first welcome to a generous house surrounded by a dense backdrop of pine forest. The path continues into the house, bisecting it as a secondary axis into two volumes. A glass passageway reconnects the two asymmetrical volumes, one with deep overhangs, one without. To the east of the path are living and bedroom areas, while the maid's room, kitchen, guest quarters, den and dining room are to the west. Subtle details enliven each façade: for example, the wood posts supporting the screened-in porch in the rear are located on the outside of the screen, lending a vertical rhythm to the elevation that reverberates in the trunks of the surrounding pine trees. The rear façade is an engaging game of selective revelation: the roof of the screened-in porch extends from the living room and stops four feet from the edge of the framing. Meanwhile, living-room joists concealed by the shipdeck tongue-and-groove ceiling are exposed as soon as they cross the boundary of the lintel beam. These joists run past the roof a few feet before each is caught and held between a pair of studs beyond the roof overhang. The effect is that the house is sequentially undressed, its architectural elements finally blending with the bare trunks of the pine-tree forest, achieving a romantic, satisfying tension unifying indoors and out.

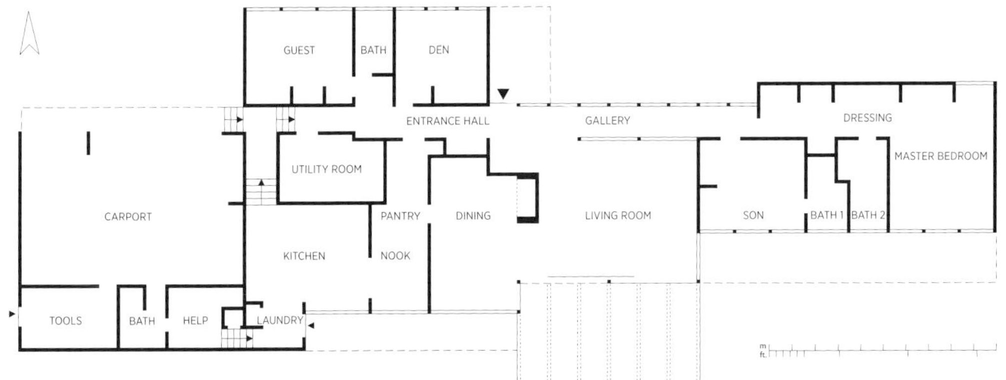

Opposite: The view faces the gallery and the living area beyond. As the plan shows, the house, sited in the middle of a double lot, was masterful in accommodating ever-changing generations of family.

Below: Opening from the living area, the screened outdoor terrace, a thoughtful gesture in light of humid Louisiana's insect populations, was supported by seven spider legs.

ABRAHAM "A.L." AND ALPHA WIRIN HOUSE

2622 Glendower Avenue
Los Angeles, California, 1950

Right: Russian-born Abraham Lincoln Wirin was a lawyer who worked on many landmark civil-rights cases. Secluded "amidst a pine grove," as Neutra put it, in the hills above Hollywood, the home's warm materials provided sanctuary from bruising days in court.

Below: Alpha Wirin relaxes on the south terrace. Seen here, the unusual balcony railing had two "rhythms" of wood. View facing west.

Opposite: Alpha in the kitchen, looking north. Behind her is the massive brick fireplace with a barbeque grill.

FREDERICK AND CECIL FISCHER HOUSE

1618 Pinecrest Road
Spokane, Washington, 1951

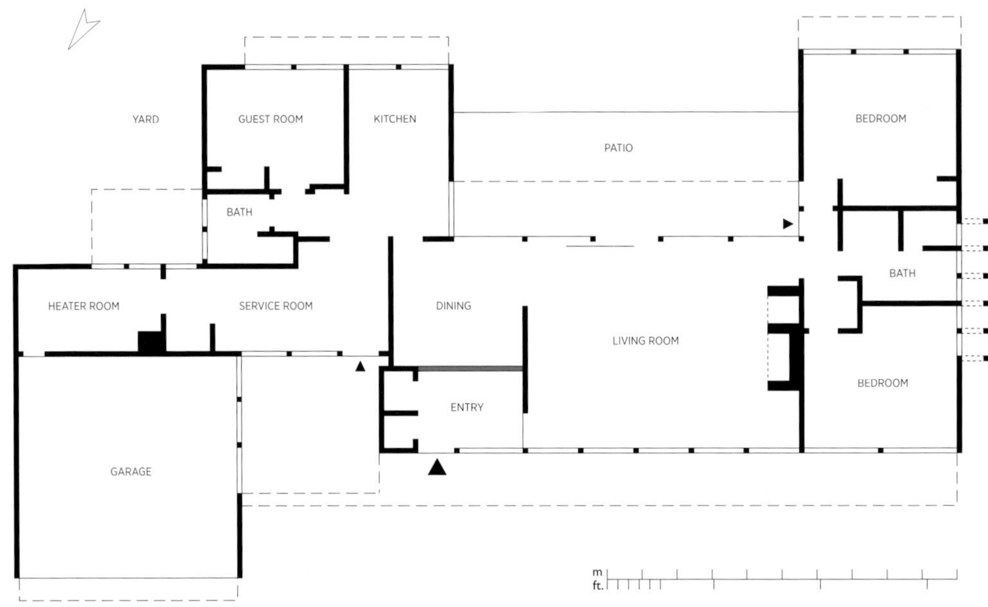

Previous: The terrazzo floors were warmed by radiant heating during the "cold, snowy winters," Neutra wrote. The mirror to the right of the fireplace makes the birch paneling, windows, and redwood ceiling appear to go on infinitely. View facing west.

Opposite: What a quintessentially mid-century image! The coiffed lady of the house, planning her busy day on the telephone, keeping an eye on the terrace with its "Knoll Hardoy Butterfly Chairs." View facing southwest.

This large, one-story house is a shallow U shape where the enclosed outdoor patio is provided with radiant heating to melt snow in winter. There are many interior mirrors to "stretch space" including one behind the dining table to ensure all could partake of the view. The exterior is clad in cedar board and batten, the interior in birch plywood. The garage volume stands in front of the strongly horizontal house, while its west wall appears to extend into the landscape. Apart from terrazzo in the living room, colored and waxed concrete is used throughout for the flooring. This was a musical family and acoustic studies were done to accommodate the built-in organ. A window in front of a built-in desk in the kitchen allows a parent to supervise children on the living room deck. The Fischers said they were more comfortable in winter in their house "than in summers on the Riviera."

JAY AND CATHARINE HINDS HOUSE

3940 San Raphael Avenue
Los Angeles, California, 1951

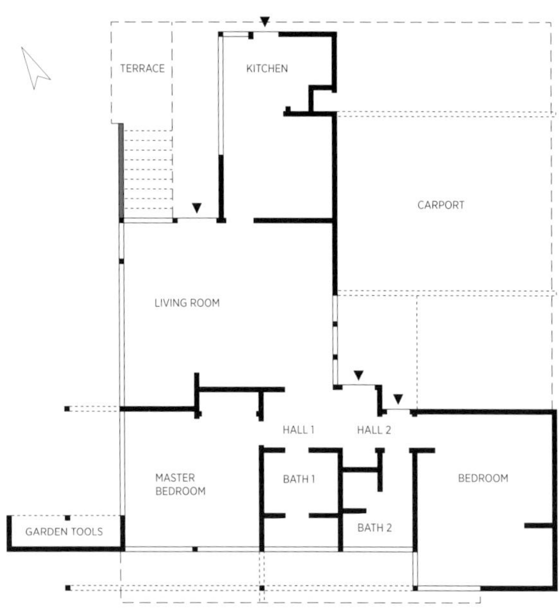
TERRACE
KITCHEN
CARPORT
LIVING ROOM
HALL 1
HALL 2
MASTER BEDROOM
BATH 1
BEDROOM
GARDEN TOOLS
BATH 2
m
ft.

Neutra reduced the rear façade to three planes: wood, glass windows 12-foot long and 42-inch high, and stucco. Below, where the rest of the house steps down the hillside, a tall, narrow storage shed stands at a right angle to the main volume. Just beyond that, a spider leg, parallel to the shed and stretching beyond it, delicately reinforces the anchoring gesture of the smaller volume. "We look back with very deep gratification at the many conferences we had with you, the numerous trips you made to the site during construction, and the several visits you have made to our home since it was completed ... the house brings us as much excitement now as it did a year [ago] ..." the Hinds wrote Neutra on March 12, 1952. Fordyce "Red" Marsh built the house and did an addition for them two years later.

Opposite: Just 1,082 square feet, the Hinds House yet conveys self-assured clarity. A rare example of an intact Neutra design, its new stewards value the history embedded in patina: a good match. View facing northwest.

Below: The master bedroom overlooks the spider leg and the humble perpendicular volume (for garden tools) beyond, which anchors the composition. Clever venting above the windows and hidden in the cabinetry. View facing southeast.

MAX AND ARLENE GOODMAN HOUSE

4227 Golden Avenue
San Bernardino, California, 1952

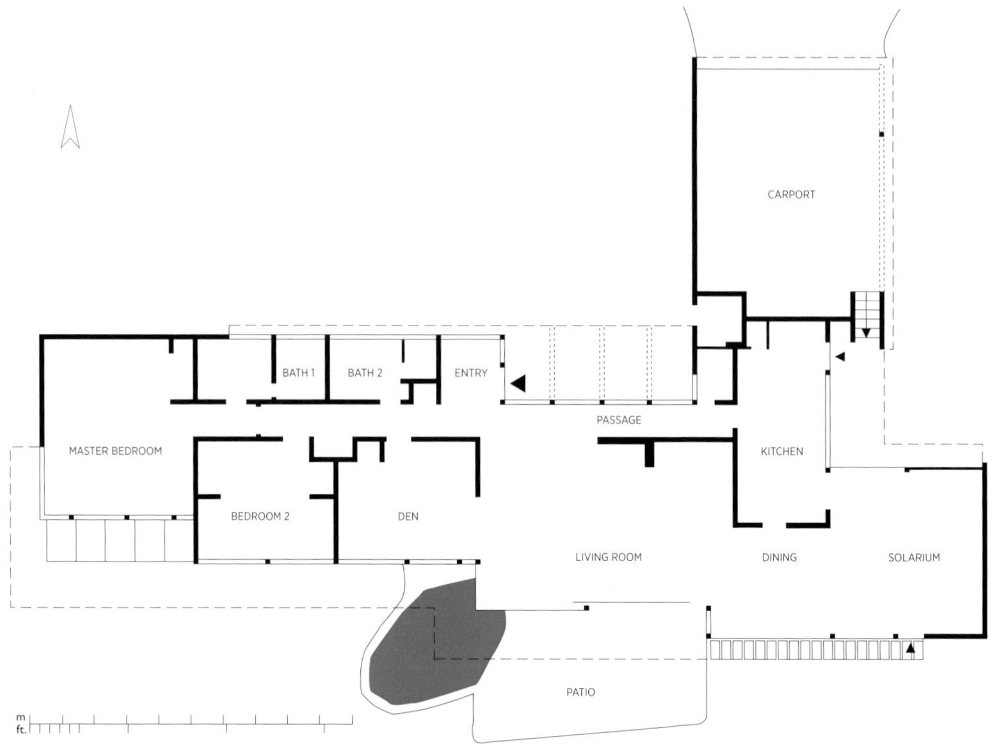

Opposite: A bevy of Neutra furniture waits patiently for the program to begin. The central actor here, the television-on-a-pole, has made this a favorite photo for Neutra cognoscenti. Sited at the lip of the San Bernardino Mountains, the house was lost in a 2003 wildfire.

This house was built for the man later instrumental in commissioning Neutra for the San Bernardino Medical Center. Except for the carport it is a simple rectangle in its footprint, a building rendered in wood. Its relationship to nature is remarkably intimate, and exceptional in its self-assumed didactic role to make Neutra's vision of biorealism in architecture a reality, yet aesthetically self-assured and creative. For example, Neutra used clerestories at the *bottom* of a glass wall, which open out to an intimate reflecting pool, so that the air wafting over the water and plants is cleaned and cooled as it enters the house. Above the floor clerestories Neutra uses steel casement windows with clear glass in addition to large translucent lights, so that the geometry of the glass is reminiscent of the subtle rhythms of traditional residential Japanese architecture. The ceiling plane of redwood planking is a monolithic sweep throughout the house, unifying the floor plan. Curtains acting as shoji screens separate social spaces, harking back to earlier work such as the 1940 Jan DeGraaf House. A portion of the living room steps out beyond the overall mass and its glass corners are mitered, making diagonal vision and "nature near" not only possible but inescapable.

MAURICE AND ESTELLE HELLER HOUSE

811 Camden Drive
Beverly Hills, California, 1952

Opposite: Stairs leading up to the guest apartment featured the same semicircular terminus as seen in many other houses such as the Beard House; a short spider leg framed the upper landing.

Below: Demolished in 1979, the U-shaped house was one of Neutra's best, with elegant spaces and appointments that flowed into a variety of gardens and terraces of buff Utah flagstone.

One leg of the handsome 2,000-square-foot, U-shaped house is a two-story volume. A bridge over the pool leads to the front entrance, marking the transition from street to house. A planter runs into the house from the garden patio, linking indoors and out. Neutra designed the house to be prepared for long-term visitors. A private bedroom wing for children or grandchildren was zoned so it could be closed off when the couple was on their own; one guest room had its own tiny refrigerator hidden by solid birch plywood paneling. Radiant heating under the cork floors and the tongue-and-groove redwood ceiling created a sense of warmth and dignity. The Hellers were devoted to Neutra. "Even when we differed, we never felt fenced-in by your ideas," Mr. Heller wrote him on April 6, 1952.

JAMES AND ORLINE MOORE HOUSE

512 North Foothill Road
Ojai, California, 1952

This memorable house is inextricably linked to its setting, one of the reasons it won a first honor award from the American Institute of Architects. Neutra described the site's context in the fertile Ojai Valley as "a lovely subtropical landscape of orange groves between mountain ranges." It is also a very private site, since the Moore ranch covered 30 acres. The $70,362.41 dwelling consists of a main house, connected with stone stairs and a pergola overgrown with vines to a studio and guesthouse. Two "private quarters," as Neutra referred to the bedrooms, are bordered on the west by an unusual exhibition gallery corridor with rounded plaster coving. Of all Neutra's houses, this house in particular reveals a complicated, rich spatial relationship with the lush landscaping and the large, erratically shaped pool wrapping the northeast corner

Opposite: View facing north, across the bridge that leads to the front door. The projecting stone pier separates public from private space.

Below: View of the main house from the guest studio. The articulation of the roof overhang defines the spatial transitions.

of the house, a relationship that both draws the outdoors in and reaches out to it. Neutra wrote about its fluid quality: "The north end of the social quarters opens into a party glazed, partly screened porch and into a fireplace-enriched day room which in turn flows into the dining nook and kitchen." The entire glazed east front looks down the length of the valley. Framing a different view, the north opens to the distant mountains and to the intimacy of a stone deck, which in turn extends to a "psychologically cooling" L-shaped pool that also serves as an irrigation system for the plants.

Throughout the composition, the sophisticated use of asymmetric, sliding lines and planes placed at right angles to one another (seen in the overhangs, spider legs and extended lintel beam) work together to weave house and

Opposite: The glazed northeast corner looks toward the rugged Santa Ynez Mountains.

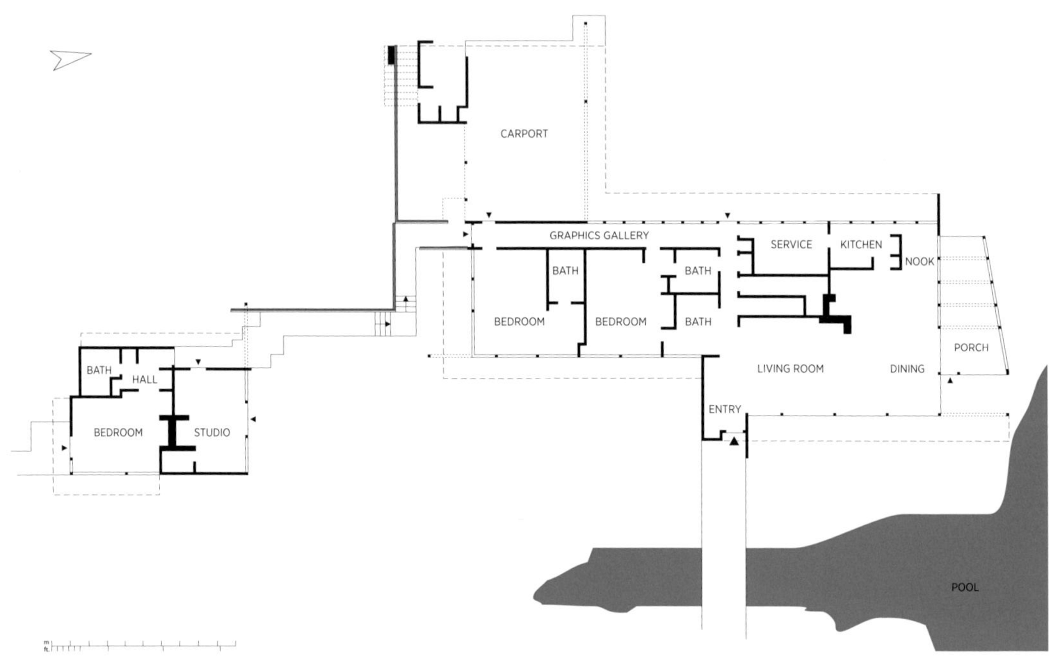

site together. The effect is that of a De Stijl raft moored to both water and land. The floors, warmed by radiant heating, extend into the deck, further linking indoors and out. The high ceilings (11-feet-tall in the living area) are staggered-board redwood, walls and built-ins of birch, the windows aluminum sash. "Real Wood" Formica countertops match cabinet fronts. Mrs. Moore did her own landscaping, including cattails, Louisiana iris, water hyacinths, lotus, waterlilies, creeping cottoneast; native shrubs such as ceanothus, toyon, giant buckwheat, sage, and rhus; four kinds of eucalyptus trees as well as pepper, live oak, carob and pine.

The roof of the detached carport in the east was designed as a pool to reflect the surrounding mountains and trees. Because it is at a lower elevation than the rest of the house, in essence Neutra made the carport disappear for those looking down from above.

FRED AND BEA VAN SICKLEN HOUSE

Rancho Santa Fe, California, 1952

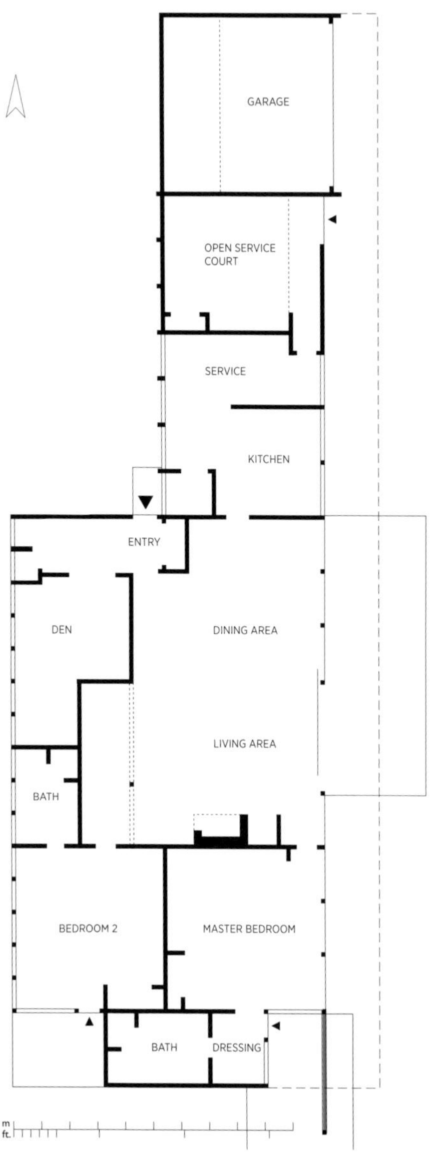

A sweeping, steep shed roof is the main gesture in this long rectangular building, with the high point of the roof facing the street. Its disciplined, minimalist redwood façade conceals an open service yard and the kitchen with exceptionally tall windows, tied together rhythmically by the vertical posts supporting the sustained lintel beam. Inside, the kitchen ceiling soars, its large translucent windows rising above the datum line of the cabinetry. The long house had an all-wood interior, with redwood tongue-and-groove ceiling and birch plywood walls and built-ins, while the fireplace was rendered in white plaster. Radiant heating extended into the three outdoor patios, according to Neutra's description of the two-bedroom house.

Opposite: The extraordinary kitchen featured translucent glass and bamboo drapes. Neutra wrote that the owner "fortunately had very decided and clear ideas" about the design of her kitchen, which included rotary-cut plywood cabinetry, walls of dark green, and countertops of deep green Formica.

FREDERICK AND MARY JANE AUERBACHER HOUSE

121 Sierra Vista Drive
Redlands, California, 1953

Sited well above orange layers of suburban sprawl and pollution, and just below the grade of the winding street, this 2,300-square-foot house is oriented so that the prominent view, almost non-stop glass, looks to the mountains beyond, while the street side is primarily closed except for clerestories. Interior walls running perpendicular to this long rectangle end in floor-to-ceiling glass along the edge of the view wall, which steps out two feet. This move creates a long visual corridor and sense of transparency through the house and demonstrates Neutra's ideas on the role of peripheral vision in accessing nature. While the house is aesthetically *longitudinally* bisected, it is *laterally* divided up in terms of function. The interior is

Above: View to the southeast, from the dining room to the living room. Opposite: The same view orientation, but here a little to the north; the solarium/play room is in the foreground.

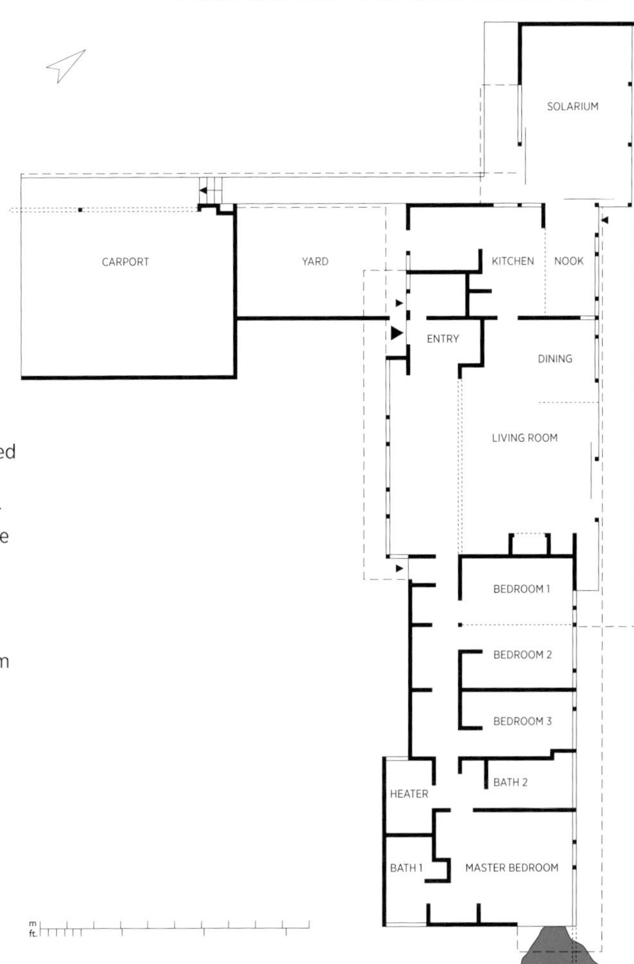

Opposite top: A carefully sequenced set up spaces separated an entry area for music and Mary Jane's organ, complete with a corner source of daylight. View facing east.

Opposite bottom: Now that the landscaping has grown, the seamless corner window in the bedroom with its own tiny reflecting pool is very private. View northeast to the Redlands Country Club.

a carefully orchestrated spine of spaces, terminating in a tranquil master bedroom at one end, whose mitered glass corner leads the eye out into leafy landscaping and a quiet corner pool, and a sturdy, light-filled work and play room off the kitchen (with the sink the central command post for watching children in any direction) at the other end. While the bedrooms are painted in flat whites, dark browns and greens, the living and dining area combine birch paneling, redwood tongue-and-groove ceiling, and a flagstone fireplace. (Mary Jane Auerbacher said that Neutra ordered that the flagstone, inadvertently laid symmetrically, be redone so that no large stone commanded a central position.) In this space Neutra also provided a space in the living area for her, the professional musician, that was serene and yet attuned to every possible need for sheet music and instrument storage, as well as for the phonograph, Fred's "instrument." In the dining area, Neutra placed a low mirror behind the dining room table (aligned along the window wall) so that all guests could enjoy the mountain view.

JOSEPH W. KRAMER HOUSE

108 West 8th Street
Norco, California, 1953

Opposite: The birch plywood cabinetry was carefully designed to be book-matched or to "flow" over the top and continue down the face of the cabinets. Dr. Kramer's site was quite isolated; the rugged finishes of concrete block and brick, matched the rural setting.

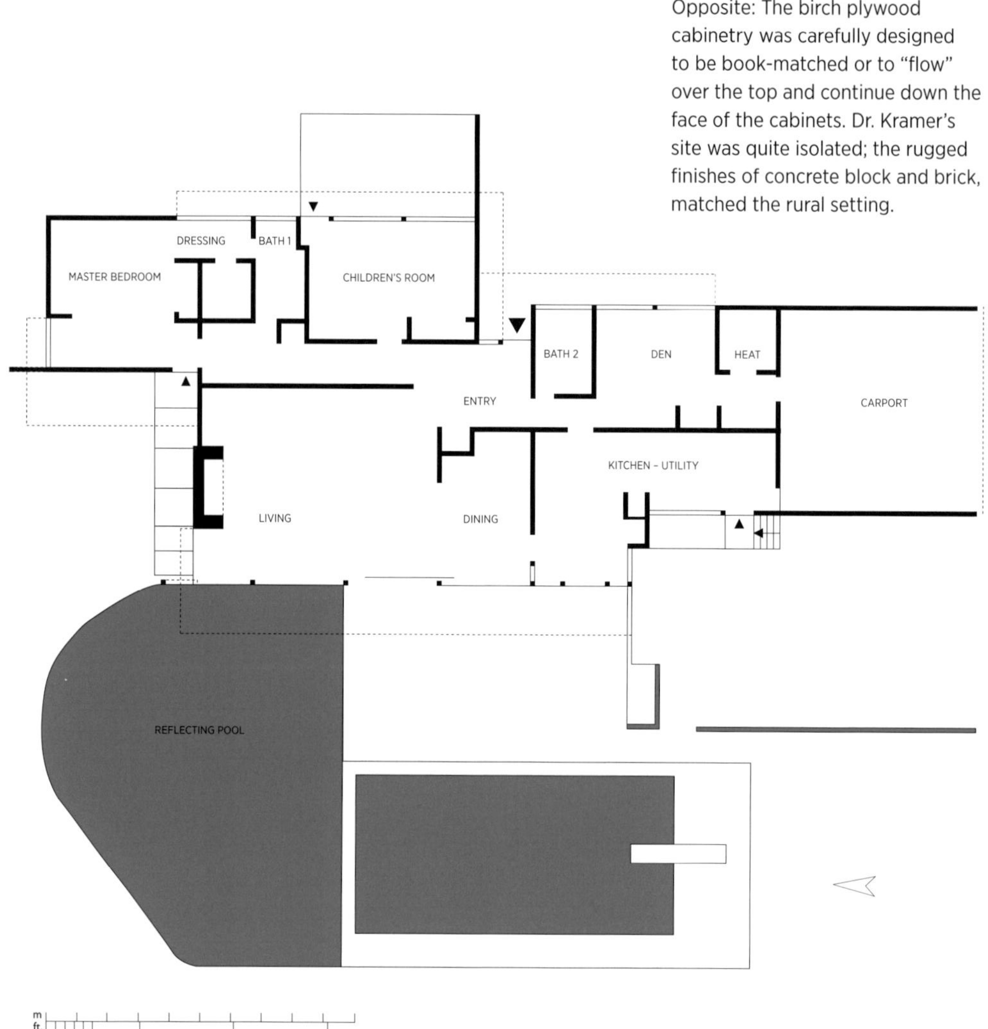

"If the busy country doctor has to make several night calls and does not want to disturb his wife, he sleeps in a guest room so conveniently near his faithful car," Neutra wrote. The guest room for the doctor is well away from the master bedroom, which pops out on the north so it too has diagonal visual access to the curved pool that runs up to the end of the west-facing living room. Putting this bedroom here also ensured it is surrounded by greenery and is very private.

The land is arid and desert-like; the ground is decomposed granite and "it will be difficult to get a garden started on this windswept plateau." Neutra addressed the climate by creating many transitions to the outdoors through terraces, patios, landscaping and a brick wall windbreak. Other features include radiant heating and a monolithic tongue-and-groove ceiling throughout the house.

ORANGE COAST COLLEGE SPEECH ARTS BUILDING

Neutra and Alexander
2701 Fairview Road
Costa Mesa, California, 1953

This large group of buildings included an auditorium, ancillary stage production areas, band and orchestra rooms, choral and instrument practice rooms and dressing areas, and is the most successful of the Neutra and Alexander designs for the campus. The auditorium is a rounded and clipped ellipse in plan, its footprint was shaped specifically to allow "theater-in-the-round" and "audience-in-the-round" techniques. It is placed at a tangent to a long outdoor entrance walkway, which is aligned to the larger grid of the campus and partially sheathed in translucent panels. Neutra and Alexander responded to the brief for a flexible environment by designing tables of different heights as adjustable and removable seating platforms; they also incorporated a pair of revolving stages and two side stages to permit dramatic action to extend around the audience. Massive motor-driven doors open the stage to the outdoor amphitheater.

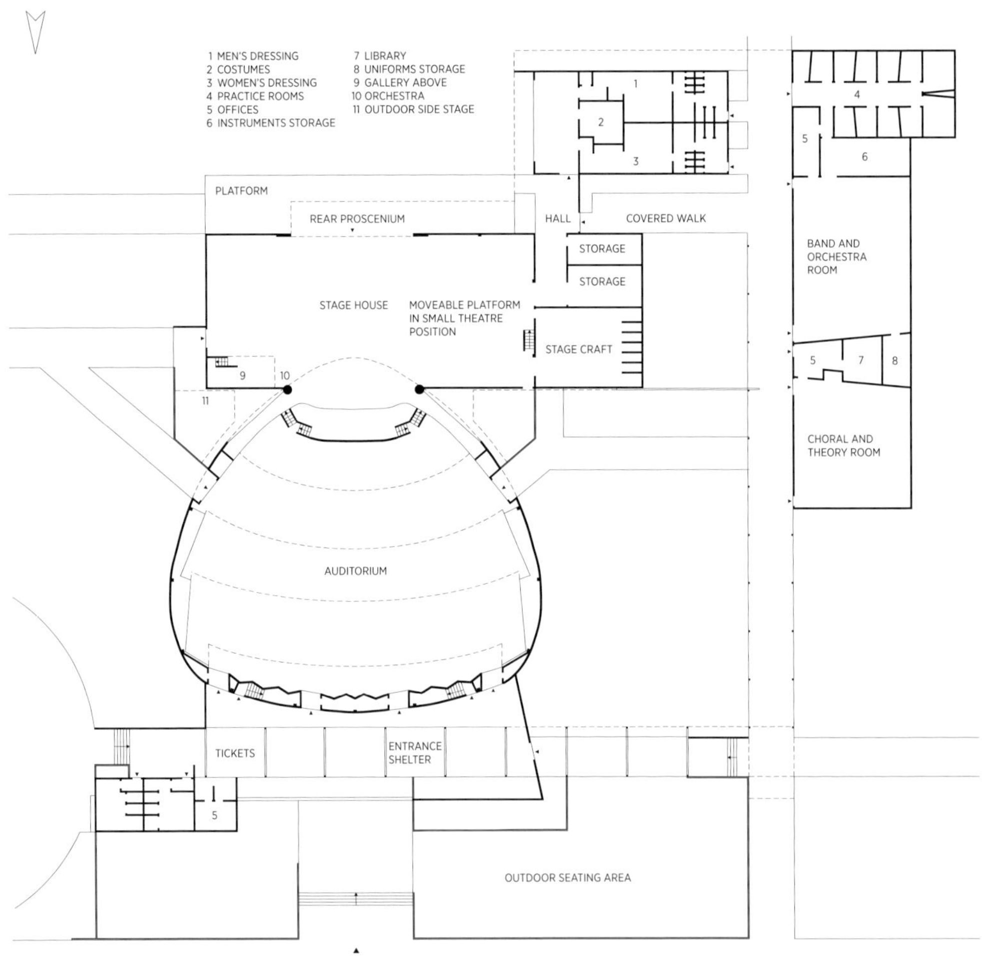

Right: The translucent glass panels at the entrance walkway acted as both a windbreak and as a privacy screen.

Below: The band room's curves, soffits, and materials supported excellent acoustics.

SAN BERNARDINO MEDICAL CENTER

1700 Waterman Avenue
San Bernardino, California, 1953

This group of small medical buildings was sited near two hospitals and included parking space for 120 cars. Neutra's first move was to set the buildings back 100 feet from the street and to plant fig, magnolia, and walnut trees to act as sound buffers. A structure of wood studs and plaster, the volumes are broken down to increase interior daylight and views of nature, with many large patio gardens which penetrate deep into the building "to avoid claustrophobia ... The patient feels more like in a botanical exhibition hall than in a medical building." He was not only concerned with the patient: "Because each speciality is different, requiring different amounts of time per patient exchange, the clinic is not simply a row of offices in space but a layout in time as well ... a well laid out group practice clinic keeps the doctor away from his own sickbed or mental institution ...," he wrote in 1955. Not only does nature percolate through the one-story, 20,000-square-foot compound (estimated at $343,000), Neutra also designed a clear system

of daylit corridors specifically for easy way-finding and stress reduction. The group expected to expand, and so Neutra placed storage spaces for archives, X-rays, files and pharmaceutical suppplies at the periphery of the building where they would be easily accessible in case of expansion. Though an unadorned composition of white stucco planes and vertical metal louvers, one intriguing detail looks as though it were designed 40 years later: to create an intermediary zone between the harsh sun and the interior, he attached a gridded framework of metal studs, supporting a perforated metal screen placed high on the studs, to the deep overhangs.

Opposite: The white, boxy volumes surround a large grassy atrium. Aluminum louvers served to calibrate the area's intense sun and heat.

Above: While humbler than the Mariners Medical Arts Center, the San Bernardino Medical Center aimed to allay patient anxieties by providing waiting areas whose full-height glass walls looked out to the greenery of lawns and plants.

ROBERT AND OPAL KESLER HOUSE

1367 Monument Street
Pacific Palisades, California, 1954

This design had a ingenious solution for frequent overnight visitors: in an alcove off the living area, a clever seating arrangement was devised with a double bunk. When one half is lowered it forms a sofa with a comfortable back rest, when raised it supplies two beds. The living room of this 1,840-square-foot house was on the lower level; the upper level is devoted to the two-car garage and children's rooms.

Below: Destroyed in the 2025 Los Angeles fires, the Kesler House made use of every square inch of the small, awkward site. View facing southeast.

Opposite: The multifunctional living area looked northwest to Temescal Gateway Park.

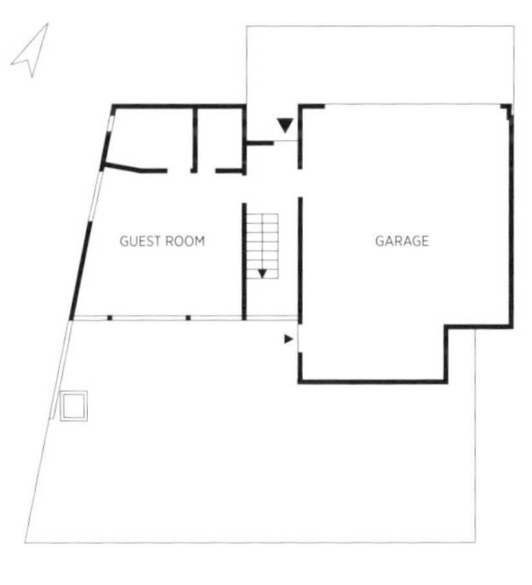

STREET LEVEL PLAN

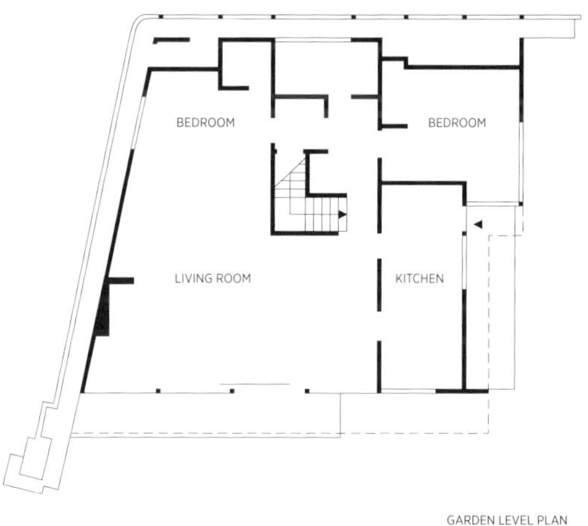

GARDEN LEVEL PLAN

CAROL WESTON HOUSE

3220 Durand Drive
Los Angeles, California, 1954

This minuscule gem of a house was designed for a single school teacher on an "unbuildable" site she bought at a tax sale for under $1000. The budget was extremely tight as was space, so the carport was designed as an extension of the social quarters by means of a wide doorway past the kitchen. A guest room was later added down below.

Below: A small budget propelled a super-efficient floor plan. But whatever the budget, rotary-cut plywood cabinetry seemed always to have a place. Ms. Weston enjoyed an incomparable view from her sink.

Opposite: One of most windy and hilly streets in Los Angeles, the house seems to cling to a hairpin turn. View facing east.

SIDNEY AND SONJA BROWN HOUSE

10801 Chalon Road
Bel Air, California, 1955

In the 1950s Neutra commanded a large residential base of prosperous upper-middle-class clients in contrast with the not-as-monied but avant-garde clients of the 1930s and 1940s. This house has fine finishes and weaves lowly and expensive materials. As with many of his surburban homes during this period, Neutra convinced the Browns of his principle of paralleling the contours of a hill; here a standard move is to raise the body of the house up and out from the slope and place service areas beneath. Perpendicular wall planes separate the house into three distinct masses of private, semi-private and public areas. (In contrast, see how the Slavin House is handled in this regard: there a spider leg, and not a heavy plane, performs the necessary articulations but far more delicately.) The living room is the *pièce de résistance*, opening to a height of 11′ 6″, terminating in a semi-freestanding fireplace raked by light, its light brickwork puncturing the slope of

The (square) posts on the left are clad in stainless steel, a first in the Neutra canon: he sometimes clad (round) columns in steel to pick up load where he needed it. View facing southwest.

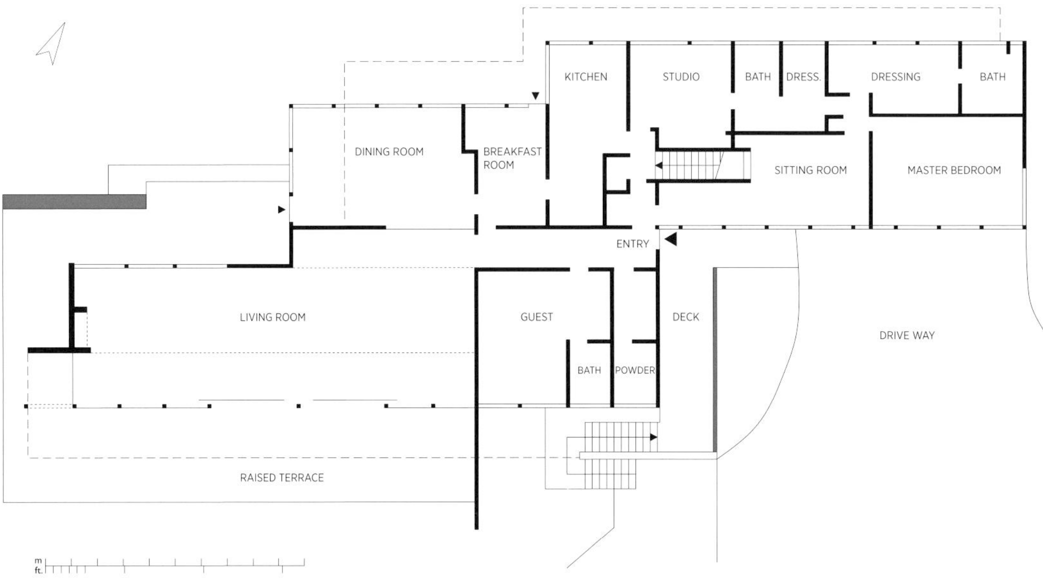

the roof. One of Neutra's ruling ideas was the integration of all elements to make a whole, an idea that eluded this house as originally designed and since remodeled. There are beautiful mini-compositions of geometry and positive and negative voids within a larger framework in which the awkward space planning seemed to be an afterthought, odd because usually his designs make traffic patterns flow easily.

After a carefully nuanced procession to the front door, the house trapped the visitor at the cramped entry, which terminated a long tall ash plywood-clad hall leading from the living room. One must also make many turns to traverse the kitchen and bedroom areas, where typically Neutra might "peel off" the bedrooms from a generous spine. But there are several whimsical details throughout, such as how rain is handled. The roof gutter on the long, terraced side of the living room extends west from the building. Rather than directing water to the back of the house, Dion Neutra suggested an outdoor corner waterfall, falling into the center of a four-foot-diameter circle of gravel placed just beyond the far mitred glass corner of the living room. Inside, a column between dining and living areas is clad in stainless steel to "dematerialize it," as Neutra wrote to the Browns. He worked hard with the plasterers so that the inside and outside of the living room soffit were uniform in color and texture "to ensure the visual expansion of the room."

However, the poolhouse is a three-dimensional Mondrian jewel of planes and lines, beginning with a delicate series of stainless-steel clad spider legs that descend from the structure to the heavily wooded hillside below. Roberto Burle Marx, who had earlier worked on the Tremaine House with Oscar Niemeyer, made suggestions for the landscaping including "one rhythm but with many different heights and colors in massing," he wrote to Neutra on July 14, 1955.

HENRY AND BETTY CORWIN HOUSE

25 Huckleberry Lane
Weston, Connecticut, 1955

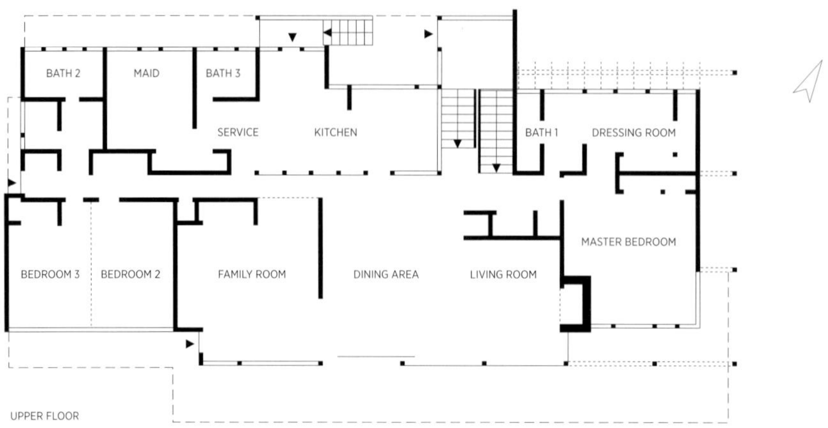

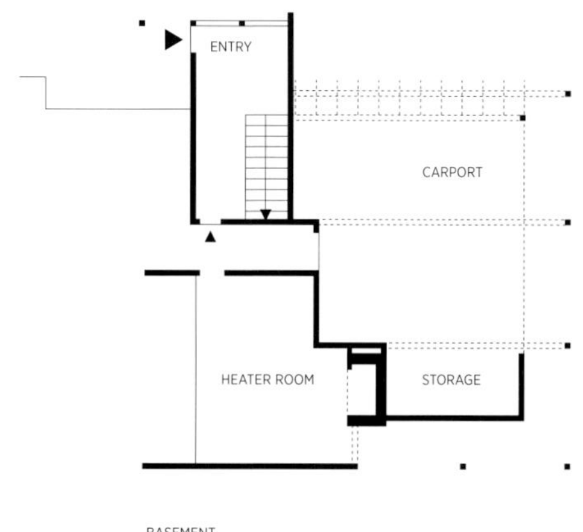

Opposite: Set on 4.3 acres above the Saugatuck River, the house was sold in 2020 by Betty Corwin herself, fortunately finding new stewards who were intent on preserving and restoring the home. The one-and-a-half story glass, stucco, and wood-clad house provides a myriad of interactions with nature in every season, but it seems most arresting in the winter.

The sense of procession here is very strong, and the two-story gallery entrance is reminiscent of some of Neutra's early houses. This is a house of strong geometries rendered in brick, glass, and tongue-and-groove redwood. The fireplace is a void below smooth white plaster which also terminates a horizontal plane of brick and vertical grain ash cabinetry. The pattern of the dark slate flagstone floors is the same indoors and out, the only difference is that the exterior stone is ungrouted. The relationship between the client and Neutra – as well those architects and assistants in Neutra's office – was typically intense and manifested in thick sheaves of letters back and forth, sometimes almost daily, between the office and the client. Neutra would go through the client's letters – their biographical essays describing their daily habits – or the office forms they had filled out, and underline preferences or items he believed important in each of these letters, usually in red. By the 1950s, all this information was by then distilled into a grid titled "Abstract of Client's Requirements" while two decades earlier it was titled simply, "My Questions to You." Those wishes, precisely documented as to time and place of occurrence, were then "hard-lined" into architectural responses in a category for how those requirements were to be addressed, in furnishings or appliances, or whether they must be addressed in elevation, plan, or details. The next step was invariably Neutra's request for a contour map. In the Corwin House, the office file reveals an exhaustive interchange between Neutra and Henry Corwin on where, exactly, the corner of the living room should be placed in this heavily wooded landscape filled with huge rock outcrops. The Corwins objected to Neutra's plan for a long, rectangular house, calling it a "railroad type room arrangement"; Neutra then shortened the interior cross walls to allow corridors on both sides of the house. He, in turn, warned them that placing the children's bedrooms right next to theirs and near the kitchen would not bode well in the future when they would "want to have their late night parties without disturbing you." But often client letters were even more intimate, possibly because frankness led to a more responsive design. Henry wrote confidently that they are a popular couple who "entertain frequently, are trim and athletic," and that he loves his wife. He also made sure that Neutra knew and responded to all his needs: "When defecating I like to read and would like to have a magazine rack next to the toilet," he wrote ... a fairly frequent combination of two activities but rarely voiced so matter-of-factly.

CORWIN AND GLORIA HANSCH HOUSE

4070 Olive Knoll
Claremont, California, 1955

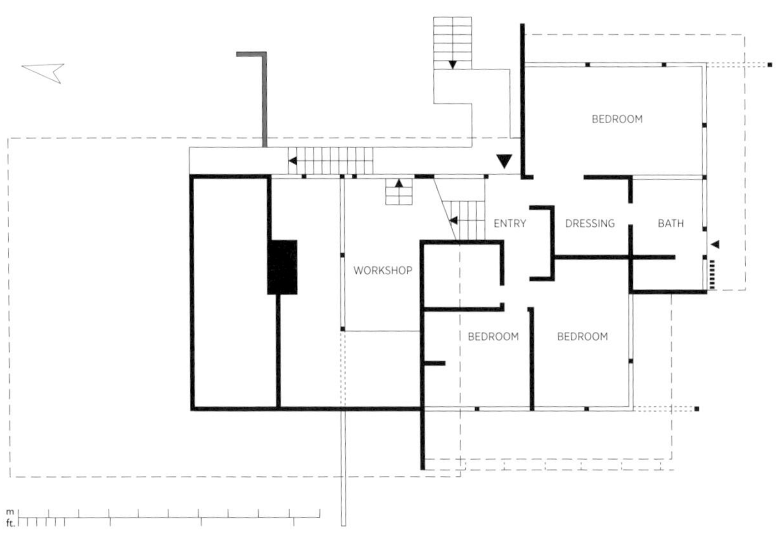
BEDROOM
ENTRY
DRESSING
BATH
WORKSHOP
BEDROOM
BEDROOM
m
ft.

Opposite: Like Betty Corwin, Gloria outlived her husband and also found excellent new stewards for the house, sited high above Claremont in the Padua Hills. View looking over the roof deck, facing southwest.

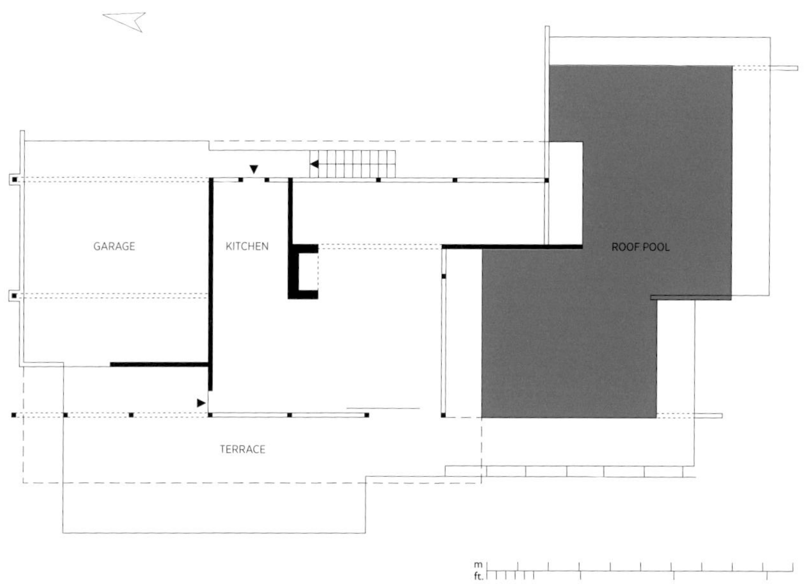

This house sits on a tight, narrow promontory surrounded by curving roads in an idyllic olive grove, just where the San Bernardino Mountains start to rise quickly behind it. The site was so sharp in profile that Dr. Hansch wanted a retaining wall to stop dirt from washing away but Neutra preferred "planting fortissimo" instead. One enters the split-level house from the lower floor, where there is a 13-foot-tall entry hall. Here there is an awkward moment, odd given Neutra's usual care for who is allowed to see what, because a visitor can see right into one of the bedrooms when the door is open. Stairs lead to the main living room where brick paving continues from the outdoor terrace to the interior. A southern rooftop terrace at the top of the lower floor is at eye level while one stands in the living room. Its height feels uneasy, neither high enough to enclose nor low enough for the eye to grasp the roof terrace. When flooded with water and windows were open, it was meant to cool the interior and reflect light patterns on the inside, but it proved difficult to maintain because bacteria and mold quickly took over. The interior wall finishes, in strong contrasts to make forms recede or come forward, include Japanese ash plywood, a favorite of Neutra's, and plaster, painted in citrus tones or in white or in the familiar Neutra tone of brown. The concrete slab has radiant water heating, and the west side of the simple, functional galley kitchen leading from the carport overlooks wonderful views of the mountains.

HERBERT AND HAZEL KRONISH HOUSE

9439 Sunset Boulevard
Beverly Hills, California, 1955

Opposite: At 6,891 square feet, one of Neutra's largest homes, the house included a glassed-in garden. The son of a Brooklyn banker, Herbert Kronish was a successful home builder and part owner of a Beverly Hills hotel, among other ventures.

Right: The house is on a two-acre, wooded flag lot, completely secluded from busy Sunset Boulevard. Demolition proceedings had already begun in 2011 before community outcry stopped it and a new owner stepped forward at the suggestion of the architects Marmol Radziner, who in turn led a renovation and rehabilitation.

Neutra seemed to be an odd choice for this couple – in an October 14, 1953, letter they stated that they didn't want a design that looked like a wooden box, they didn't like flat roofs (or even shed roofs), and they didn't want radiant heating or sliding doors. In any case they went ahead. The result is a very formal, pinwheel-shaped one-story villa (with radiant heating) exhibiting a very different perception of nature's role: here nature is no longer an equal and possibly unpredictable partner but thoroughly tamed and cleaned up. For example, at the entrance a landscaped garden is technically "inside" the house but is confined to a "fish bowl" of glass. Elsewhere the sense of texture in materials is suppressed so that surfaces feel slick and hard. There is a wealth of amenities: the kitchen alone included double built-in ovens, an elaborate phone system, a rotisserie, a shallow series of base cabinets at less than standard depths with six gas burners in a single line for perfect access. Neutra suggested Utah stone. "Its main interest," he wrote to them, "is the lack of mortar which would cheapen the appearance and compete with the real precious mineral surface." In a later letter dated January 31, 1955, he shared the basis of his architectural convictions in a poignant paragraph: "Every major project like this takes a good deal of 'starch' out of me, my life-strength, but there is always deep satisfaction. ... This production would not have been possible if I had been a little more casual about what concerns you, or take it all less to heart than I did. After all and in the end, life is a lonely business for each human being even when there is a crowd around us, and an architect and a client must naturally come close and stay in mutual sympathy while a new and a little happier life can start after all the troubles and noise of building."

ORANGE COAST COLLEGE SCIENCE BUILDING

Neutra and Alexander
2701 Fairview Road
Costa Mesa, California, 1955

Like the Business Education Building, the Science Buildings were also composed as a T-shaped compound and included laboratories and classrooms. A small planetarium partially surrounded by a curving pool was located in the northwest portion of the T. Broad overhangs around the two long buildings to the northeast suppressed the visual impact of the slight pitch of the gabled roofs.

Above: Richard Neutra and Robert Alexander began their ten-year partnership on large projects with the many handsome, low-scale campus buildings they designed for Orange Coast College, many of which have been demolished, including the planetarium.

Opposite: View of the simple layout for science students. Clerestories let in ambient daylight.

CONSTANCE PERKINS HOUSE

1540 Poppy Peak Drive
Pasadena, California, 1955

The almost-daily letters between Neutra, his project architects, including Dion Neutra and John Blanton, and Constance Perkins show a depth of reciprocity that is amazing even in Neutra's circle of deep client relationships. The house is in a quiet, hilly part of southwest Pasadena, 20 minutes to Silver Lake for Perkins or Neutra, and it was built when both were very clear about who they were and what they wanted and had to offer. He was at the height of his fame. She was a tart, opinionated, intellectual art historian who had lived a big life filled with travel and teaching at Occidental College, but Perkins also had longed for "a home that is a part of my own living, [something] I will feel homesick for."

It is no accident that this project, on a very tight lot and on the $17,000 budget of a single (but hardly solitary) academic, is well-known. The spirited 1,310-square-foot house gamely steps up its steep site in a taut, open interlocking system of white stucco planes and Douglas fir posts and beams. At the entry, the eye is immediately

drawn to the garden on the east and the famous tiny pool winding in and out of the mitered glass corner. Above, the lintel beam propels the gaze outward as the beam is pulled across the window wall, changing identity and stretching space as it becomes a spider leg reaching down into the pool. To the north, the glass wall opens to the view of the San Gabriel Mountains and to the roof deck above the carport, illuminated at night by the exterior soffit lighting. The corner is a sensuous part of a house that speaks to the literal body of the client, not in a disrespectful way, but in that intense, unique way good architecture caresses the whole life of a client. Her bed is not in a bedroom, but is located in short leg of the L-shaped living room, facing alternately the mountains or her desk piled with papers. A reading light above the bed is next to the wood bookcases, whose detailing is standard Neutra. The shelves stand proud of the vertical supports, emphasizing the horizontal line, and their edges are tapered, giving the bookcase a subtle, inexpensive grace. The palette of glass, redwood decking, burnished concrete floors, rubbed and waxed tempered Masonite (used in the cheapest way possible for sliding kitchen cabinet doors) and white plaster was enlivened by the choices by "Professor Perkins on Poppy Peak" of bright yellow and vibrant persimmon on some doors and walls. The kitchen has a long service yellow Formica countertop under the suspended cabinets to entertain student gatherings.

Opposite: The spirited little house is a wonderful demonstration of Neutra's brilliantly employed line and plane "pulling apart" what could have been a stolid volume on a hill. View facing southeast.

Above: Professor Perkins did have a lovely bedroom tucked away amidst greenery, but she preferred her day bed, next to her books and looking out to the San Gabriel Mountains.

Above: Inexpensive tempered and oiled Masonite upper cabinets had sliding panels, rather than doors, to make the tiny kitchen a little more ergonomically friendly. The countertop is clad with a bright yellow Formica, while the opening to the living area made it easy for the professor to socialize with her guests.

Opposite: One of Neutra's most famous spider legs terminates in the tiny biomorphic pool that Perkins designed with the architect's team to run under the glass and into the living area. View facing west.

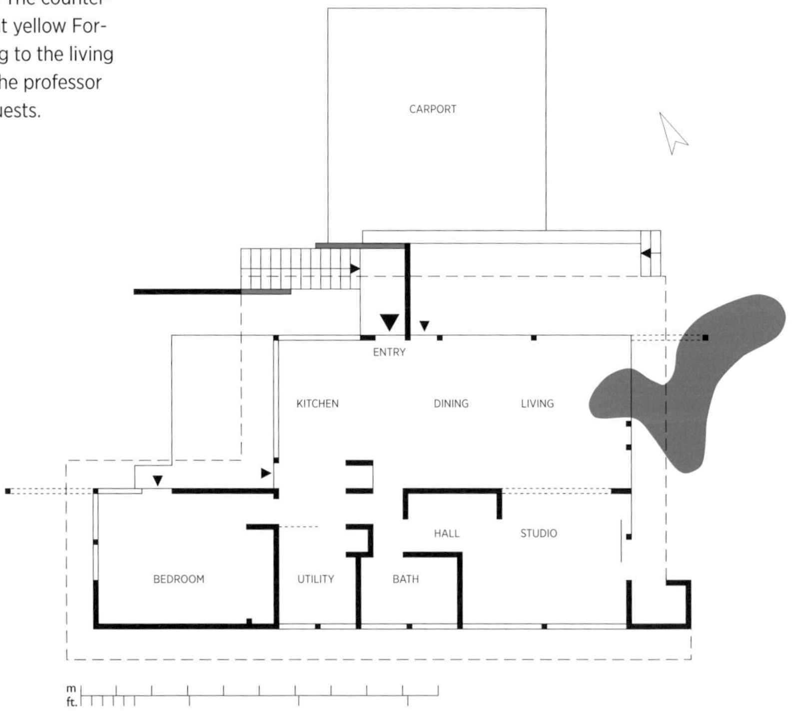

GEORGE AND DOROTHY SERULNIC HOUSE

3947 Markridge Road
Glendale, California, 1955

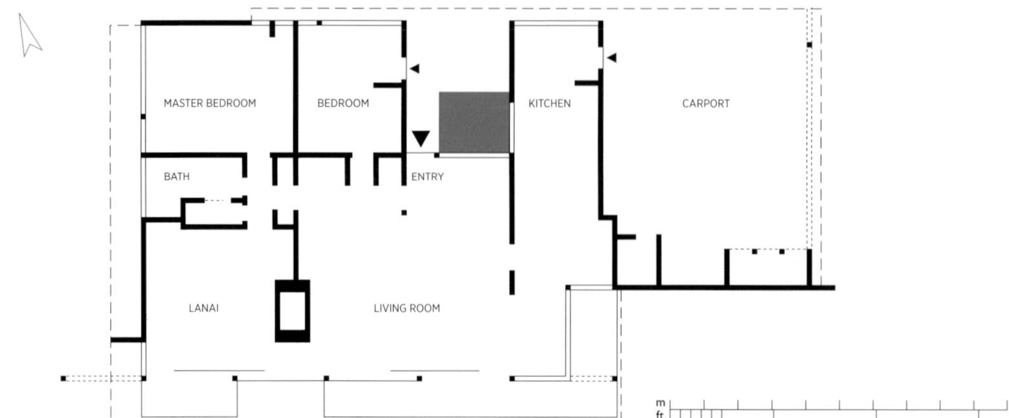

This is the beloved house of an associate close to both Richard and Dione. Neutra was dubious about the sheer slope of the site near the Angeles National Forest, writing that when he first visited the site, all he saw were "simply several acres of precipitous slope ... there seemed, and was, no possible way to get up." Today, one sees the house from below quite easily, against a hill covered in blazing purple succulents. The approach flanks the hill, then doubles back into the carport. The 1,360-square-foot house, almost square in plan, was built for Neutra's secretary, a poet whose passion overcame severe budget constraints and her husband, a violist with the Los Angeles Philharmonic. Neutra delivered plans with exhaustive cost estimates and a design which could be accomplished over time, and at her insistence, the savvy, conscientious Fordyce "Red" Marsh, well known to Mrs. Serulnic, was the contractor who delivered the building. "Bear Valley" stone quarried from Big Bear, "cut for small scale to fit the proportions of the environment," was selected for the fireplace that bisects the main interior space to define the living room and lanai. Light-colored brick was chosen to blend with the birch cabinetry and to match the stone which ranged from buff to deep maroon. To reduce energy costs Neutra placed an awning that was attached to the extreme end of the deep overhang of the south-facing living room, keeping the low afternoon sun off the glass; at the same time, air circulates behind the awning and into the living room through three sliding-glass sections, keeping the interior cooler. The living room is a good example of two Neutra conventions: the living room settee (cantilevered so it floats above the ground) is located so the user simultaneously participates in the fireplace and in the stunning view, aided by mitered glass corners; the back of the settee is not only a 36-inch-tall cabinet but also defines the hallway leading to the bedroom and bath. This is one of the few Neutra homes in which access to the narrow galley kitchen from the living area feels cramped and awkward.

Opposite: Dorothy was a force of nature; even Neutra, used to building on impossible slopes, was taken aback when she showed him her land. The living room overlooks a truly breathtaking view of Los Angeles. View facing west.

RICHARD NEUTRA

JOSEPH AND SONIA STALLER HOUSE

901 Bel Air Road
Los Angeles, California, 1955

This is a large house with a three-car garage and two servants' rooms in addition to the family bedrooms. On a steep hillside with a background of tall trees, the long two-story house (32′ 6″ wide by 15 bays at 8′ on center, or 120′) digs into the slope behind it. Its broken roof is gabled: although each roof shares the same seven-foot starting point (the plate line at the building's perimeter), the southern roof is longer and meets the ridge beam at a higher point than the northern roof, affording north ambient daylight and a view of the hill. The structural posts are clad in stainless steel. Living quarters are separated from the library to the east by a double fireplace clad in Texas shellstone; both areas open by sliding glass doors to a wide terrace overlooking the pool, so that the terrace reconnects the semi-separated interior spaces. Neutra had not met Sonia Staller who remained behind in Illinois when her husband came to the

Opposite: In Neutra's hands, the long horizontal sweep of the house was divided only by a vertical plane that firmly distinguished the public area, on the right, from the private, on the left. Now a large glass-and-stucco volume disrupts that sweep; the wood beams and columns have been painted white. View facing north.

Below: As ever, Neutra uses the slope of a hill to his advantage, gracefully navigating the rhythm down from living room terrace to the pool. View facing west.

Silver Lake office. On November 9, 1953, Neutra wrote her a letter asking for her preferences in materials for cladding the fireplaces and other elements. "May we ask a rather personal question?" he continued, "That is, what do you prefer in your own dressing area – a regular dressing table on which you can sit down for make up, or do you prefer to do this standing up, as some ladies have asked us to provide for?" The letter is a surprise, imagine Neutra asking Sonia Staller what materials he should choose, but very predictable in revealing the architect's knowledge of this member of *Homo sapiens*; in this case, leading to the intimate details of the rituals of the female toilette.

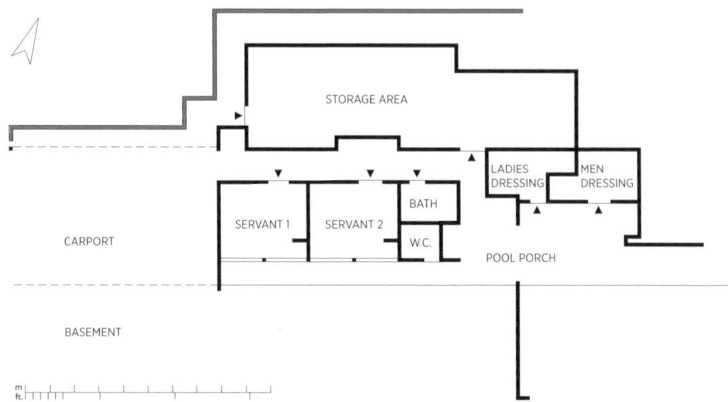

Below: Neutra demonstrates his mastery of the section here in a play of varying ceiling and floor heights, finishes, and sources of daylight. The library is tucked behind the living area. View facing east.

Opposite: Large circular skylights were popular with mid-century architects, giving a dramatic touch in a potentially dark area (the hill-side rearing up behind the house beyond). Here it also illuminates the steps down to the fireplace.

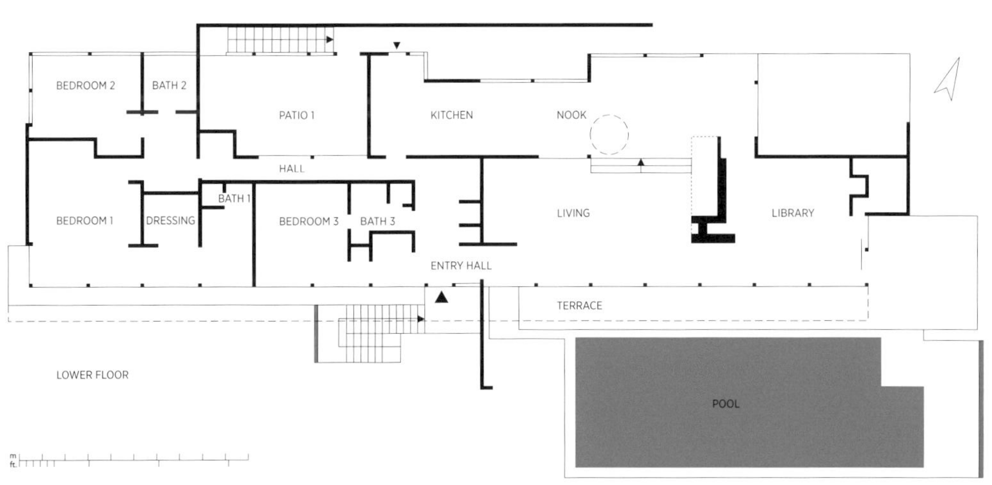
BEDROOM 2
BATH 2
PATIO 1
KITCHEN
NOOK
HALL
BEDROOM 1
DRESSING
BATH 1
BEDROOM 3
BATH 3
LIVING
LIBRARY
ENTRY HALL
TERRACE
LOWER FLOOR
POOL
m
ft.

ROBERT AND JOSEPHINE CHUEY HOUSE

2460 Sunset Plaza Drive
Los Angeles, California, 1956

Opposite: The Chueys were poets, painters, thinkers. Their belongings were simple, and their site was high up, between Coldwater and Laurel canyons. Robert's paintbrushes and oils were always at the ready.

Above: Josephine had known Neutra since the late 1920s, when the Schindlers and Kings Road were the center of the arts and culture scene in Los Angeles. The flawless beauty sitting on the sisal rug on the terrace, Josephine, had been Gregory Ain's second wife.

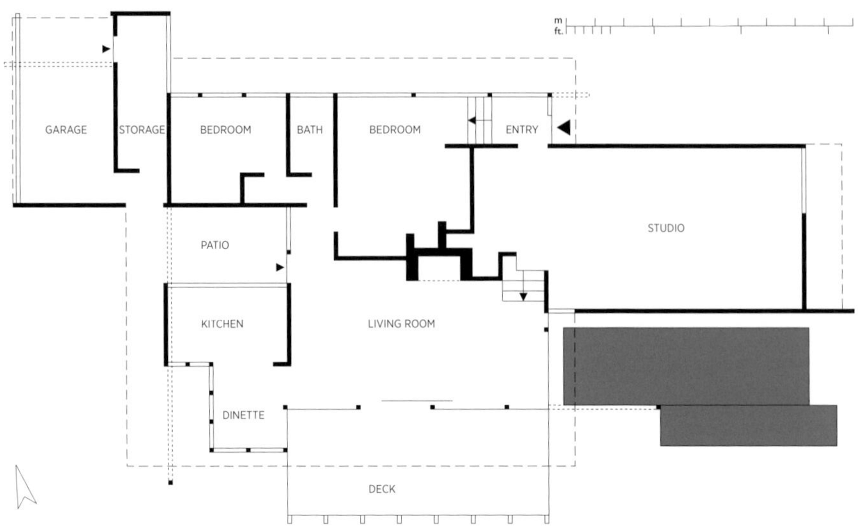

Without question this hilltop house enjoys one of the best sites and the most spectacular views in Los Angeles. Built for a poet and an artist, the beautiful Josephine (once married to Gregory Ain, whom she met at Galka Scheyer's Neutra house) and Robert Chuey, the home was an intellectual and cultural gathering place for years. Here nature runs everywhere, surrounding the 1,896-square-foot house with lemon, olive, flowering apple and orange trees, narcissus, lilac, eucalyptus and cypress trees. The house was blessed, in a sense, by the names involved: Walter Johnson, who, like Red Marsh, was a general contractor who worked on many Neutra houses; the gifted and patient project architect John Blanton; Jocelyn Domela, a landscape architect whose name frequently comes up on Neutra projects. While the letters between the Chueys and Neutra reveal a passionate zeal for their house and for Neutra's genius, like most of his clients they too learned how to read drawings and to analyze their site, so that a great deal of time was spent determining the precise orientation of the house. The studio is a spectacular space. It maintains the same ceiling height as the living room but steps down create a ten-foot-high room with glazing on two sides; casement windows for circulation float in larger panes of fixed glass. "Both my husband and I are allergic to low ceilings covering a broad expanse of space, especially as one is more aware of ceiling heights when one is almost continually standing at the easel," she wrote to Neutra, who often dropped by unexpectedly to see his work and how his clients were using their space. He once implored her, through a late night telephone call from Dione, to let him sleep on the terrace one night to soothe his anxieties. Including the land, the project cost about $50,000.

Opposite: The famous nighttime Shulman photograph of the dramatic spider leg amidst the two stepped reflecting pools, elongating space and cooling the house. Both have been filled in. View facing west.

FRANK AND BETTY MILLER HOUSE

with Thaddeus Longstreth
109 South Whitehall Road
Norristown, Pennsylvania, 1956

This long house faced in rough blonde brick is sited well back from the street, and overlooks a wide sweep of gently sinking meadowland rimmed by distant woods. From the entry, around a walnut partition five feet high, one steps into the rear glass-fronted living quarters. Double fireplaces in the same asymmetrically laid big shaggy blonde bricks and back-to-back separate the informal living room and den, areas with dark walnut cabinetry under sloping, finished pine ceilings. The entry separates the master bedroom from the three others at the front of the house, while the living and family areas to the north are combined. There is a pop-out screened porch in back.

Soffit lighting hidden in the lower, plastered ceiling illuminates the beautiful wood ceiling, a play of Gestalt aesthetics, light and dark, solid and void.

ALFRED AND HARRIET DE SCHULTHESS HOUSE

with Raul Alvarez
15012 Avenida Quijano
Havana, Cuba, 1956

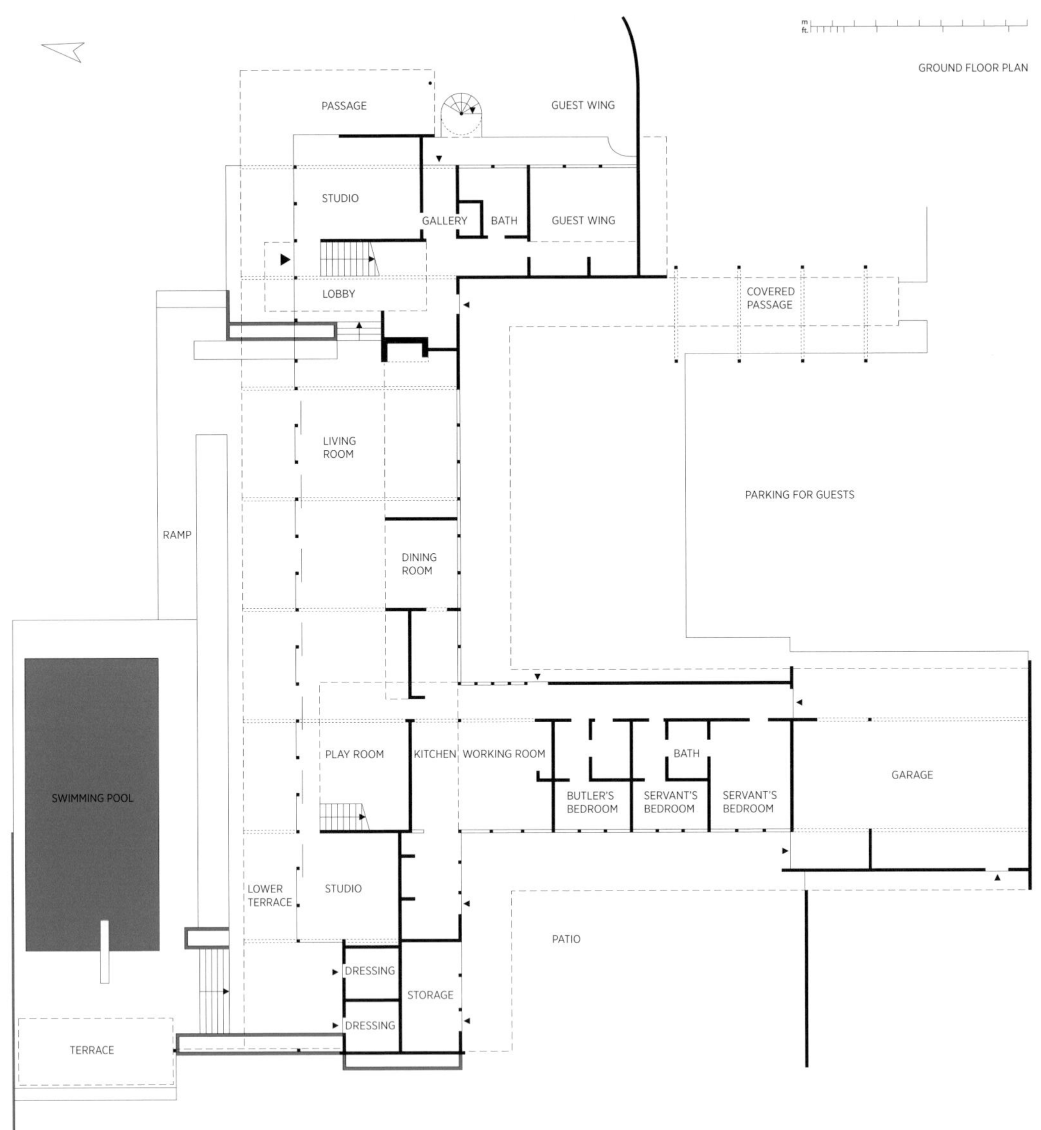

One of the largest residential built commissions for Neutra, the large 8,000-square-foot "residence" is located in an exclusive gently hilly suburb and country club area. Mr. De Schulthess' choice of materials indicates a generous budget, including tropical woods such as majagua wood for the interior, and sabicu (resembling mahogany) for the exterior. Once again Neutra educated himself from afar by writing to several local contractors, asking them about tropical hardwoods, whether they come only in solid stock, how is fiberglass safely attached to the soffits, how drastic hurricanes are. He treated these clients very carefully, asking them in

This Janus-faced, U-shaped plan for a wealthy, international client presents a stately rectilinear elevation on the north, while the entry façade, on the south, featured a long processional entrance across from the projecting servants' wing, together creating the U.

December 1954 for permission to step the house down with the site, because he "did not want to lose contact with the ground," telling them also that the house has to have a certain dignity in its relationship to the suburban street and therefore should not sit too low. The east end of the two-story building is closed by walls for privacy against the street while the north and south sides are primarily glass. The pool was situated on the northwest "for mirroring clouds and landscape of the valley view." Neutra made sure the house was as hurricane-proof as possible using concrete-clad fire-proofed steel framing.

FREDERIC AND ANNETTE SLAVIN HOUSE

1322 Dover Road
Santa Barbara, California, 1956

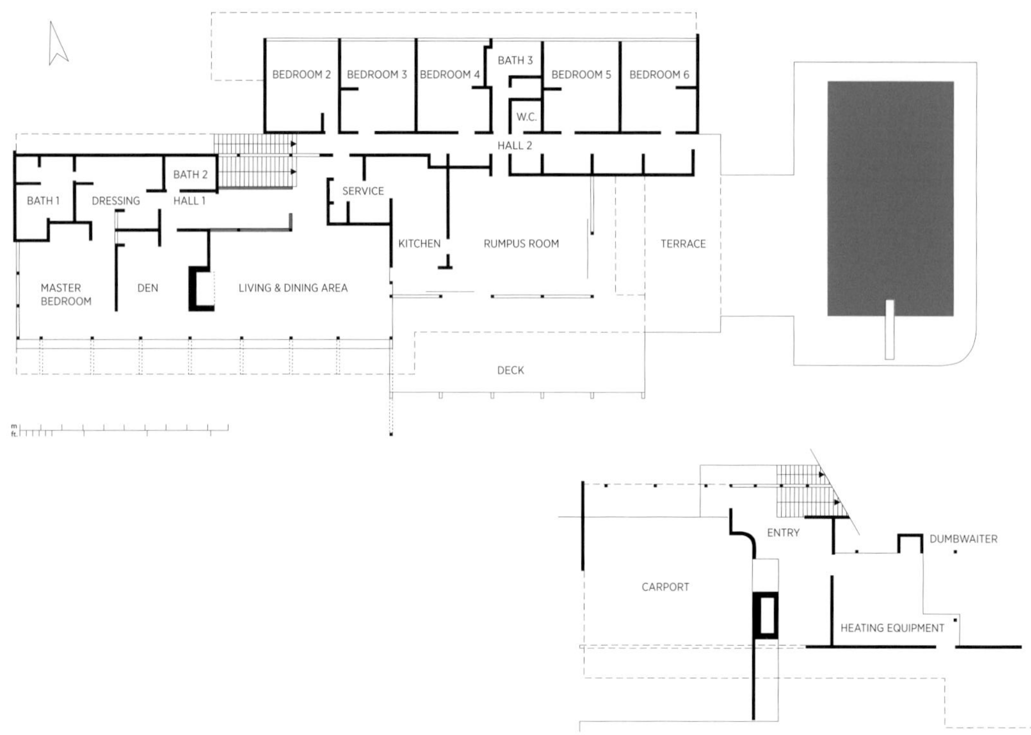

This is one of many houses Neutra designed as a long rectangle lifted up and out from its steep hillside site. Usually the volume is split by a perpendicular freestanding wall that simultaneously defines entry and protects the privacy of the bedroom wing, typically a volume that recedes or steps forward. What often distinguishes these houses is the entry. Sometimes the front door is reached via stairs outside the house, as with the Sidney Brown House. Other times it is up through the belly of the house, as it is here, which led to many subtle transitions from public to private before reaching the living room above, so the concept of "entrance" is enriched. One walks under the house, past large storage closets (in protected but outdoor space) and to a front door flanked by a glass wall with plantings on both sides, brightly daylit from a glass wall on the hill side of the house. Now one is in an "interior" space, uncarpeted, open, just the place to take off wet boots, and then one turns to mount the stairs up to the living area. Just beyond the glass wall adjacent to the stair, a second, exterior concrete stair mirrors the interior one: the Slavins had many children, and Neutra provided ways to keep primary areas tidy or quiet(er). Having the entrance below had other consequences: there was no longer any need to have an opaque wall to protect the private quarters, so that the eight-foot window and beam module could be read through the horizontal sweep of the entire front façade. The Slavins wanted a means to keep the kitchen noise separate from the living area, so Neutra and his team, in this case led by architect John Blanton, resolved that with a glass door which could slide out perpendicularly to the house and out into the valley; Blanton also suggested that the kitchen/rumpus

Sadly, the house was destroyed in a spectacular fire in 2021. The imposing primary façade faced south. Neutra and lead project architect John Blanton devised acoustic solutions to ensure a quiet home, including putting ballasts for the fluorescent lights in the basement and a glass door to separate kitchen noise from the living area.

room volume be stepped back to enliven the façade. A single, beautifully detailed spider leg denotes the change in the two volumes but it is not only there for formal reasons. It has work to do, because it holds the track for the glass door. Behind the kitchen volume to the north is the long march of the five-bedroom children's wing, away from the master bedroom to the west. The post and lintel system continues to run east, beyond the building envelope, to engage the pool. "It's odd, but you feel like you're falling off the hill without it," one of the current owners said. The house is also technologically sophisticated: all the ballasts for the multitude of fluorescent lighting is located in the basement, so that the annoying hum of the fixtures is negated; one more way Neutra made this an acoustically astute home.

SIDNEY AND ARILLA TROXELL HOUSE

766 Paseo Miramar
Los Angeles, California, 1956

"House" seems an uncomfortable word for this setting high on the top of Paseo Miramar, where there are many carefully blended transitions between indoors and out. Architectural elements extend into the landscape; the land, studded with olive and laurel trees, ceanothus and ribes, flows back into the house, rendering a calm, multivalent equilibrium. A good example of this takes place at the crotch of the L-shaped house. Here a large pond is shaped like a quarter-circle which echoes the shape of the hill below it, as though the pond constituted the last line on the contour map. The water is edged in exposed aggregate concrete pavers and is protected by

Above: The house burned down in the Paseo Miramar fire in 2021. It embodied a sensual response to nature, the driveway-cum-walkway curling around the building's foot-print to slip into the garage below.

Opposite: In Neutra's hands, the eclectic group of elements became a carefully choreographed composition.

The signature glass-and-wood walls looked out to the view and an eccentrically shaped pool.

an unusually deep overhang, drawing the land inside. More concrete pavers laid in a stepped pattern separate that larger, curving pool from a small, crisply rectangular pool. Along one straight edge of the larger pool, parallel to one glass wall of the house, a long strip of plants edged by a concrete curb is echoed on the other side of the glass wall inside. Here, indoors, the same shape is cut out of the floor, which is the same exposed aggregate as that of the exterior pavers. Thus, in a very tiny area, a lively conversation between indoors and out occurs. This entire scene is laid out for the visitor who approaches from the west side of the house by a long switchback path to the curved pool.

Just in front of the small pond lies the curved flight of concrete steps leading to another terrace connecting the "garden room" (overlooking the curved pond), the kitchen, and access to the carport down to the freestanding garage below. Neutra thoughtfully provided a catwalk at one corner of the terrace so that the "housewife could more easily clean the south window" above this cantilevered corner. (He neglected to include a railing, which aided in making this idiosyncratic corner a wonderful event compositionally, at any rate.) It is no wonder the house won two awards. Sidney Troxell, after reading *Survival Through Design* soon after it was published, promptly accused Neutra of being a behaviorist, noted a mild-mannered internal office memo. Arilla Troxell, on the other hand, was far more pragmatic in her writings, in which she describes wanting to buy

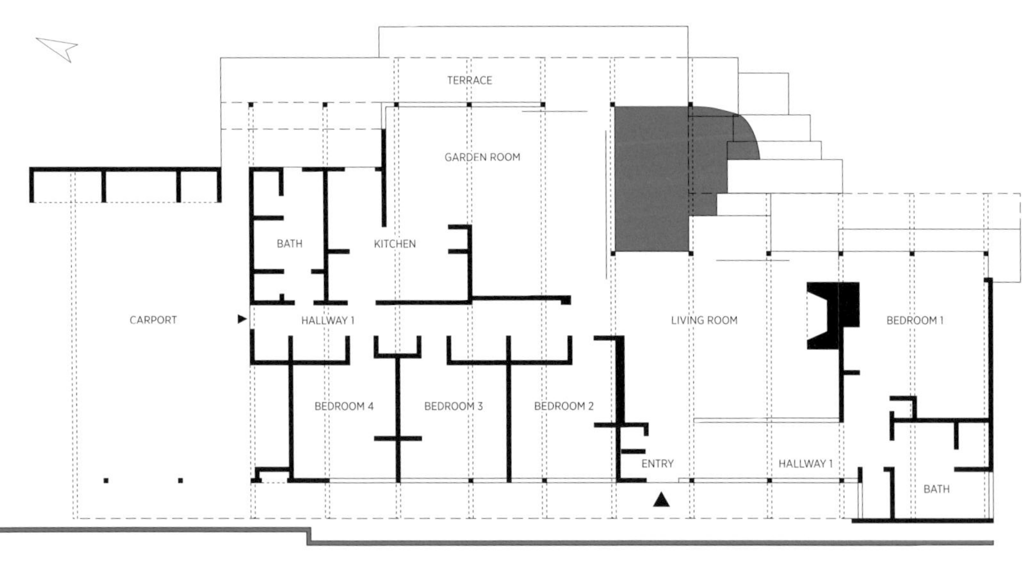
TERRACE
GARDEN ROOM
BATH
KITCHEN
CARPORT
HALLWAY 1
LIVING ROOM
BEDROOM 1
BEDROOM 4
BEDROOM 3
BEDROOM 2
ENTRY
HALLWAY 1
BATH
m
ft.

enough food to last "four to six months," and above all a U-shaped kitchen not in line with foot traffic. Landscape architect Jocelyn Domela used native plants for low maintenance. She shared Neutra's vision of the integration of house and site: "It is very important to know what people want because if they interject false notes into the rhythm of the forms and textures that I visualize, the discord is more obvious than the rhythm," she wrote to Neutra on August 10, 1955.

An interesting throwback to Neutra's early experimental work is a memo dated March 21, 1955, from the Los Angeles Building Department denying Neutra the right to use tempered Masonite over 15 pounds felt as an exterior wall surface. According to builder Fordyce "Red" Marsh, the house cost $58,157.57.

Opposite: The view south from the huge garden room looked across broad stepping stones around the curved portion of the pool.

Below: The open shelving above a classic Thermador range allowed easy entertaining.

ALAMITOS INTERMEDIATE SCHOOL

Neutra and Alexander
Dale and Lampson Streets
Garden Grove, California, 1957

Neutra and Alexander designed the school to be residentially scaled. Occupying an old orange grove, they retained several citrus trees. One of many innovations included alternating quartets of classrooms with grassy, landscaped courts.

The entrance to the school grounds.

ERNEST LAWRENCE ELEMENTARY SCHOOL

Neutra and Alexander
12521 Monroe Street
Garden Grove, California, 1957

Although the school is informed by the same principles as Neutra's early schools, this commission was part of a larger national need to create new classrooms quickly for the childen of World War II American veterans. It afforded Neutra a rich opportunity to exploit cheap, prefabricated, modular materials in a bolder, more daring design strategy than his earlier designs, but that now harnessed the capabilities of later 20th-century materials. It was situated in an orange grove, and discrete classroom buildings were punctuated by garden courts where existing orange trees in their original grid were to remain. Wide walkways covered by corrugated plastic or metal were pulled away from the ganged classrooms. Supported by beams extending from the buildings, they became a protective horizontal thread running through

the relaxed compound of airy, one-story gabled buildings. Frankly exposed, angled steel bents are the primary structural support for the grouped classrooms with a secondary infill wood post-and-beam system. These modules of "bent plus infill plus cladding" could be added on the end as needed in the future. The tapered ends of the beam portion of the bent appear to pierce each building's envelope, comprised of a series of clerestories above tall, sliding glass-and-infill panels. These elegant tapers support lightweight panels running parallel to and outside the building, evenly spaced apart so strong sunlight is broken up but not barricaded from the children. At about the same time Albert Frey was applying similar ideas to school buildings in Palm Springs, though the two architects knew little of each other's work.

Opposite: Southern California's intense summer heat made covered walkways a must for students navigating new, expansive, one-story school campuses.

Above: The luxury of classrooms and open landscapes on the ground floor dictated a frugal approach to materials: corrugated metal, brick, stucco, glass.

FERRO CHEMICAL COMPANY

Neutra and Alexander
450 Krick Road
Bedford, Ohio, 1957

This haunting photograph, of a delicate glass-and-steel volume sliding out from a brick frame, immortalizes this little-known Neutra project in a small industrial city outside of Cleveland.

The building is oriented east-west and the sequence of spider legs is in the south. Here the large steel beams are lightly but firmly terminated by two slender aluminum columns. The roof slab asymmetrically covers a portion of the spider legs and does not line up with the beam, giving a sensation that the roof has been temporarily laid and may slide around at any moment. The spread metal letters at the top of the building are their own decorative element. Only an inexplicable gesture, a long single steel bar placed toward the end of the bold stroke of the spider legs, mars the composition.

HACIENDA MOTOR HOTEL

Neutra and Alexander
1st Street and Miraleste Avenue
San Pedro, California, 1957

Below: Adjacent to its own golf course, the "motor hotel" had 80 rooms and promised a "secluded country club atmosphere" according to an advertisement, which promised rates starting at "$9 per couple."

Opposite: Abundant landscaping adorned terraces whose privacy was ensured with separation walls.

In an undated essay titled, "Hotels – Man's Intermittent Habitat," Neutra wrote: "The weekend and the vacations hold their own social significance and have their own manner of human get-together. The soul impact of the extraordinary occasion – the holiday – calls, according to Neutra's studies of natural patterns, for architectural solutions and layouts which perhaps surpass in significance what the architect can and must offer on behalf of daily habituation and routine ..."

The entry to this now-demolished resort spa is unmistakably oriented to the automobile. A triangular canopy joins the two wings of the hotel where passengers alight; beyond the main building, detached rows of units stepped down the sloping site to maximize the ocean view for each unit. While the guest rooms themselves were surprisingly humble and even rustic, given this upscale venue, the lobbies and dining areas held some surprises. In the 400-person dining room, Neutra used lighting in a painterly way by illuminating the web and flanges of exposed, tapered steel bents, so that their lines glow to great effect above tables heavy with white linen napkins and the big, brass-studded leather club chairs. The gigantic room could be made more intimate by gorgeous massive sliding doors of aluminum louvers (thus allowing light to filter through). And while wealthy diners might require solutions that surpassed the routine, Neutra treated the restaurant to the same thinking he applied to grammar schools: there is a primary window wall on one side, with clerestories between the beams. Its parallel wall on the other side is solid except for a strip of clerestories. In other public areas, a fireplace with a raised brick hearth was set asymmetrically into a large white wall with a long expansive brick firebox whose back wall was curved. Neutra and Alexander used lowered floating planes in the lounge areas to define spaces and to create opportunities to light-wash walls and ceilings; in these planes, the

wood module was 1″ x 2″, contrasting with the 1″ x 6″ module of the higher tongue-and-groove ceilings, further distinguishing the planes.

Like the Pitcairn House, the Hacienda also boasted a minimalist fish aquarium – except here it is 30 feet long, separating the dining and bar areas. The bar had unusual columns of heavy brushed aluminum; they were shaped like elongated ellipses whose ends are clipped. The guest rooms were much more rugged, with one glass wall facing the ocean. The other three were exposed, smoothed concrete block masonry walls that supported tongue-and-groove knotty pine ceilings contrasting with dark-stained Douglas fir beams.

Above: The golden brick walls connected interior to exterior. The handsomely appointed rooms included Neutra-designed chairs and, of course, a "Camel Table."

Opposite: There is an air about the dining room, with its walls of fishes and rounded pink leather booths, that recalls the halcyon days of the Rat Pack, cocktail dresses, and cigarettes.

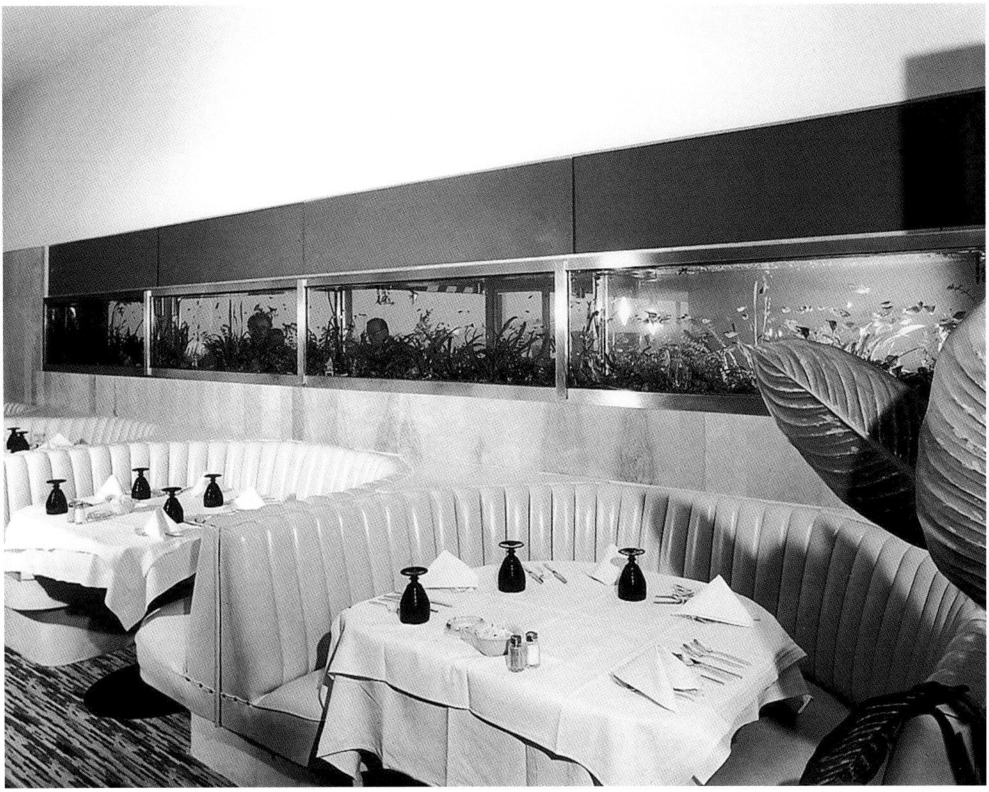

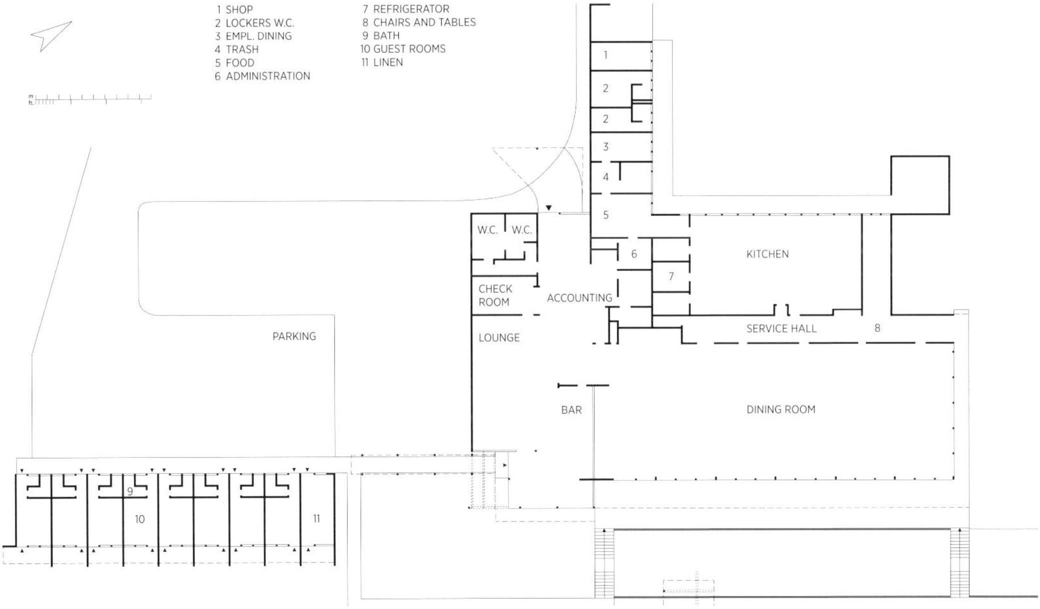
1 SHOP
2 LOCKERS W.C.
3 EMPL. DINING
4 TRASH
5 FOOD
6 ADMINISTRATION
7 REFRIGERATOR
8 CHAIRS AND TABLES
9 BATH
10 GUEST ROOMS
11 LINEN
m
ft.
PARKING
W.C.
W.C.
CHECK ROOM
ACCOUNTING
LOUNGE
KITCHEN
SERVICE HALL
BAR
DINING ROOM

AIRMAN MEMORIAL CHAPEL

Neutra and Alexander
Marine Corps Air Station (MCAS)
Miramar, California, 1957

Right: The chapel at the former Naval Air Station features a rhythm of custom prefabricated concrete bents and is illuminated by continuous sky and side lighting. View facing west.

Opposite: The unique suspended staircase and the chapel's other dramatic elements honor the drama in the air, in the exceptional fighting and training skills this base is known for, home to the real *Top Gun* flight school.

The 600-seat all-faith chapel at a U.S. Naval Air Station is the primary building of a Z-shaped compound including classrooms and a smaller morning chapel on the north. While the exterior is a rectangular box, the inside is far more animated. Ten massive concrete buttress-like frames serve as the larger chapel's structure, soaring up and curving over a V-shaped hung ceiling in the nave. The ceiling also hides lighting that illuminates the frames and spills over the sides. The artificial light is balanced by the daylight coming through vertical slits in the infill panels between each frame, as well as from the wall of glass on the chancel end to the west, where the altar is also illuminated by a continuous strip of skylight. One principal feature is the exterior open staircase that leads to the vestibule on the east, meant to symbolize spiritual ascent. It is a dramatic sight at night, illuminated from above and mirrored in the reflecting pool below. The half-round concrete shell above the bell here, though, seems an unfortunate inclusion, one decorative element too many. The drawings for the church show, even for Neutra, a thoroughness of detail, down to the curved revolving altar sheathed in 1" x 2" wood slats, the handsome molded plywood pews, and the huge cross at the stair, which doubles as a downspout.

MAURY AND BERNICE SORRELLS HOUSE

Old CA-127
Shoshone, California, 1957

In his writings Neutra appeared to be fascinated by the "primeval solitude" of the house in the "colossally spacious Inyo County ... a region of fantastic contrast, where many a wanderer lost his life far from human help." The Sorrells owned and operated a general merchandise store, gas station and cafe in Shoshone, a town that serves as one of the primary entrances to the famous Death Valley. In this barren, sometimes surreal scene, the walls of the house run out freely into the landscape. Planes and lines are stretched, partly in response to the fierce dusty winds but in any case creating a strong composition whose verticals and horizontals are effectively interwoven. Like some other Neutra houses, this was to be a "three-generation house." The guest room had its own entrance just before the front door of the Z-shaped, 1,500-square-foot house, which meant a guest could discreetly arrive or depart. The south wall of this room is glazed, opening to a large walled landscaped court which forms the southwest quadrant of the bedroom wing. There are several types of outdoor areas, each with its own character, such as the terrace formed by the living room and the family room (a separate volume to the northeast) as well as a more informal patio to the north, where a double-backed fireplace serves both the patio and the family room. In the carport, just before one entered the family room en route to the kitchen, Neutra included a small bathroom where one could quickly wash off the grime of the desert day.

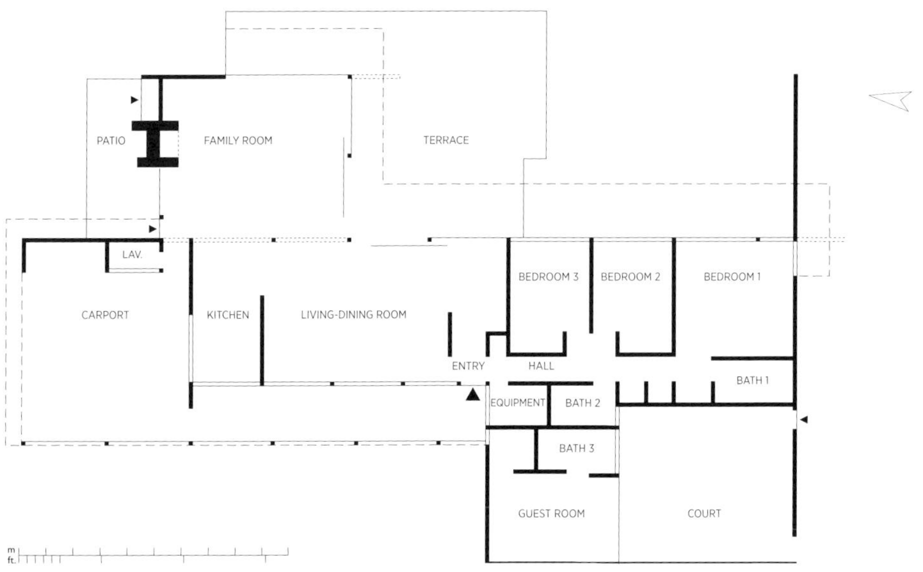

Opposite: Easily one of the most exciting images of Neutra's genius in "breaking the box." Lines, planes, and volumes recede and project, playing off materials, colors, and textures to protect this sleek box in the middle of an old rugged West. View facing southwest.

Below: The Sorrells met Neutra through reform politician John Anson Ford, one of the illustrious dinner guests to the Neutra's home in Silver Lake. View facing north.

GEORGE AND PAT WISE HOUSE

1371 Paseo Del Mar
San Pedro, California, 1957

Of George Wise the office notes by John Blanton read, "He wants to build at the edge of bluff – which might be dangerous – it looks steeper than 45 degrees – it would be a shame not to be able to see the coastline, however." The 50-foot-wide lot ran 100 level feet toward the ocean before it dropped to a lower level, and it was that level which looked over the sea near San Pedro.

The Wises, a couple in their early 30s with three young boys, were hesitant in approaching Neutra because of cost constraints. They loved the Weihe House, though, especially the beamed ceiling and "the continuation of the fireplace into the bedroom." Neutra maintained their budget, and they got their wish: the house is humble but looks out directly over the precipice. Beyond the lush landscaping the ocean lies at your feet.

The eight-inch beam at the foot of the children's room permitted them a full gaze of the ocean while providing just enough of an obstruction to feel secure.

EDWARD AND FAY FLAVIN HOUSE

2218 Neutra Place
Los Angeles, California, 1958

Below: The Flavin House is one of four Neutra-designed homes on wooded Neutra Place. View facing southeast.

Opposite: The private, shaded interior courtyard of this U-shaped floor plan provides an easy-going gathering space for family or friends. View facing east.

A member of the Silver Lake Colony, this three-bedroom, 1,587-square-foot house on the slope above Neutra Place has an unusual plan and section that salutes a difficult site. It is a U in which the south end of the U is broken to step up the slope where the bedrooms are located on the upper split level. The clients were typical in their ten pages of notes and diagrams, carefully notated with dimensions. Sophisticated in contemporary architecture, they admired Marcel Breuer's work on the East Coast, as well as Ain, Eames and Wright, but "Mr. Neutra's houses represent to us the organic wholeness we have been looking for." In 1953 they tried to buy first the Meltzer House for $ 26,000 and then the Sokol House for $ 35,000. Finally the Flavins hired Neutra to build their own. "We have two streams in our lives, one active, one passive – a striving for peace and quiet, a place to read, think and talk. This desire probably manifests itself

in small, instinctive moves such as removing all bric-a-brac ... The second is active, the desire to plan mentally, to design and then finally to build, is a fundamental one ... we want a large anonymous space for someone to use whether at the piano or shop bench." This second imperative is reflected in the workshop at the northeast end of the house, which Flavin asked Neutra to bring out to the same line as the master bedroom on the south, resulting in an equilateral U with a sheltered outdoor room. The cost was probably lower than the bid of $27,803.92 by one contractor since the detail-oriented Mr. Flavin successfully assumed the role of general contractor.

JACK AND ANNETTE FRIEDLAND HOUSE

with Thaddeus Longstreth
1020 North Lane
Gladwyn, Pennsylvania, 1958

The long approach to this grand, 8,153-square-foot house leads to a *porte cochère* placed some distance from the house. In the two-story hall, a spiral stair rises above an underlit pool which extends to the outdoors. Just as at the California Military Academy, there is a large overhang but here it seems lifelessly attached to the building rather than charging from it. As originally built, the building lacks that sense of coherence so typical of a Neutra dwelling, because of the heavy-handed use of many elements and materials all squeezed together. There are some wonderful moments, such as the horizontal steel edge band at the fireplace which runs beyond its brick boundary to become a glistening miniature spider leg, visually far too delicate to transfer the weight of the fireplace down to the floor. The wood-sheathed stainless-steel staircase, whose treads cantilever from a slender curving Mobius strip of a stalk, is finely detailed. The primary materials used for the kitchen are walnut and stainless steel.

Opposite: This two-story home has more in common with Neutra's grand villas in Europe. The entry alone, with the *porte cochère* canopy marked by a circular reflecting pool, speaks to luxe indoors and out.

Below: Terminating in a marble floor, the spiral stair's angled, open-tread steps cantilever over an interior pool. At night, the pool is illuminated from underwater.

ALFRED HUGHES HOUSE

1560 Oriole Lane
Los Angeles, California, 1958

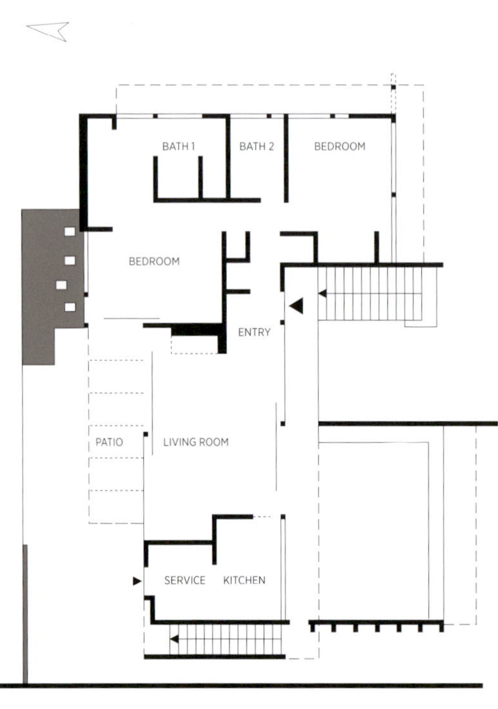

The 1,396-square-foot house is hidden at the end of a cul-de-sac in "The Bird Streets" of West Hollywood, high above the Sunset Strip. It's a neighborhood dotted with pedigreed dwellings.

GEORGE KRAIGHER HOUSE #2

234 Litchfield Road
Litchfield, Connecticut, 1958

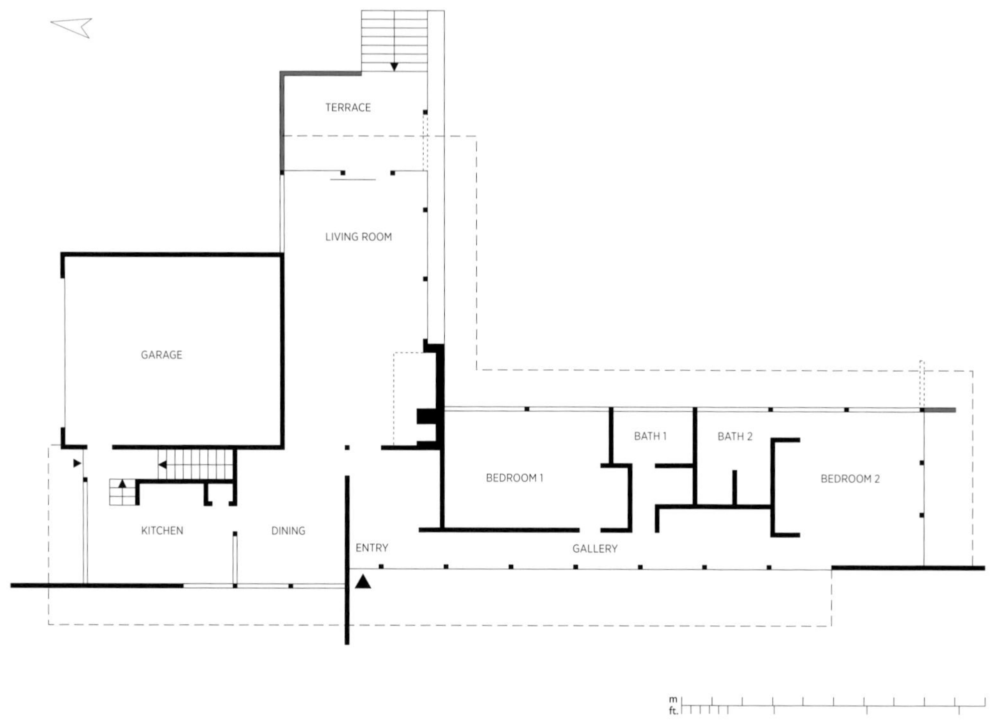

Neutra designed George Kraigher's first house on open country in Texas, and the Connecticut setting for the oil man's retirement dream could not have been more different. The second design was to complement his now-substantial collection of Modernist art and furniture designed by Eames, Nelson and others. Kraigher wanted nine-foot-tall ceilings so Neutra ordered special plywood rather than having to make a horizontal cut in standard eight-foot sheets; Kraigher asked for 1,900 square feet not including the garage, and contrasting light and dark stains, and he got that too. Neutra's office made him responsible for determining the best sheathing, as they were concerned about the durability of cement plaster on studs in a wet and winter climate; Kraigher

The clever angle of all the publicity photographs hides the hipped roof, Kraigher's defense against winter snow loads.

decided on cedar. In plan the house is T-shaped with a strong, linear entry that runs straight up to the front door with a transparent view to the east straight through the living room. Neutra used radiant heating coiled in the basement, telling Kraigher that it eliminated the need for expensive double-glazing. A superb front façade with clean notes of solids and voids is underscored at the entrance where a lightweight spider leg rests on a heavy brick base. Given their long history there was a curious lack of faith between client and architect: Neutra was agitated because Kraigher instructed his contractor to insert a post where a mitered corner glass was to be placed; Kraigher also added a hipped roof because of his concern for snow loads.

JOHN AND ETTA RADOS HOUSE

2209 West Daladier Drive
Rancho Palos Verdes, California, 1958

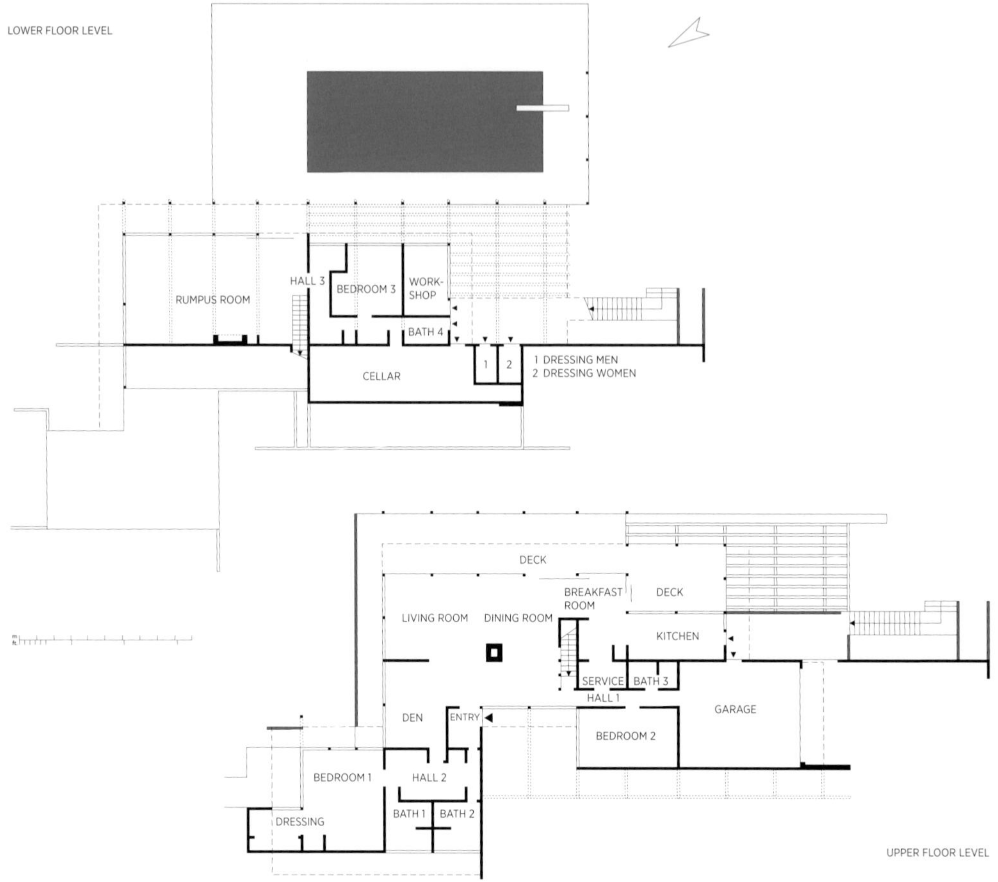

The site steps down the rocky east slope of the Palos Verdes Hills at the end of a private road. This provided not only privacy but a fantastic view, day or night, which included the busy shiplife of San Pedro Harbor, the Port of Long Beach, the horizon of the Pacific Ocean and the Los Angeles and San Gabriel mountains. Here the sea is its own urbanscape of inlets and sea channels, with tiny sailboats dancing in the sun not far from massive tankers sitting at dock, the scene peppered with the gawky vertical detritus of oil refining equipment. Quite the appropriate vista for the head of a shipbuilding firm whose son became a naval architect.

This is an exciting house, first because certain architectural problems, problems Neutra set himself and which could only be problems in the context of Neutra's ideas about architecture, are resolved in the flawless details that are everywhere. Second, the house is rewarding because these solutions are rendered in the richest of materials and with unprecedented craftsmanship: stainless steel, mahogany, glass, aluminum and ruddy, veined marble from Italy. There was no specific budget for the 4,000-square-foot, two-story house that took two years to build, with its acres of walnut cabinetry and miles of terrazzo floors used indoors and around the

Beyond the interior's exquisite finishes and Neutra's "Camel Table" in the foreground, the view faces southeast to San Pedro Harbor and the ocean, a vista perfect for a shipbuilder.

entire pool. The shipbuilder-owner brought his own world of materials and methods to bear, using his own master shipwrights and metalsmiths alongside the venerable Fordyce "Red" Marsh, builder of 25 Neutra homes. Mahogany used for his ships' ballast, for example, was fashioned as highly varnished 14-inch-deep laminated beams with alternating boards of light and dark wood that support the upper floor, and as the square-cut tongue-and-groove sheathing for the exterior. Some other materials were exotic in a progressive, technological sense: "As a whole the house is built like a ship with many calculated economies, in weight and material. The decking material is fiberglass, the upholstery plastic ... a rust-colored plastic fabric for the reverse-curve accordion doors near the den and master bedrooms; 'primrose yellow' linoleum countertops," Neutra wrote in his description.

God is in the details: between huge sheets of glass, ranging from a 3⁄16-inch to 5⁄16-inch in thickness and some as wide as 11′ 6″, Neutra no longer needed to paint supporting wood posts silver so that they posed no visual impediment to the eye as it sought the horizon. Here, the columns are 2¾-inch square structural aluminum and jacketed in brushed aluminum so they are utterly streamlined. In the master bedroom, the huge sliding glass-and-steel doors are hung behind a large beam. The top of the door frame is hidden from the eye so that all one sees is glass disappearing into wood. In the small adjacent dressing room, Neutra pulled back a ceiling just enough from the taller glass wall it would have met, thus providing a "hiding space" for the unsightly tops of Venetian blinds: again, a detail which resolves the problem of what one sees (now only the trees and sky). It is a detail whose thoughtfulness is best appreciated while lying on the master bed. The round freestanding living room fireplace is made of polished stainless steel; the aluminum pans of the outdoor aluminum staircase are welded to the trunk of the stair with diagonal flanges that just hint at similar, tiny flanges supporting the glass shelves in a suspended glass display case at the entry.

John and Etta Rados entertained frequently, and every conceivable storage need has been accommodated, e.g., the cabinetry for ice cream sundae glassware (for the grandchildren) or for folding card tables, designed at the exact height and depth necessary to get a hand around an object without bruising knuckles. There is a state-of-the-art stereo sound system with concealed speakers in every room, a bomb shelter, glass windbreaks for the pool, a huge, open lower level with an Arizona stone fireplace, bar, play room, guest and pool dressing rooms. The radiantly heated poolside terrazzo cracked badly and was recycled by the owners as a step path around the perimeter of the site.

Below: Many of Neutra's exterior staircases are understated but carefully detailed, with just a touch of a curve, as seen in the Beard and Bucerius dwellings as well as in the Rados House.

Opposite: The ground floor was devoted to pool, family, fun, and water. Upstairs was formality, views, and entertaining. View facing north.

ST. JOHN'S COLLEGE ART AND SCIENCE BUILDING

Neutra and Alexander
with Cochran, Stephenson and Wing
Annapolis, Maryland, 1958

St. John's was founded in 1696 and is one of America's oldest and most prestigious educational institutions. Neutra had previously lectured there to a very enthusiastic response, and the Neutra and Alexander partnership seemed the obvious choice to continue its rationalist tradition in a Modernist architectural vocabulary. Their brief included responding to a tradition that sought to show the connections among disparate academic disciplines rather than to perceive them as isolated fields. They were also to sensitively relate new designs to the existing red-brick, hipped-roof Colonial-era buildings.

Thus, in good Socratic tradition, an agora – open or "negative" space – is the heart of the design surrounded by a U-shaped group of buildings in which physics and chemistry classrooms were not far from music rooms. The program also called for a discussion hall for "Socratic Dialectics" and an auditorium to handle theater or music events. What emerged was a reasoned group of buildings that combined materials such as steel, translucent and clear glass, red brick, poured-in-place concrete, concrete tiles and aluminum louvers rendered in disciplined rhythms with a strong emphasis on the horizontal, yet always exploiting asymmetry in the service of the overall composition.

Sometimes exterior planes overlap each other and/or run perpendicularly to one another, puncturing an interior. Volumes and their uses read clearly, such as the front façade of the library, whose staircase volume at one end becomes a glowing beacon of translucent glass panels at night, or even the elegant façade of the loading dock. Here, a part of the façade is treated as an independent "picture" attached to, and which steps out from the façade of a long, concrete tile building (the tiles are combed vertically) in its own concrete "frame." Below, a long base of vertically oriented Roman brick anchors the rest of the "picture" which includes an expanse of vertical louvers and a stepped-back section of concrete wall. The "picture" terminates succinctly with a huge pair of metal doors faced with tightly corrugated sheet metal.

On the interior, special attention was paid to color, acoustics (especially important in this setting dedicated to verbal discourse) and lighting. In classrooms Neutra and Alexander balanced day and artificial light; in the auditorium and conference rooms they designed multi-level curving ceilings to create opportunites for wall and ceiling light washing. Walnut partititions were zigzagged to aid multi-directional acoustics and persimmon-red accents were used on side walls and on some of the chairs to "provide stimulation against white backgrounds." Outdoor landscaping, breezeways and walkways were inspired by the Aristotelian method of teaching at the Stoa Poikile, in which "vital thoughts are often developed in ambulation, by a promenading group of conversing persons," wrote Neutra, so that progress was achieved through "dialectic conversational stimulation."

Mellon Hall, the college's main academic building, has been rehabilitated and expanded in ways that both enlarged the building and made it more flexible while restoring some of Neutra's signature strategies, including Neutra and Alexander's exterior planters with low-level plantings and the expansive glass that connects inner and outside spaces.

UCLA EXPERIMENTAL AND TRAINING SCHOOL

Neutra and Alexander
10636 Sunset Boulevard
Westwood, California, 1958

Although part of the original design was demolished, much remains of Neutra and Alexander's relaxed group of simple one-story brick buildings. They are located on the northwest edge of the UCLA campus on a pastoral site amidst oak trees and overlooking a ravine with a creek. Its program was unusual in that it was designed and built in a series of separate contracts not only as an elementary, kindergarten and nursery school but also as a research and training venue for teachers. The plan consisted of two types of spatially experimental classroom arrangements. One was a "fingerplan" arrangement, with rooms placed between courts and fanning out from a curved corridor. The courts were meant for more relaxed groupings and play. The second arrangement was a more compact layout of four classrooms clustered around a central, skylit hall, which was to be used for exhibitions and group activities. Smaller work and preparation rooms

are inserted between adjacent classrooms. The two plans were connected by a covered walkway. In both arrangements, the classrooms were designed to be especially large to accommodate student groups and observers. As with all Neutra schools, large glass sliding doors for access to the outdoors, generous overhangs, cross-ventilation, bilateral lighting and movable furniture and equipment were a given.

Buildings and landscapes of gardens, lawns, bridges, ponds, and even a small forest are interwoven here. Classrooms include interstitial spaces for teachers and smaller teacher-student interactions. Tuition is subsidized for some families at this outstanding school.

CLAREMONT UNITED METHODIST CHURCH

Neutra and Alexander
211 West Foothill Boulevard
Claremont, California, 1959

On February 14, 1960, when the new church celebrated its first Sunday in its new home, the Rev. Pierce Johnson preached a sermon based on Psalm 118:5, which in one translation reads, "I called to the Lord from my narrow prison and he answered me in the freedom of space." The design of the church speaks to that freedom by opening up the west end as an almost solid wall of glass facing the San Gabriel Mountains, so that parishioners can participate in nature, here embraced as one aspect of God and not as God's antithesis.

Below: The sanctuary is on the right; to the left are administrative rooms and classrooms. As in many of Neutra's civic entrances, the roof is off-center, exposing the longer supporting spider legs. View facing northwest.

Opposite: When interviewed, the minister was asked if he minded if parishioners paid more attention to nature and a bird feeder beyond the massive glass wall. He laughed. "God is in nature!" he said. View facing north.

An austere brushed-steel altar and cross, designed by Neutra, are deliberately spare so there is no obstruction between eye and nature. The church's ceiling is a V, like the keel of a ship: it is both an acoustic baffle and a symbol of the "nave" of the church as holding a body of believers. The interior is one of strong contrasts. On the east side, the white walls cant out and have high clerestories revealing the sky. On the west, the vertical wall is painted in that familiar Neutra brown-black.

A row of large orb lamps, a Neutra standard, bring the ceiling level down. On this side a clerestory at floor height runs the length of the nave, "illuminating one's path," to quote from the Bible, so that one can see the earth and the roots of trees and bushes; the two clerestories work to show the link and contrast between heaven and earth. The nave aisle is asymmetrically divided so that there are short and long pews, giving the congregation the opportunity to group themselves in various ways. The church also incorporates a one-story office and community wing at right angles to the nave. A long walkway outside the church consists of light post-and-beam bents supporting an asymmetrically laid roof.

CHARLES LEE DAILEY HOUSE

953 Granvia Altamira
Palos Verdes, California, 1959

In contrast to other sloped roof houses in Palos Verdes, this design's mix of angles and materials and shapes leads to a less than harmonious composition. On the interior, the ridge line of the living room bisects the room in plan. Internal perpendicular walls and structures in the living and dining area do not cross this invisible line. Neutra often pulls such spatially defining walls back to create a continuous window wall. Usually the "invisible line" is not the same line as the ridge line but asymmetrically placed closer to the window wall. This time the leftover space is so large it became vacant and ill-defined.

Opposite: The living area opens out to the pool. Dr. Dailey, a distinguished physicist and Caltech graduate, was a devoted swimmer. View facing west.

Above: Palos Verdes had strict laws regarding roof slopes; Neutra and Alexander employed slopes again at the Palos Verdes High School, 1961. View facing west.

DAYTON PLANETARIUM AND MUSEUM OF NATURAL HISTORY

Neutra and Alexander
with Nick Athens
2629 Ridge Avenue
Dayton, Ohio, 1959

The brief for the design included exhibition spaces, a small planetarium and areas for public education and activities. Using a four-foot module, Neutra created a series of boxes in this T-shaped building whose auditorium forms the leg of the T, where the site falls away sharply. The west elevation of this long building has vertical louvered aluminum windows for sun protection. In section the museum shows a great deal of hierarchy assigned to different spaces: a 14-foot ceiling height for the multi-purpose room, ten-foot for work and activity rooms and eight-foot for corridors. Neutra's programming included using glass walls on work spaces so visitors could watch museum processes as well as solutions for possible expansion. He presented his programming ideas in a simple, but serious cartoon fashion to make them easier to understand for the layperson.

The little planetarium is still a beloved member of the community, offsetting the low brick building, surrounded by a wooded park on the banks of the Stillwater River. View facing west.

EUGENE LORING HOUSE

2456 Astral Drive
Los Angeles, California, 1959

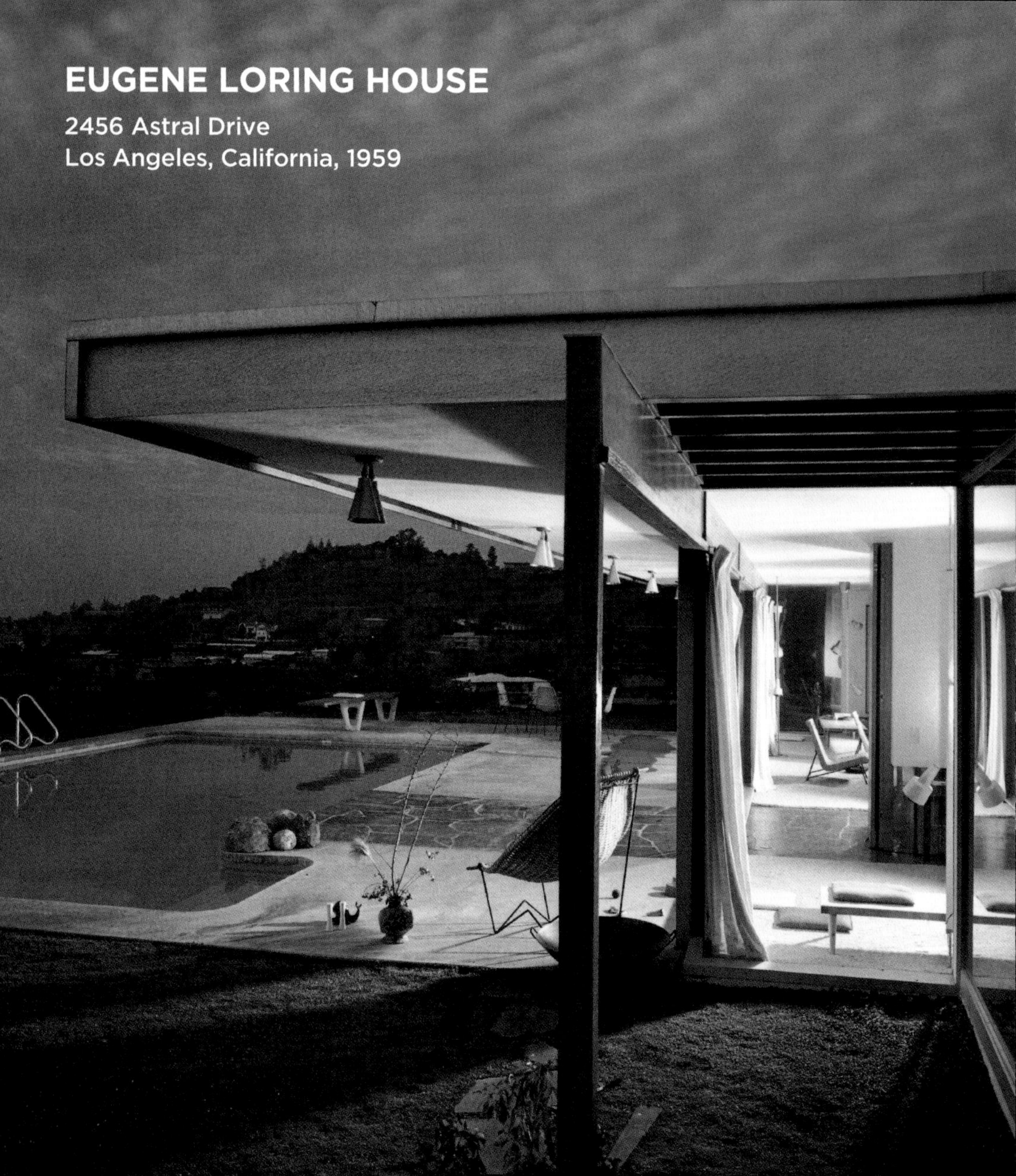

In many houses Neutra used thin Roman brick to help assert the contrast between the positive quality of the wall above the fireplace and the void of the firebox. Here he uses common brick with white mortar, both diminishing the contrast's impact. The master bathroom in this small two-bedroom house is beautiful, with black slate floors and floor-to-ceiling glass overlooking the pool. The generous mirrors suspend any visual termination to a gorgeous panorama.

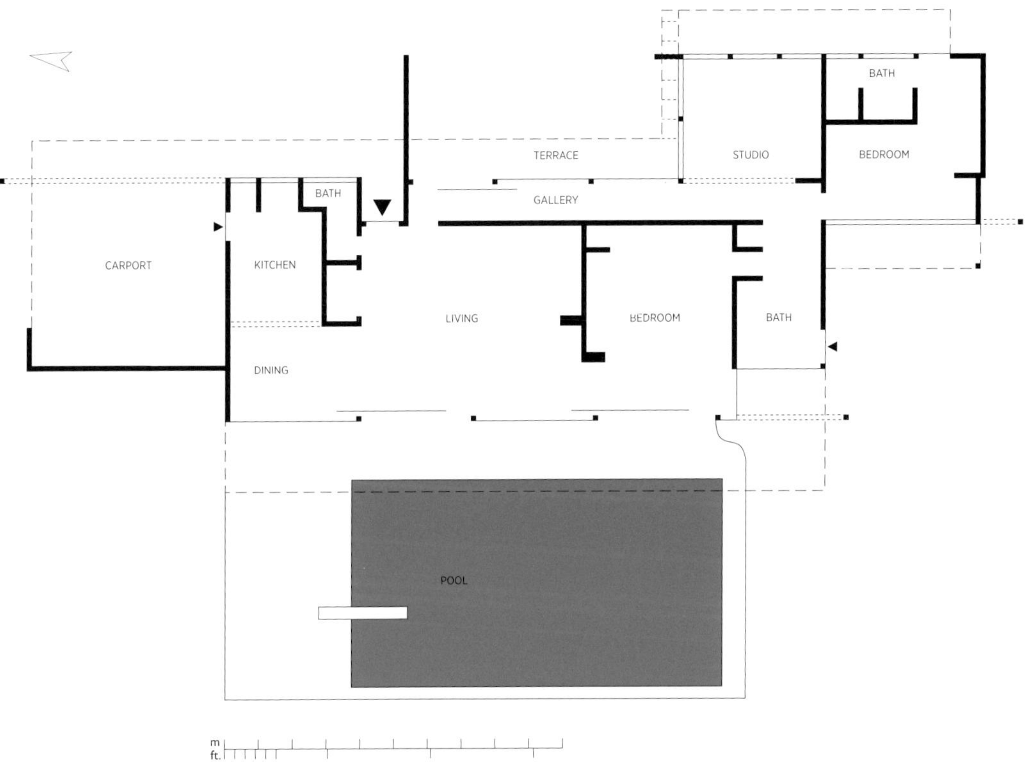

Following: This very private house, above a steep slope, is completely open to the pool and site. View facing east.

Opposite top: The fireplace is a composition unto itself, one of Neutra's best. View facing south.

Opposite bottom: Even the bedroom is enveloped in nature, with no loss of privacy. View facing south. Out of sight, a sensitive and deferential addition was executed by Escher GuneWardena Architecture.

Above: The bathroom featured a jalousie (louvered) window, a type popular in mid-century homes.

RICHARD AND LENORE OYLER HOUSE

771 Thundercloud Lane
Lone Pine, California, 1959

Compared to the James and Orlene Moore House that grows out of its site, murmuring in close conversation with the water and plants around it, the Oyler House and its backdrop of barren Mount Whitney Mountains throw each other into sharp relief. The dialectic is one of complete conviction: the unsparing horizontal line and the eight-foot column/beam/glass module of the house look ever more a controlled, intentional human intervention while the jagged mountains seem to twist ever more frantically against the resolute lines of the house. Two mighty rocks rearing up between the house and the hills have their own secondary dialogue with a thin short horizontal wall at the rear of the house, a wall clad in stone collected by the owners from the site. The two lone spider legs, like long notes suspended in the air, have vital work to do in being a medium for the current running back and forth between the land and the house that seems to hover above it. Even so, the strange landscape is so overpowering that in the file labeled "interior shots," all the shots really are of ... the landscape. Features such as the birch and steel kitchen or the rock fireplace pale as mere lightweight human requisites. Somewhat surprisingly, the pool at one corner of the house is not a further right-angled imposition into the land but cut of the same cloth: Neutra simply blasted out the top of a huge rock so that the six Oyler children played in their own private wonderland. Above the datum line at the top of the fixed and casement windows, clerestory windows between the exposed beams

provide additional ventilation. The overhangs do double duty in that they protect not only from overhead sun but from the brutal light and heat bouncing up from the desert floor.

The family was Mormon (Church of the Latter Day Saints), a belief system that is very American yet stands apart from it, somewhat metaphorically like the relationship between house and its site. They had long lived in Lone Pine and learned to love the extremes of climate. They embarked on architectural research "with many special requests to the County Librarian" which led them to the now world-famous Neutra. Would the architect design a house for them, a "simple, unknown family of modest income?" The man came, along with Benno Fischer, Sergei Koschin and John Blanton, three of his best designers. They planned carefully for this courageous couple; there was no money for a dining room so the big generous kitchen table, with storage underneath, was used all the time. The kitchen flanks the children's wing (so that when they grew older their gatherings were somewhat acoustically constrained) to the south, with their bathroom at the extreme wall (the first wall of defense against the sun) while the parents' bedroom is at the north; here the bathroom is in the west taking the brunt of the late afternoon sun. Thus, programmatic needs overruled the more efficient consolidation of mechanical services. Every interior north-south wall is pulled back from the 52-foot east window wall, so that the view is everywhere and family traffic is open and easy in this central portion of the house.

While the primary façade faces the beautiful Eastern Sierras, the rear looks east to the extraordinary ancestors protecting the house.

HENRY AND CAROLINE SINGLETON HOUSE

15000 Mulholland Drive
Los Angeles, California, 1959

The Singletons knew what they liked, such as exposed structure, easy housekeeping and minimum yard work. Henry Singleton was the ambitious young chairman of Teledyne Corporation; he was on the cover of *Forbes* in January 1968, and the large, expensive home with its wealth of terraces reflected sophisticated tastes. There is a long procession up wide steps of exposed aggregate concrete panels; at the top, a white-painted freestanding masonry wall on the left (hiding a private portion of the house) runs out to greet the visitor. Here three outrigger spider legs, purely decorative in that they spring out from the wall, frame the last part of the journey to the door. The south walls of the living area are transparent, so the first thing the visitor sees is the distant valley beyond, with a reflecting pool which was to resonate with the Hollywood Lake in the distance to "continue and bring the lake close to the house," Neutra wrote. Inside, the children's wing lies to the west while the master bedroom is to the extreme east. Terrazzo floors throughout add qualities of precision and hardness to the long house, softened by exposed redwood ceilings and walnut or birch cabinetry. The contrasts here of light and dark are particularly strong, most evident in the original dark stained beams against the whitewashed ceilings. Because it sums up Neutra's thesis in a single image, the southeast corner of the living room with its spider leg and pool with three step stones, has become famous. Julius Shulman's photograph of this quiet moment has been reproduced many times. Jocelyn Domela, who often worked on Neutra houses, was the landscape architect for the Japanese-inspired plantings.

Opposite: Five acres of verdant greenery surrounds the house to-day. Once a masterpiece constructed by Neutra's legendary contractor, Red Marsh, it was renovated in the mid-2000s. View facing east.

Above: One of Shulman's best-known photographs, the spider leg frames both the reflecting pool and the view south, across Stone Canyon Reservoir all the way to Catalina Island. (A fun aside: Julius scolded anyone who described taking a photograph as "shooting." "I am not a violent man, I do not shoot buildings," he said.)

View north through the living area to the original library/den for a completely transparent view through the house. The original bedroom wing, now significantly altered, is on the right.

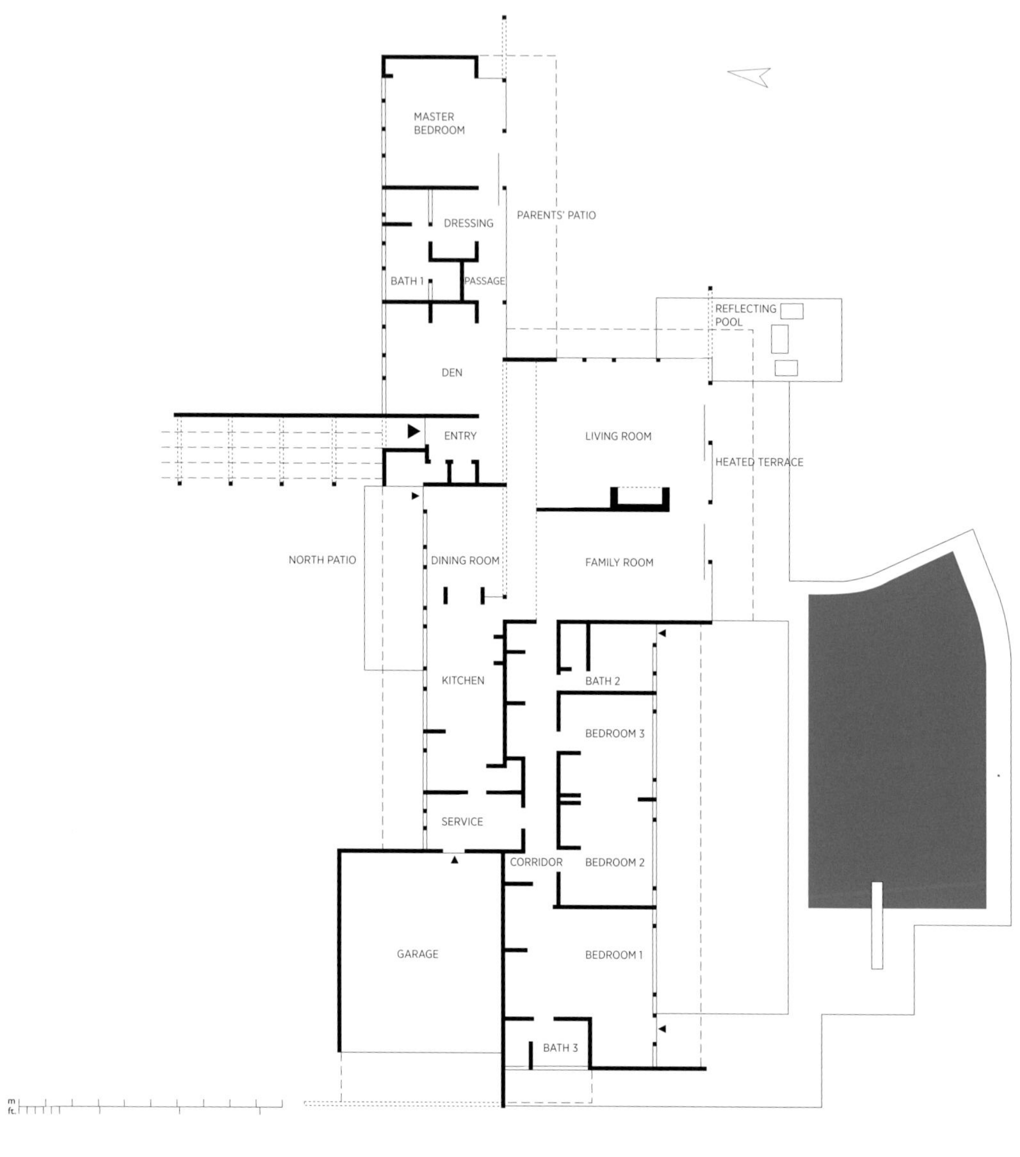

Opposite top: Whoever was in the kitchen could quickly see who might be approaching. The ashlar masonry is a theme that runs through the house. View facing northeast to the San Gabriel Mountains.

Opposite bottom: A breathtaking corner, with opposing axes crossing to create a moment charged with tension and serenity, where the house seems to dissolve into the undulating landscape. View facing southeast.

Above: View south from dining area through the family room that in turn opened out to the terrace with radiant floor heating.

Opposite: The original clean white terrazzo tile throughout unified the villa. It's hard to see, but note how the direction of the wood grain on the desk is book-matched and flows down the side panel.

Opposite: Oddly, the "Camel Table" blocks the easy openness between dining area and family room, probably staged for the camera. Neutra also designed the chairs, later reproduced by VS International.

Above: The clarity of views, the lightness of the glass, is matched by the palette of materials, enduring and majestic, that jumped from surface to surface.

DAVID AND SARA COVENEY HOUSE

301 Hughes Road
King of Prussia, Pennsylvania, 1960

Much like Neutra's Bewobau developments in its compact, straightforward sturdiness, this inexpensive house still has some interesting custom details. For example, in a discreet play of crossing axes, a gutter slides in one direction over a small header beam at the corner of the living room, along whose length a light trough runs which ends by delineating a cozy protected reading area. The terrace is supported by a grid-work of rough-textured wood planters, beams and girders. There is a big skylight in the large open kitchen, which in its dominating centrality in plan is reminiscent of the radical role Catherine Beecher Stowe, educator and proponent of women's suffrage, assigned to kitchens in her house designs of 1856.

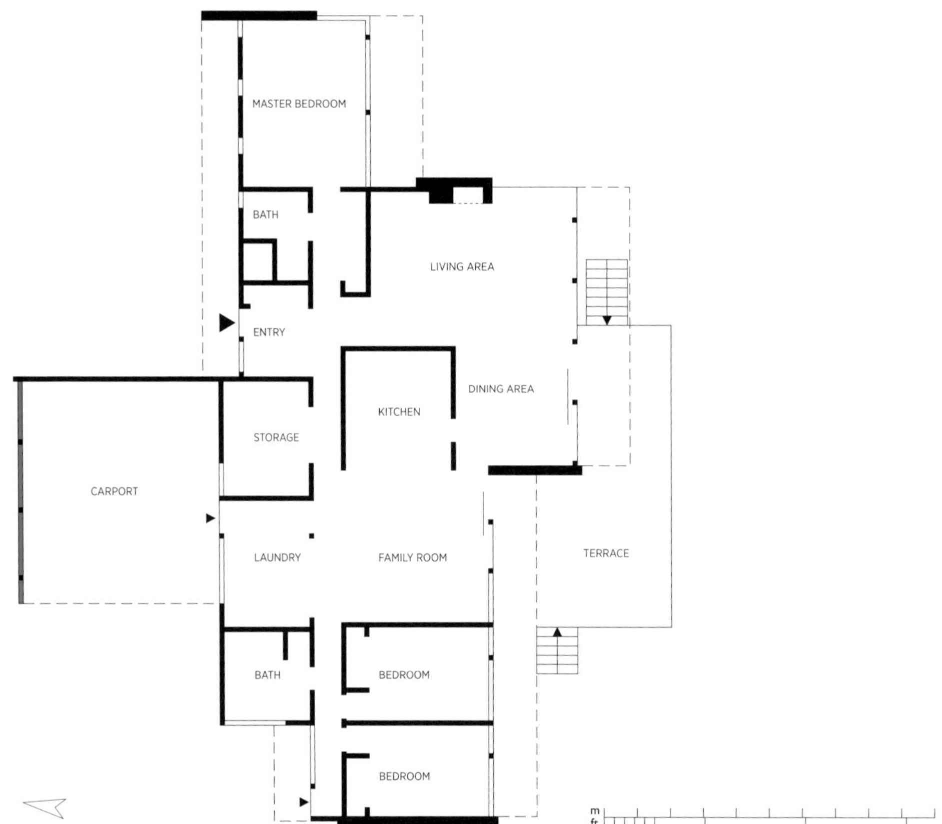

Neutra often placed the master bedroom (as the primary bedroom was called in the 1950s) at the opposite end of the house as the children's bedrooms, typically equipping the house with intercom systems to alleviate parental concerns while preserving a little privacy.

Neutra is often photographed seated on the floor, conveying an informality amidst the disciplined interior, a master class in integrating very different spaces: sheltered and open, dark and light, rough and smooth.

ROBERT AND ELSA SALE HOUSE

1531 Tigertail Road
Los Angeles, California, 1960

The young owners were an engineer and an "artist-craftsman" wife who purchased a lot on a shelf of land on a dauntingly steep slope overlooking the Pacific coastline with another view of pastoral farmland to the north. They desired a home of woodsy, quiet serenity; they "hiked for miles free from evidence of the city," Neutra wrote in his description. Built by Walter Johnson (like Red Marsh, Johnson built many Neutra designs) the footprint of the 2,230-square-foot house had to fit to the level bit of land for budget reasons. Neutra designed an entry which included a skylit gallery for her art work; like artists Josephine and Robert Chuey, this couple requested that the acoustic plaster ceilings be raised one foot. The foundations were designed to sustain the loads of a prospective second floor. Neutra lavished much design work

Opposite: High in one of the most rugged and inaccessible areas of Los Angeles, the views from the house are especially wonderful. View facing south.

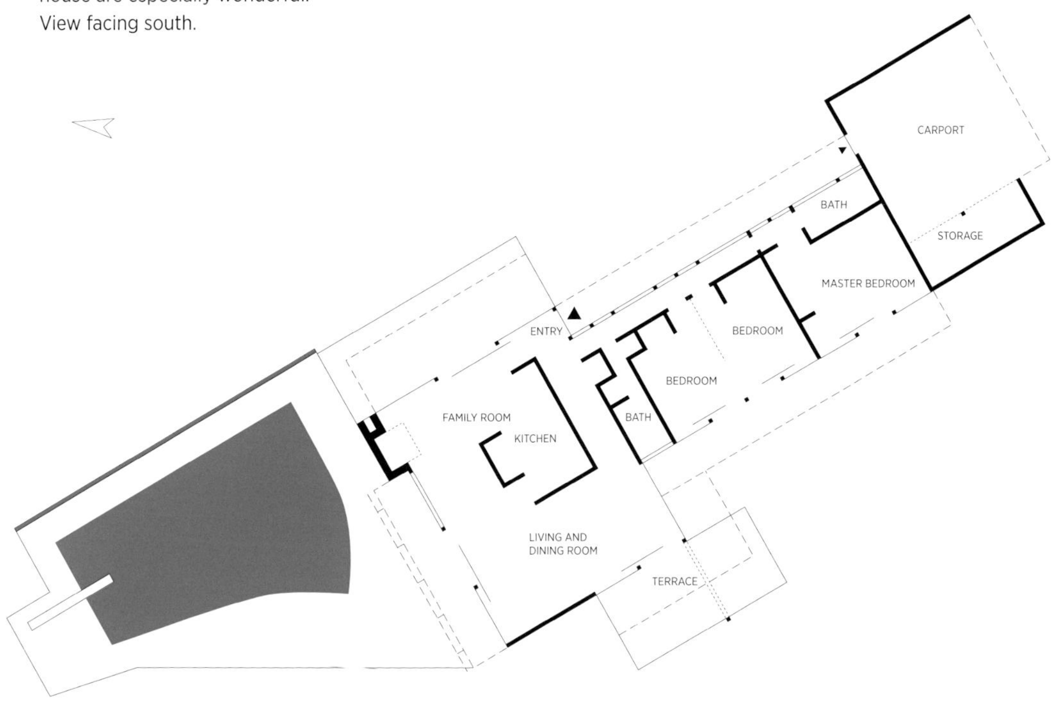

on orchestrating artificial lighting in the houses with not only his standard exterior soffit lighting but strip lighting in the art gallery and lighting under the hall windows that continued into the master bath to provide a "warm glow of light to the entrance walk" on the opposite side of this wall. "The family room and kitchen open to a wind-sheltered brick barbecue terrace adjacent to the pool area where a picnic table can stand without [visually] interfering with the far landscape," wrote Neutra, clearly concerned about any impediment between eye and horizon. He tied the dwelling to its site with an entrance pergola on the northeast side of the house, facing the hills. This was planted with bougainvillea to extend the sense of procession up to the house.

Paul Klee

Neutra designed a great deal of informality into the house, with the pool just a sliding glass wall away from the combined family, living, and kitchen space.

GETTYSBURG CYCLORAMA CENTER

Neutra and Alexander
with Thaddeus Longstreth
The Abraham Lincoln “Shrine of the Nation”
Gettysburg, Pennsylvania, 1961

Neutra and Alexander's uncondescending and finely detailed Modernist design signaled a paradigm shift in the nature of the interaction between the visitor and America's national parks. The design was a showpiece of the "Mission 66" building program of the late 1950s and early 1960s, when the Park Service introduced the "visitor center" as a new building type, designed to gather auditorium, interpretive exhibits, bookstores, and staff offices in one centralized structure. The centers would not only celebrate America's historic sites but also engage and regulate their visitors. Its legacy was a series of progressive modern architectural designs representative of post-World War II prosperity and optimism in the future.

From one side, the huge round drum appears as a pure white cylinder floating above massive stone piers extending radially out into the landscape. On the other, the volume is attached to a long horizontal glass spine with vertical metal louvers housing Park Service administrative offices, terminating in a giant spider leg penetrating a rough masonry wall. It is the cylinder which houses the 1883 "Cyclorama" painting of the bloody Battle of Gettysburg, a circular panorama by Paul Philippoteaux. Neutra and Alexander used the site to advantage to heighten the drama of procession to view this painting symbolizing a nation's moment of crisis. A landscaped exterior ramp leads to an overlook above the battlefield before folding back toward the

Cyclorama building. Inside, a ramp spirals up to a dark viewing platform in the center of the Cyclorama, where, viewing the painting, one can hear and see a light and sound interpretation of the three-day battle. Below, the auditorium side-wall and glazed panels in the exhibition area slide away in a symbolic gesture to a proposed annual celebration of Lincoln's famous 90-second speech to be delivered from the historic rostrum to seated visitors inside and out on the lawn.

In 1997, a new initiative was announced by the Park Service; it would build non-descript mega-mall-like "boxes" off-center to channel visitors to food, entertainment and transportation centers. Gettysburg was to be the pilot program to test the viability of this approach, and as such the Cyclorama Center would have to be demolished, for fear it might compete for visitation with the new mall. Championed by Dion Neutra, the Cyclorama's project architect, the center has now been listed on the country's National Register for Historic Places. It has also been deemed eligible for National Landmark status, a status that would protect the building from being demolished by the Park Service as it is the highest honor which can be bestowed on an American momument.

Opposite: Despite its status as a National Landmark, this majestic monument and visitor center was tragically demolished by the National Park Service on a muddy, cloudy day in February 2013.

Below: Permitting a larger audience to take part in events, part of the Cyclorama wall slid away to reveal the famous battlefield.

NAVAL AIR STATION LEMOORE RICHARD J. NEUTRA ELEMENTARY SCHOOL

Neutra and Alexander
with Donald Francis Haines
Lemoore, California, 1961

Neutra gave the dedication address for the Richard J. Neutra Elementary School at the heart of Lemoore Naval Air Station on March 25, 1962. It was 37 years after he had first conceived of the idea of a ring as a theoretical plan for a school back in 1925, a model of which was commissioned by the Museum of Modern Art for its 1932 exhibition on modern architecture. (Collaborators on the Ring School included Gregory Ain, Harry Dovell, Raphael Soriano and Alfred Weidler.) In the built project two arcs of nine classrooms branch out from a core of administrative offices and kitchen to enclose a multi-purpose room. Storage space and two kindergarten rooms, near a 100-car lot, project in the opposite direction from the core. Each of the classrooms opens onto the playground by means of a sliding glass door, one-half the length of the classroom. Neutra was able to exploit new glass technology in new non-glare glass that allowed schoolchildren to see out but was visually impenetrable from the outside, lessening potential disruptions, Neutra believed, from would-be pranksters passing outside. One of the most important facets of the building was the huge, high multi-purpose room with multiple folding doors and movable indoor-outdoor platforms.

In one of the photographs of the school, Neutra is seen entering one of the finished classrooms next to six brand-new plastic chairs. The chairs are lined up and placed to defy the boundary between indoors and out, just as photographs of the Corona school had shown with old-fashioned wood chairs. The perimeter of the ring was a broad hallway, with glass doors separating classrooms. Here colored concrete was used for foot traffic along the ring or for access to the outdoor play areas, while asphalt tile was used for the classrooms proper. In built contrast to the theoretical Ring School, however, Neutra broke up each formerly curved unit in the ring into wedge-shaped pieces with straight lines, achieving the same effect but at lower cost. It also permitted him to introduce another long wedge for foot traffic and storage space that leads from the perimeter of the ring to the center between each classroom, ensuring greater quiet for teaching.

Opposite: The adaptation of the 1925 design from a ring to angled segments afforded Neutra the opportunity to extend classroom walls to create angled outdoor storage areas.

Below: The change also afforded classroom floor plans that included a rectangular class area and a triangulated walkway, wide at one end, open to the greenery outside the "circle," and narrowing at the classroom entrance, opening to the enclosed community space.

PHYLLIS BARKER HOUSE

Palos Verdes, California, 1961

Opposite: The Phyllis Barker House is a bit of a mystery, but the little-known structure is clear, strong, with wonderful resolutions in how the slope can be harnessed on behalf of good ergonomics and spaciousness. As ever, Palos Verdes' rules meant sloped roofs, which Neutra exploited to his advantage.

Right: The change in flooring material denotes a change in the function of the space.

Below: The house boasted a glorious wood ceiling; beyond lay stunning ocean views and sea air. View facing northeast.

HITOSHI AND JUNE OHARA HOUSE

2210 Neutra Place
Los Angeles, California, 1961

Raymond Neutra singled out this house as one of his favorites, because "it is three-dimensionally complex in the way it climbs stepwise up the slope it sits on. The interior space is unusually complex too, with the stair of the entrance emerging upward into the living room, which is then connected upwards to bedrooms at a higher level." Because of the different levels, all connected to outdoor rooms, it is indeed difficult to grasp that the spacious, light, open three-bedroom house is only 1,600 square feet. The familiar materials palette included pebble-dash concrete, birch cabinetry, cork tile on one bedroom wall and clear Douglas fir tongue-and-groove decking. The Oharas enjoyed their conferences with Mr. Neutra, said June Ohara, "maybe because we liked his ideas and gave him his rein. We thought he would be way beyond our budget, but that turned out to be not the case. He must have really liked this house; he would come often and sit in it." Neutra often visited his houses long after they were built, doing a personal "POE" (in architectural parlance, a Post-Occupancy Evaluation is an assessment of a building's performance). He sometimes surprised clients such as Josephine Chuey or Fred and Mary Jane Auerbacher, arriving unexpectedly at dinner time or late in the evening.

Opposite: One of Neutra's most accomplished integrations of site and home, the house on Neutra Place (the former Argent Place was renamed in 1992, thanks to the efforts of Dion Neutra) is set back into the slope. View facing east.

Below: The view north shows how, starting with the garage at the right, the dwelling steps down the hill.

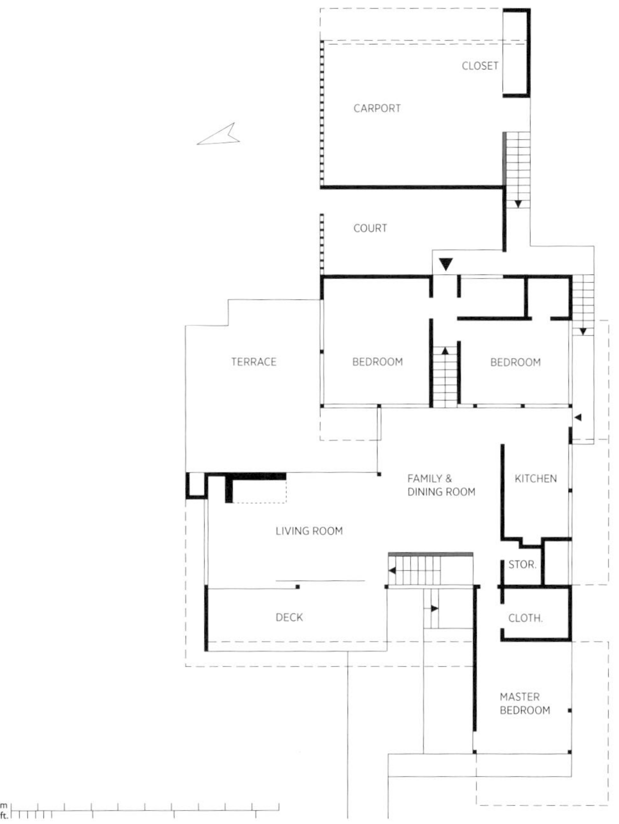

PALOS VERDES HIGH SCHOOL

Neutra and Alexander
with Carrington H. Lewis
600 Cloyden Drive
Palos Verdes, California, 1961

Below: In Palos Verdes sloped roofs and red clay tile roofs were mandatory. Just one block from the ocean, the new 37-acre school reflected the postwar population boom. As with most of the firm's schools, asymmetrically placed canopies were supported by spider legs.

Opposite: The cavernous gym's roof was supported by a steel beam whose shape, deeper in the middle, tells a story about where loads are greatest.

Sited on 37 acres in the Malaga Cove section of Palos Verdes Estates, the school is a sprawling village of buildings totaling 138,000 square feet and built at a cost of $4.5 million. The large sloping site was first graded into two plateaus separated by a pre-cast concrete retaining wall. The lower plateau provides space for the physical education building, two shop buildings and playing fields. The upper plateau contains classrooms, an auditorium, assembly rooms for 3,000 and an indoor-outdoor stage. With its strict legislation on roofs and materials, it is no surprise that the rooflines for this large school in Palos Verdes had to be pitched. "The most significant factor determining the design of the plant," Neutra wrote pointedly, "was undoubtedly the restriction requiring clay tiles except on minor areas. Because of the roof slopes resulting, the large buildings became much taller than would otherwise be necessary." Sometimes these Spanish tile roofs are expressed, other times flat overhangs above walkways slip in under the roof line so that the user's primary experience is that of flatness. The spider legs for the covered walkways are made of wood beams and square steel tubes held back from the ends of the beams.

SANTA ANA POLICE FACILITIES

Neutra and Alexander with Ramberg and Lowrey Civic Center Plaza Santa Ana, California, 1961

Above: Long demolished, the formidable structure featured several notable interior features, including a series of large round skylights, and a sculptural "floating" staircase with a voluptuous aluminum railing in the entrance.

Opposite: The façade was composed of glass and yellow-colored aluminum louvers, reflecting warm daylight into the building's interior. One exterior wall was clad in exposed aggregate of warm desert stone.

Despite its glass and aluminum louvers on the street façade and Neutra's description of the building as a "friendly enactment of cherished order ... the human counterpiece to the hated Bastille" this is a building closed to its public. Cells are pulled beyond the footprint of the rectangular box and face, in an optimistic architectural gesture, a strip of gardens planted in front of their windows. The reception and office occupy the ground floor. Upstairs, offices for police personnel surround a large locker room and auditorium.

BEWOBAU HOUSING

with Baubüro Bewobau
and Erich Schneider-Wessling, Carl Heinz Rebstock
Marienhöhe Quickborn, Germany, 1962
Mörfelden-Walldorf, Germany, 1963

Neutra's ambition to simultaneously house "the masses" and to address the needs of the individual was most comprehensively realized not in suburban American but in Germany. As chief design architect he collaborated with the Bewobau Corporation (Betreuungs- und Wohnungsbaugesellschaft mbH, Hamburg) to create a speculative multi-residential development for Bewobau Corporation Quickborn near Hamburg and in Walldorf near Frankfurt/Main. The roughly 250 well-crafted units included nine different housing types ranging from two-story flats in short rows to upscale freestanding houses in a variety of price ranges. Harking back to his early studies for Rush City Reformed dwellings, he addressed the needs of families with two- to

Opposite: The houses in these dense estates have double brick walls, dual glazing in the living room, and a roof structure of thin steel and wood beams. The flat roofs have two drains; drain pipes are hidden in the walls.

Below: Neutra made every effort to preserve as many trees as possible throughout the developments, now dense with mature landscaping.

six-bedroom dwellings; studios were designed to house single people. The sites were exceptionally beautiful, which was a strong selling point, helping to lead to startlingly quick and sustained sales of the units. (William Levitt had turned down Neutra's proposals for Levittown, fearing that flat roofs and other Modernist details wouldn't sell, a move which ultimately led to the "flat" paradigm in residential architecture America enjoys today.) The dwellings were oriented for both sun and privacy, often stepped back so that each unit had views. Neutra mixed up the building types so none would be segregated.

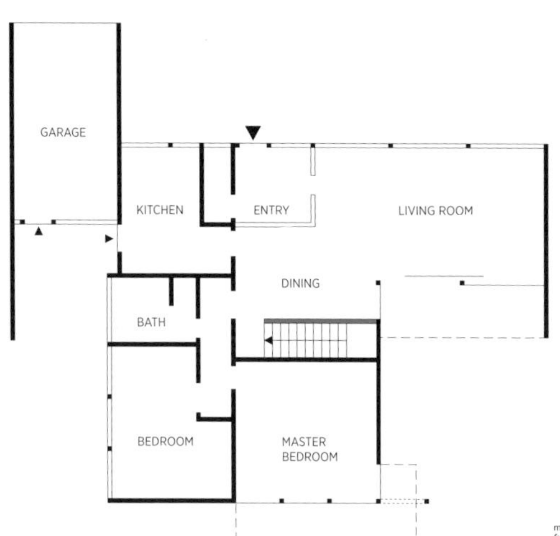

The idea was to provide a variety of housing types with the same building language, different vocabulary. Ceiling panels made of Oregon pine and Chrysler heaters, both imported from the USA, increased the construction costs; the corporation offered a free Volkswagen in 1965 to attract buyers.

The Walldorf units, which ranged from 97 to 160 square meters (1,044 to 1,722 square feet), were placed under monument protection in the early 1990s, followed by Quickborn in 2006.

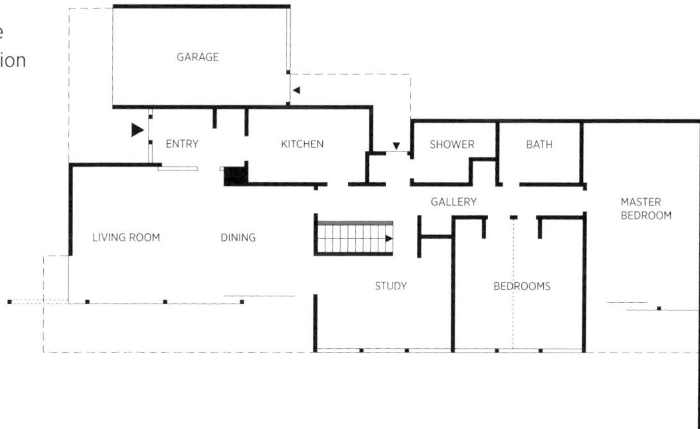

Above: Each homeowner enjoys the same solid construction, glass walls, asymmetrical floor plan, and limited palette of materials of brick and wood. Beyond that, the décor is up to the individual.

Left: "Happiness cannot be measured in square feet" ... "Individualization is an entirely different thing than just empty and arbitrary variation," Neutra wrote, with Bewobau his demonstration of that.

Above: Reflecting pools and plants were used to increase the privacy of each unit.

Right: Neutra designed the kitchens to be taut and lean without sacrificing views to nature.

GARDEN GROVE COMMUNITY CHURCH

12141 Lewis Street
Garden Grove, California, 1962

The Rev. Robert A. Shuller, the now world-famous evangelist, began his ministry by renting a drive-in movie theater and commissioned Neutra to design this church which would accommodate conventional worship with the radically new concept of worship in one's automobile, the "pew from Detroit," as Neutra called it jokingly. In later years he became a regular confidante of Richard and Dione during the architect's days of despair in the 1960s.

The Garden Grove complex is a group of buildings over ten acres in addition to the famous "drive-in church." It includes the one-story wing containing church offices and lounge, a social hall with kitchen, and a Sunday school, which surround an inner garden at the south end of the worship space. The church itself combines crisp, well-tailored steel detailing with a deep understanding of one aspect of ministry, that good theater and cadenced delivery is part of good preaching. A balcony juts just beyond the glass building envelope, floating above a long reflection pool with fountains flanking this side of the building. There is a long diagonal white staircase

Opposite: The church is shown just after construction, before Neutra's 13-story "Tower of Hope" was added to the immediate north of the bell tower in 1968, and well before the Crystal Cathedral was constructed in 1981. View facing west.

Below: Framed by the "Tower of Hope" on the north and the sanctuary on the east, classrooms and Rev. Shuller's elegantly appointed offices were part of the one-story quadrangle that was based on traditional cloister models. View facing north.

cutting across the chancel space leading to the balcony, slowing the sense of procession as the preacher ascends to simultaneously address the crowd in the nave as well as people listening in from as many as 600 cars in the outdoor amphitheater. The vertically laid stone used for the long low walls stretching into the landscape outside are used again behind the pulpit to reinforce the indoor-outdoor connection. The communion table is a "heavy brute concrete mensa" as Neutra

Left: Brilliantly rehabilitated by LGA Architects and the Diocese of Orange under Rob Neal, the sanctuary is now called "The Arboretum." The fountains symbolize the 12 apostles.

Opposite: The figure of Richard Neutra can be discerned, standing on the balcony where Rev. Shuller preached to both the congregants in pews ... and those in their cars. View facing east.

described it. It may be no surprise that the table is reminiscent of Le Corbusier's work since it was designed by Sergei Koschin, one of Neutra's principal designers. The Russian-born aristocratic Koschin had worked for Le Corbusier, drafting the Centrosoyus (Central Union of Consumer Societies), built in Moscow between 1929 and 1936.

This glass-walled building is also a cultural phenomenon in its acceptance of the car as a natural element of the urban landscape, and the steeple and tall cross are meant to be seen from the adjacent freeway. It won an award for excellence from the American Institute of Steel Construction; its exposed steel bents (which Neutra called "a fugue of one-sided steel bents") taper out on the east to the wide overhang. These bents accomplished several tasks: they were an efficient use of materials, they created a sloped ceiling which was critical to good acoustics, and they directed attention to the east, where the cars and morning sun were. Here vast sliding glass doors open and finally close slowly and solemnly at the end of services. There is a controlled, strong sense of asymmetry throughout this composition: as with many of Neutra's churches, the length of the pews are different on the east and west sides of the nave. A covered walkway leads to the church offices which have their own reflecting pools and small intimate gardens in front of glass walls. The generous open-plan lounge has an unusual sheet copper fireplace and built-in furniture.

SAMUEL AND LOUELLA MASLON HOUSE

70–900 Fairway Drive
Cathedral City, California, 1962

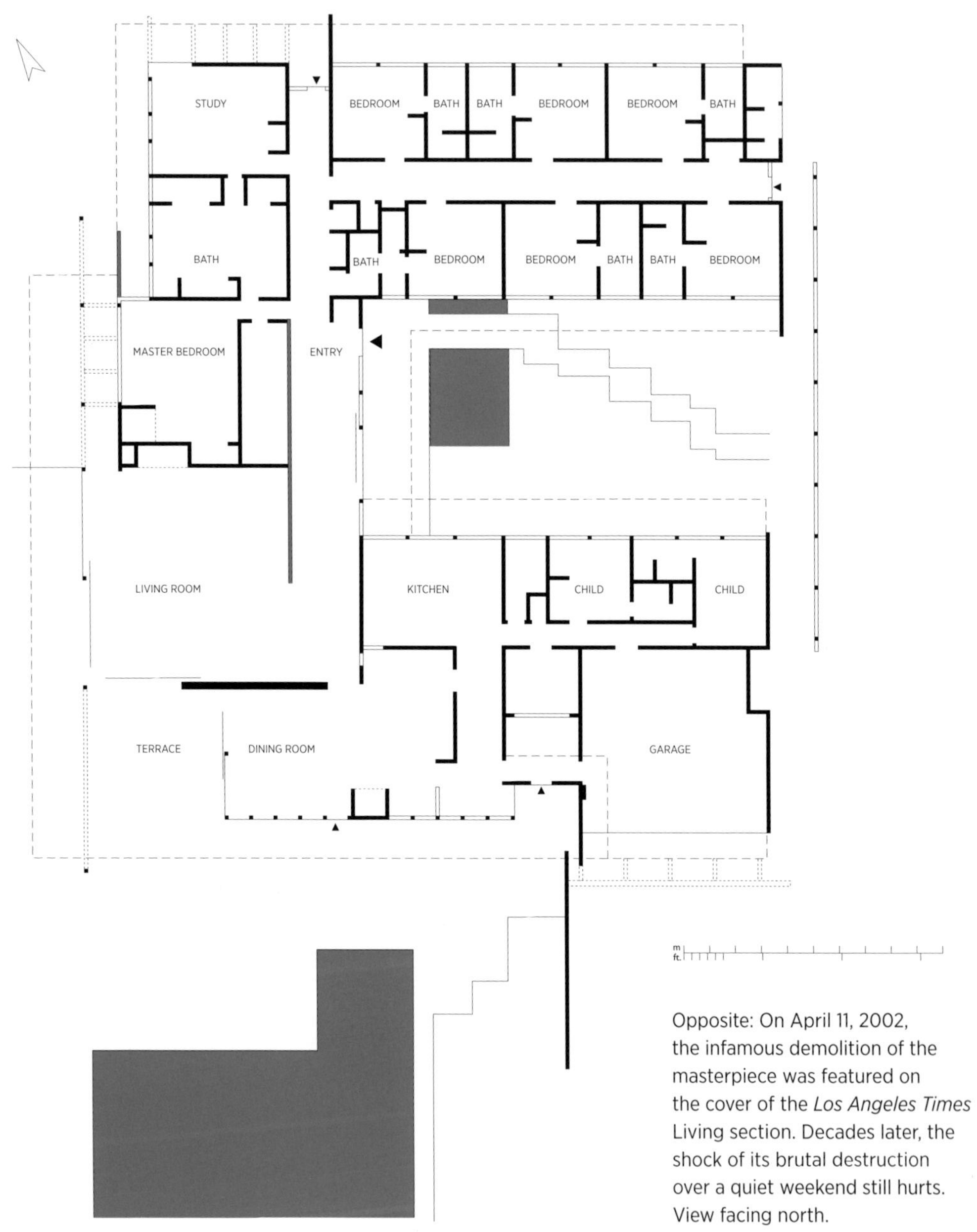

Opposite: On April 11, 2002, the infamous demolition of the masterpiece was featured on the cover of the *Los Angeles Times* Living section. Decades later, the shock of its brutal destruction over a quiet weekend still hurts. View facing north.

Palm Springs has three fine Neutra homes: the 1937 Miller House; the pivotal Kaufmann Desert House, and the Maslon House. This last is a little-known house that is of the same order as the Tremaine House in conception and execution: pure, distilled Neutra achieved on a handsome budget. The Maslon House can be described as a single horizontal line that rides very low above the immaculate lawn of a huge golf course. In the context of the architecture, the course acts as an infinite green plane parallel to the roof line of the house, while the brilliant white of the house is echoed in the occasional white sand traps of the course. In contrast to the Kaufmann Desert House, the expression of this house does not depend on the tension between machine and desert; unlike the Tremaine House, its horizontality is not mitigated by the gnarled oak trees around it. Here, the flawless lines of the house are confirmed by the flawlessly kept course. The house and its site belong to the same club. They are social peers and intimates.

Like the VDL House, this is a U-shaped compound whose two legs face southeast. Three wings are pulled apart from each other to create generous passageways and opportunities for transparency. One leg is the service wing. The other leg houses no less than six guest bedrooms on a double-loaded corridor. The choice northwest portion of the house, overlooking the golf course, is comprised by the living, dining and family areas on one side and the master suite on the other. The public enters through the inner courtyard of the U by an angled path

leading over a reflecting pond to the front door. Here Neutra firmly takes the elbow of the arriving visitor, adroitly deflecting his attention away from the bedrooms and out to the glass-walled living room. Just beyond lies a remarkable space, an outdoor room at the extreme northwest corner of the plan, a wholly "negative space" that nonetheless anchors the composition and permits spaces to meet, intertwine and continue. This grand protected terrace is separated only by sliding glass walls from the family room to the southwest and from the living room to the northeast, where the glass disappears into a wall. The large space is apparently supported on the far side only by a slender steel beam connected to a delicate steel column standing just far enough from the roof to be clearly read as a discrete element. The Maslons, formidable art collectors of 20th-century art, made it a practice to lay beautiful carpets, colluding in Neutra's constant desire to extinguish indoor-outdoor boundaries.

Opposite: The home's exquisite, pivotal siting at the intersection of two fairways was probably why – apart from ignorance – it was demolished.

Above: Louella, Samuel, and Neutra worked closely to design spaces and to hang priceless art where the Maslons wanted to enjoy their collection.

Following: Louella is seen approaching from the pool. Despite its formality, the dining area, complete with a stainless-steel hooded interior barbecue, was open to the living area. Every color, down to the vertical tile walls flanking the barbecue, was attuned to the colors of the desert.

FEODOR AND KRISTIN PITCAIRN HOUSE

with Thaddeus Longstreth
2860 Papermill Road
Bryn Athyn, Pennsylvania, 1962

Above: The 6,303-square-foot home stands deep within a forest, well back from the road, a perfect fit for the Netherlands-born Pitcairn, a naturalist, writer, banker, and ecologist.

Opposite: The formal entrance to the house combined wood and natural stone.

This is a large house with a challenging dual program: the needs of an individual, well-to-do family who also belonged to a religious society, and required spaces that could accommodate large gatherings of adults and children. In response, the architecture includes elements of both "commercial" and "residential" Neutra, first seen on the façade. Often Neutra used the same details for either sphere, but here the contrast does not enliven a conversation between elements, nor integrate them, but rather makes them uncomfortable neighbors. Here, to the right of the perpendicular plane separating public and private areas (a Neutra convention), a crisp two-story composition of windows competes with the far more domestic left side. A

Left: Neutra had a special affinity for open-tread staircases. Here, the curving ascent affords a view of the woodland beyond.

Opposite: The low cedar wall extends outdoors from the mighty, freestanding stone fireplace.

rustic wooden balcony is hoisted into the air by a series of built-up triangular wooden supports, topped by a wood-sheathed run of flower boxes. In the foyer, an exceptionally beautiful free-form staircase of floating treads cantilevered from a plaster clad steel frame is compromised by a large expanse of glass that gratuituously doubles its image. There are many other areas in the house that are far more effective. Sensitively sited amidst a thick wood, the privacy allowed for a terrazzo sunken bath immediately adjacent to the garden, with a "hot air floor grill" to make winter bathing "almost an outdoor pleasure." Walnut was the choice for built-in cabinetry in the living areas while in the bright kitchen, bleached oak plywood cabinetry (also used for facing the two refrigerators) contrasts well with the stainless-steel appliances. The space is open to a huge playroom. Rather than combining exposed beams and lowered soffits, a Neutra convention in dealing with the ceilings of gabled roofs in the primary living area, here he introduced the concept of "horizontal" though dark-painted, full-span beams that are also built-up triangular supports, with the bottoms horizontal and the tops following the gabled roofs. Pitcairn also possibly boasts one of the world's most minimalist, if not one of the largest, residential aquariums, a long unbroken sweep of glass framed in brushed stainless steel. The two-story house is framed in steel and wood, and it is interesting to note the specifications for the exterior, clad in "quarried rubble-ashlar stone of high lime, non-homogeneous content with large quantitites of ferrous oxide and quartz cleft-seam face." There is no mortar. Wood siding was two inch tongue-and-groove West Coast cedar, treated with a creosote bleaching oil. The glass is dual-pane with solar-gray tint on the west elevation.

Opposite: Bold, strong, simple moves characterize the quietly monumental Goldman House, designed for the son of Russian immigrants. View northeast.

Above: The horizontality of the design, reinforced by the thin, wide overhanging roof slab, leads the eye out from the living area. As ever, the firebox is located off-center. View northeast.

HAROLD AND KATE GOLDMAN HOUSE

3417 Southern Hills Drive
Des Moines, Iowa, 1963

Opposite: The "public" stair on the left led away from the house to a terrace in front of the living room window wall, so a visitor first faced the forest before turning around to enter the living area. View facing northeast.

Above: All the childrens' bedrooms opened to the large playroom, the longer arm of the U-shaped building, while the parents' suite wisely occupied the other, shorter arm of the U. View facing northwest.

MARINERS MEDICAL ARTS CENTER

1901 Westcliff Drive
Newport Beach, California, 1963

Above: Even the rear two-story structure is not left behind when it comes to good design. View facing southeast.

Opposite: Neutra brought all of his strategies on behalf of well-being to bear here: broad overhangs, liminal spaces afforded by the spider legs, sheltered walkways, plantings, and cooling reflecting pools. View facing southwest.

Generations of Southern Californians know this group of three small buildings on a busy shopping street. It is one of Neutra's best designs in how it functions internally and in how it exemplifies good urban design, being both resolutely Modern and neighborly. The thesis for this building was to prove that a clinic "does not have to be a forbidding intimidating institution" so nature's health-giving benefits, as well as privacy and lighting, were of prime importance. A garden between two one-story buildings on the street serves as the real "lobby" for the compound commissioned by 11 doctors. Walking past lush tropical plants and reflecting pools was to confer calm upon visitors, to slow the pace of pounding hearts. In fact, the psychiatrists' offices were

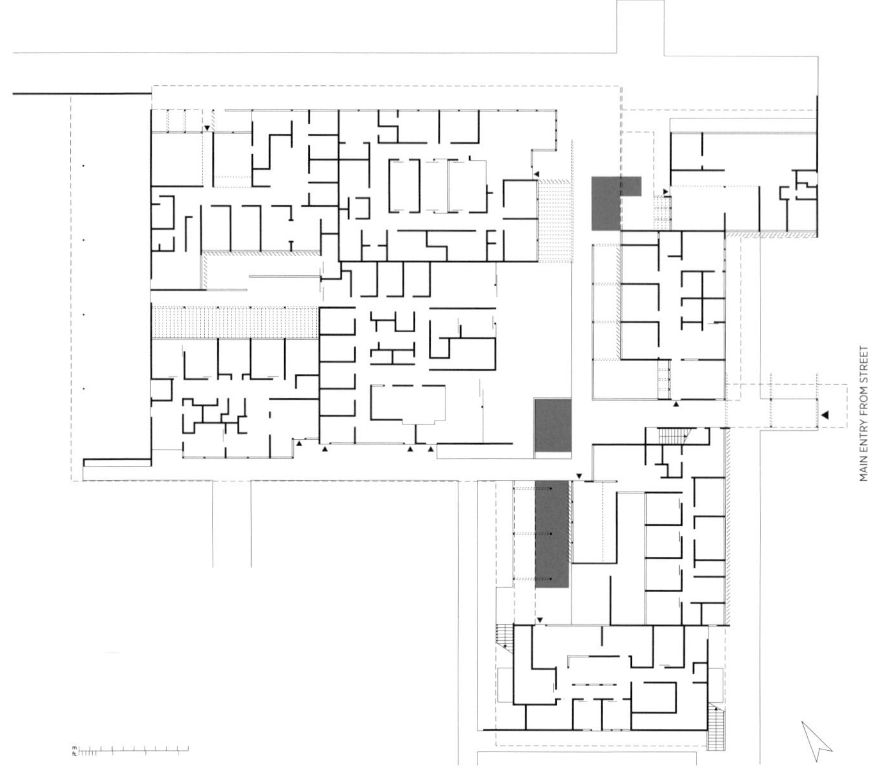

placed in the rear two-story structure, so that by the time visitors reached them they would have passed all the landscaping and reflecting pools. Neutra's clients were acutely aware of the quantifiable connection between surroundings and behavior. Citing a study of 750 rats under lighting conditions, dentist Thomas W. Doan wrote to Neutra (August 17, 1952) about the "locally illuminated spot" of the patient's mouth, and what the "scanning eye of the dentist would see peripherally as we are manipulating and working." He pointed out that "the patient had to be considered by the architect as a subject to be diverted as well as he can from the treatment impact on his nervous system ... instead of watching the fingers, the facial expression of the dentist, and expecting the worst." Ergo, Neutra's brief was to increase the focus and concentration of the surgeon dentist, and to decrease the focus of the patient.

The coverings for the walkways between the buildings are asymmetrically laid; they have some thickness and are simply not thin planes, serving to deeply connect the buildings and to provide a greater sense of protection for the visitor. Neutra elected to use vertical metal louvers rather than overhangs for shade and privacy: "The site sits 45 degrees off the North, which is the most difficult orientation for sun protection, as all four sides receive sun, with two sides receiving the hottest afternoon sun ... By plotting the sun angles, overhangs were found to be effective only in the southeast and southwest and only for very high windows ... "

Have you ever had dental work done in a garden? Glass separates the (now "antique") dental equipment from the plants and natural light beyond.

FRITZ AND TRUDI RENTSCH HOUSE

Wengen, Switzerland, 1964

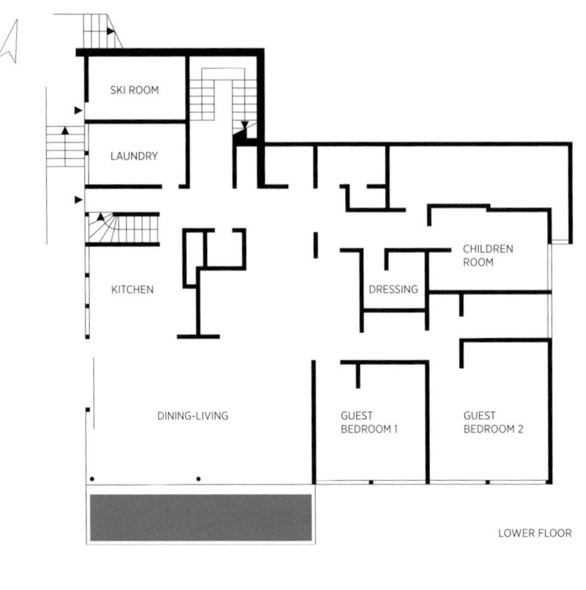

Previous: Neutra wrote of his awe in seeing the famous Jungfrau, "From a path above one would gain the first view of the structure overhanging a precipitously deep valley, embedded in a far-reaching panorama of eternal mountain and fast-racing clouds."

Opposite: When it came to flat roofs, sometimes even Neutra's most persuasive charms failed to move the authorities. Here, his description cheerfully notes that the sloped roof was "desired by the alpine community." It was actually required, but the architect seized the opportunity to use the slope to his advantage, "heightening the southerly front to an overwhelming vista of the glacier and the sometimes breathtaking dynamics of cloud shadows."

Neutra's suburban residential work is often placed in a domesticated "nature," the benign nature of artifice. The nature surrounding this house is of a terrible grandeur, and here Neutra further compounds the sense of being altogether too close to such potentially treacherous nature by successfully eradicating even the nuance of boundary between indoors and outdoors. Beyond the long thin reflecting pool flanking the terrace, the steel cable railing lies flat, not upright, so that there appears to be nothing between the viewer and the gigantic chasm beyond. The detail embodies his approach to nature: domestic or untamed, there must be as few limits to the access to nature as possible. The radiantly heated terrace and the water strip run along the principal south glass wall facing a Swiss glacier and the "breathtaking dynamics of cloud shadows," as Neutra described them. Above, large laminated beams extend beyond the roof line into the valley; a thin horizontal steel piece is attached to their ends. In turn, each beam is also met by a delicate steel column.

This house is complex in section. On the east, the roof of the house splits into two: one portion rising, the other level. Below the elevation of the flat roof, the house is clad in vertically oriented masonry or exposed concrete; above this line it is clad in wood. The vertical difference in elevation created the opportunity for clerestories that introduce daylight and views into the southwest portion of the second story. At the ridge line, located asymmetrically on the west side of the house, the roof line is broken to create two shed roofs of different heights.

To no avail, Neutra objected strenuously to the required roof pitch; he favored a flat roof and in many photographs the roof is suppressed. In addition to dwelling, the multi-purpose Rentsch House had to be part ski lodge and guest hostelry. There are also storage rooms, wine cellars, a second kitchen and a "jazz room."

The complicated section continues inside, where the *pièce de résistance* is the fireplace, pulled well back from the glass wall to create a seating and actual cooking area. It combines rough, vertically oriented masonry, copper panels, and sections of exposed concrete and common brick, all oriented vertically in an already very tall space. Each material and plane meets one another with such precision, intentionally always not quite touching, that there is not a trace of rusticity about this alpine hearth; instead there is simply unchecked vertical freedom. And yet, this fireplace, located in the heart of the house, is not only beautiful in its machined detailing. It is also a practical tool for the medieval art of cooking at the hearth. Rugged black iron stoves stand on low platforms next to the flames. An open space below the raised hearth provides a readily accessible place to store logs.

Right: Spatially, Neutra contrasted the soaring heights of the copper fireplace with the sheltering "ceiling" of the intimate wood-lined reading nook.

Opposite: Referring to them as "water guards," Neutra wrote that radiant heating, extending to the wide strip of water, "heated the entire balcony and kept it clear of snow to protect and prevent people against stepping close to the rim."

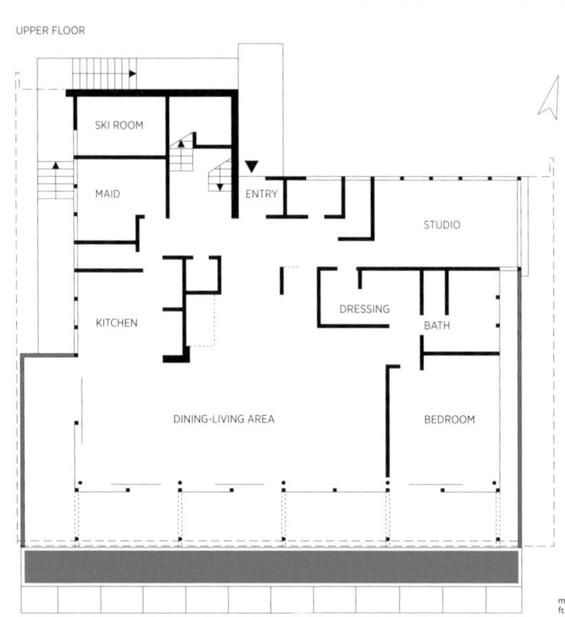

EBELIN BUCERIUS HOUSE

Navegna, Switzerland, 1966

A word must be said about Martin Hesse, the photographer of the haunting primary image of the house. Son of poet Hermann Hesse, he studied under iconoclast Johannes Itten before enrolling at the Bauhaus, where he combined architecture with his unparalleled gift for photography. The Bucerius House is the most elaborate and complex of all Neutra's European "villas."

Some of Neutra's most compelling houses are in Europe. Among these is the Bucerius House, a commission which allowed Neutra to show with extraordinary means a far more intimate, and terrifying relationship to nature, than anything in the United States. Its site invokes awe. From the western shore of Lago Maggiore, steep mountain slopes rise above the medieval coastal city of Ascona; the house faces the lake 2,000 feet below. Finely detailed, its interiors glowing with shiny surfaces in floors and stainless-steel fireplace, it reflects a handsome budget: here even the slats of the highly varnished tongue-and-groove wood ceiling in the living room are so narrow and refined that it becomes a slick monolithic plane above the beams. Terraces with radiant heating and reflecting pools maintain the extension of indoors to out even in winter. But at the edges of the terraces there are no balconies to obstruct the eye or to provide any psychological security from a powerful "nature" that here is hardly benign. Instead, Neutra inserts "water guards," wide, shallow linear strips of water at the terrace edges; these strips are

Above: A sliding glass wall separates the indoor and outdoor portions of this extraordinary pool. With its tropical plants and palms, the interior atrium recalls a primal paradise, eons and miles away from Switzerland.

Following: By contrast to the Rentsch House roof, here Neutra had control. Shifting straight planes and lines create the lightest of shelters in this glass-walled pavilion, the pool reflecting the jagged majesty of the surroundings.

flanked on the lake side by a horizontally laid "railing" of parallel steel cables. Thus the water becomes a mirror reflecting the clouds and the sky. On the ground floor, his most extraordinary pool occurs, somewhat reminiscent of the pool at the Lovell Health House in intention if far more sophisticated in execution. The larger portion of the pool is open to the ever-changing mountainscape, the other angles indoors, to the human artifice of smooth stone walls, where it wraps around an interior "winter garden." Large movable glass partitions, above and below the water, seal off the heated interior portion of the pool from the outdoors. At the roof Neutra created a European "gloriette": a small volume of three rooms connected to a wide roof terrace, partially covered by a pergola, inviting quiet contemplation; a dumbwaiter afforded "rooftop sociability" as he called it.

NEUTRA VDL STUDIO AND RESIDENCES

Van der Leeuw Research House II
2300 Silver Lake Boulevard
Los Angeles, California, 1966

VDL II responded to a very different program to that of its predecessor. Los Angeles had grown up. Neutra's nemesis, "rolling traffic" and accompanying pollution, was now a noisy fact of life just beyond the front door. With the additional destruction of the fast-growing acacia and sycamore trees Neutra planted years earlier in front of the street façade, there were no buffers to shield the house from the strong western sun. Silver Lake itself had been remodeled and made smaller, its cooling presence now 600 feet away rather than the 100 feet of the 1930s. Where the ground floor had once been devoted to a busy office and a studio apartment, after the fire Richard and Dion's practice moved to the nearby Glendale office.

In response, the new house turns into itself more without completely severing its urban identification with the street. It gained an internal sense of transparency, heightened opportunities for family community, and a more resolute connection to the interior garden.

The new design eliminated the solid walls of the interior staircase leading to the second

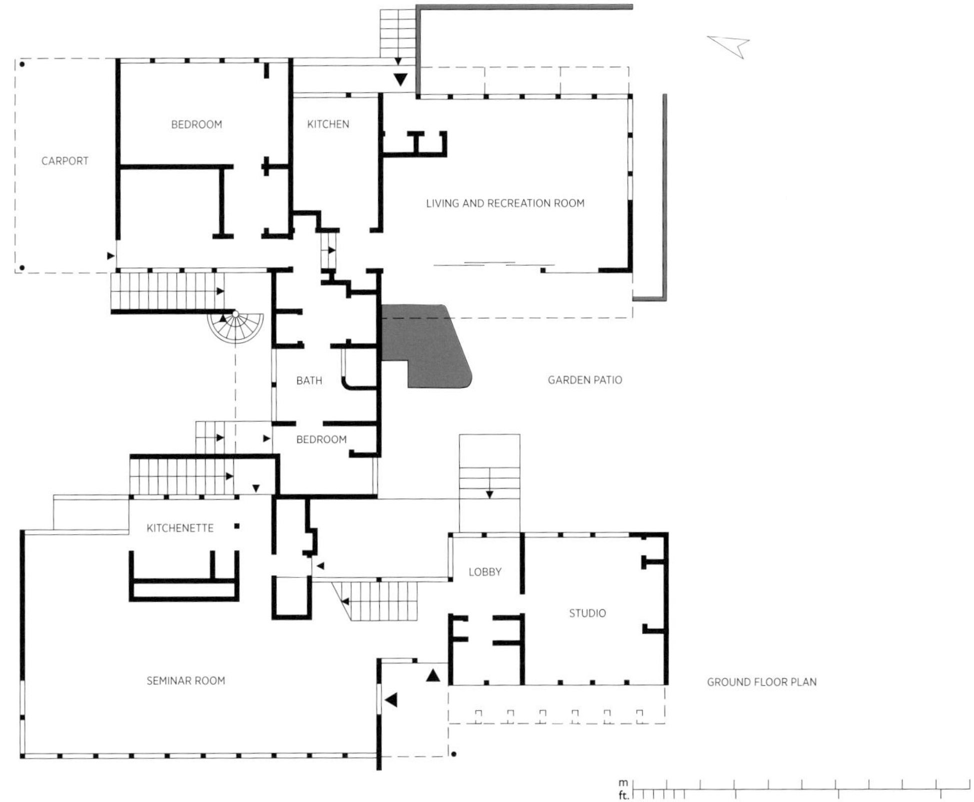

Opposite: The 1966 version of VDL I, 1932, was called VDL II until it was declared a National Historic Landmark in 2016, thanks to the efforts of Raymond Neutra, who sought a title that better fitted the compound's multivalent nature. The little penthouse looked west; the reflecting pool was intended to visually link with the reservoir beyond.

floor, linking the garden to the ground floor. It was replaced by an open-tread staircase supported by a steel stringer on one side and suspended from a balustrade of thin steel rods on the other.

A huge ten-foot-wide, screened window near the upstairs breakfast nook slides entirely outside the building, bringing trees and sky into the interior, in response to Dione's request to her son for an old-fashioned "screened-in porch."

A balcony was added to the south bedroom (Neutra's bedroom) to overlook the garden; most window sills on the east were lowered to a 30-inch height. The kitchen was cantilevered out to the rear three feet. Glass walls rise like clerestories above the built-in birch cabinets, which are pushed out as well to achieve a better-lit countertop space and a sense of openness. The kitchen is also connected to the living room with folding bypass doors for easy entertaining in contrast to the approach in VDL I, where items mysteriously appeared in the living area, passed through 20-gauge metal-lined drawers, with no contact between the hostess and her guests.

Left: The living room's transparent east wall reveals the guesthouse, 1939, and the courtyard, where the ashes of Richard, Dione, and sons Frank and Dion lie beneath the great Chinese elm.

Page 493: A sliding glass wall replaced the 1932 glass folding doors that led to the terrace. View facing south.

The physical presence of water is a precious component in Neutra's biorealism. Since the lake was now a distant sliver of silver, water was integrated into each of the three stories. At the ground-floor entrance, a small dark pool and the short elevated walkway bridging sidewalk and house serve the same vital purpose of transition from public to private – albeit now compressed – as in Neutra's larger houses, where the sense of procession could be elaborated. (The walkway is original and was saved from demolition.) As Dion Neutra wrote in the introduction to *Senses and the Setting,* the entrance here "has a great affinity to pulsatory life ..." Another smaller pool sits in the interior courtyard, near where Richard and Dione's ashes lie. On the second floor, a pool was added to the outdoor sitting room. Its source of water is the roof surrounding the penthouse, which can be sheeted in two inches of water to provide a reminiscence of the lake view and to also cool the house. Later confined to a wheelchair and sitting in the living room, Dione Neutra would listen intently to the movements of first-time visitors above in the penthouse, calling to them to insist they sit on the low seating facing the lake. Only there could they perceive rooftop water and lake as one single shimmering body of water; only then was she satisfied.

Built on the existing footprint, the original 4″ x 7″ prefabricated concrete joists laid 2′ 8″ on center with their poured-in-place slab were reused, since the fire had not caused the

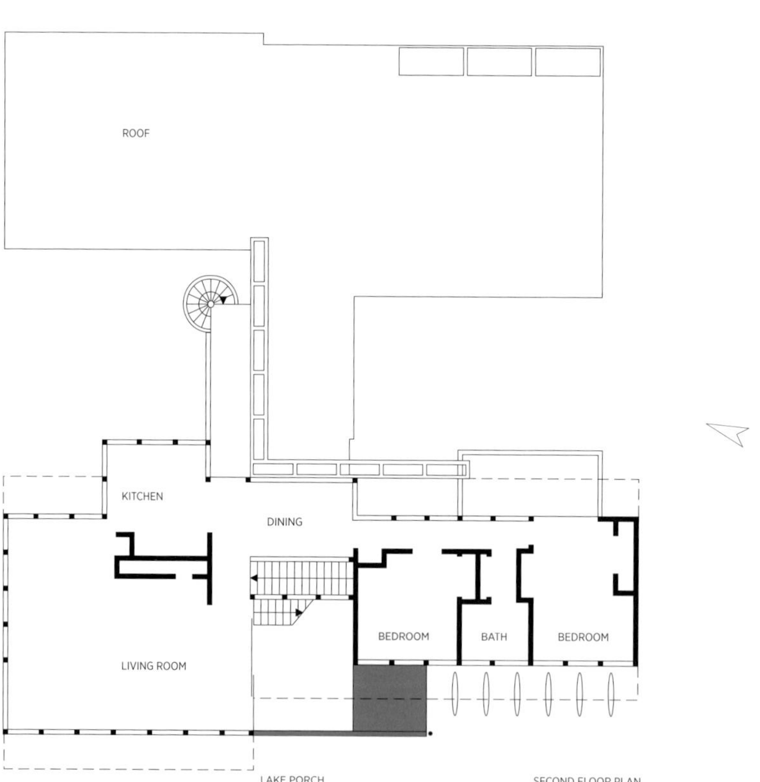

SECOND FLOOR PLAN

concrete to spall and become unsound. While maintaining the original spatial character of the house, the spirit of experimentaton continued in a state-of-the-art low voltage system, which proved difficult to maintain because the system failed to win public acceptance and the manufacturer went out of business. Two-story, electronically controlled aluminum "airplane" louvers above the entrance pool, similar to those used for the County of Los Angeles Hall of Records, provided immediate relief from the strong afternoon sun. Maintenance-free Formica paneling in a rosewood pattern substituted for the original waxed and rubbed Masonite. Gold heat-reflecting privacy glass, now fixed to avoid introducing dusty street winds and pollution, was used for the bed- and bathroom windows on the street façade. Inside, mirrors were incorporated, typically above head height, to stretch space. A freestanding panel of refelecting glass stands outside the south side of the penthouse, here primarily to shut out views of neighboring rooftops.

The result is a tree house with layered balconies, pungent with the smell of eucalyptus, yet not a house but an environment, a three-dimensional interlocking puzzle. Dione Neutra willed the house and its contents to the School of Environmental Design at the California State Polytechnic University Pomona, which is now seeking funds for its restoration and the archives in order that the house realize a more public presence in the urban canvas of Los Angeles.

Like the roof pavilion of the Bucerius House, here there are few barriers between the decks, the reflecting pool, and the world beyond. As was typical, Neutra is pictured sitting without formality, here looking west to Silver Lake Reservoir. View facing south.

GUENTER PESCHER HOUSE

Am Freudenberg 75
Wuppertal, Germany, 1968

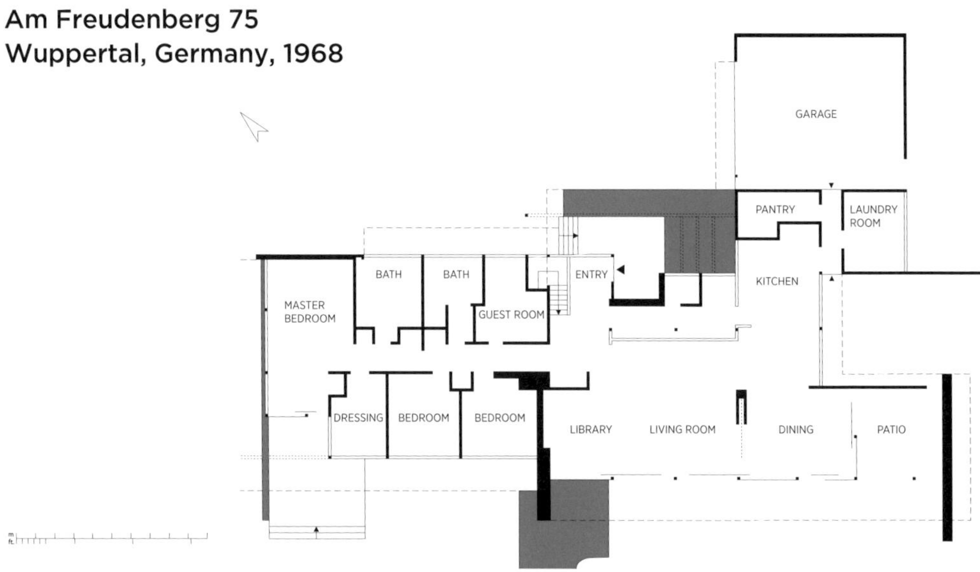

Opposite: Pescher and Neutra had an argument. (Bear in mind that Pescher was the head of a stone and masonry company and the son of a stonemason.) Neutra wanted to orient Pescher's stonework vertically, as he had in many other projects. "That is not how stone lies in the ground," retorted Pescher. And that was the end of it.

Above: There is a remarkable sense of serenity here in this long horizontal stroke of a house amidst the largesse of an unending lawn.

Frank Lloyd Wright once complained that Neutra's work was "cheap and thin," referring to his early work which was indeed a search for lightness in materials. But like other Neutra houses in Germany, this is a large house distinguished by sound craftsmanship and a sense of solidity. On the rear southwest façade, thick masonry walls perpendicular to the planes of glass define interior spaces; here they appear to be structural buttresses, giving the composition weight and balance. On the northeast façade facing the street, the masonry walls run parallel to the lighter wood-and-glass walls, so that here the masonry acts as another type of cladding. There are two reflecting pools, one at the entry, one at the rear, extending into the landscape.

Previous: The south floor-to-ceiling glass wall opens to landscape, protected by a broad overhang. The lowered soffit, a narrow clerestory above, provides a more intimate area for socializing and reading. In the evenings, the cantilevered sofa exuded light from below. Walls, tucked into cabinetry, could be pulled out to separate the dining area.

Opposite top: Framed in glass, the dining/breakfast area, on the east side of the house, is surrounded by Pescher's stone. Chairs by Eero Saarinen, commissioned by Hans Knoll himself. View facing southwest.

Opposite bottom: The house was listed in 2001; *Baukunst* magazine called it an "outstanding example of the bungalow building type of the 1960s." (A *bungalow* in Germany refers not to a Craftsman house, as it does in the U.S., but to low-slung, flat-roofed houses that became popular after World War II.)

Below: A reflecting pool frames the long wall separating living areas from the bedroom wing.

One brick wall juts out into the middle of the rear pool, which extends farther into the garden, a strategy that also creates a second level of privacy for the bedroom wing; privacy not just from the street but from the living/dining area as well. This northwest wing steps back and is surrounded by more landscaping, creating a world of its own. The spacious master suite opens to its own large terrace.

ORANGE COUNTY COURTHOUSE

with Ramberg and Lowrey
Civic Center Plaza, 6th and Main Streets
Santa Ana, California, 1968

The courthouse was one of a number of civic structures planned for Orange County, including a library and city hall in addition to the completed two-story police headquarters. For this project Neutra's "client interrogations" reached a new level. He interviewed bailiffs and judges, clerks and guards, district attorneys and public defenders, generating a wealth of planning information to ascertain the simultaneous needs of a freely moving public as well as those of prisoners under guard. The result is a handsomely detailed building, if somewhat formulaically handled. The narrow 12-story tower is oriented north-south, with a massive order of fixed vertical louvers for "skyglare" on the north and broader movable louvers on the south rising up behind a "base" of a secondary two-story court building, this fronted by larger louvers. The staircase on the east is treated like a "server" element à la Louis Kahn, articulated in white and slightly pulled away from the building.

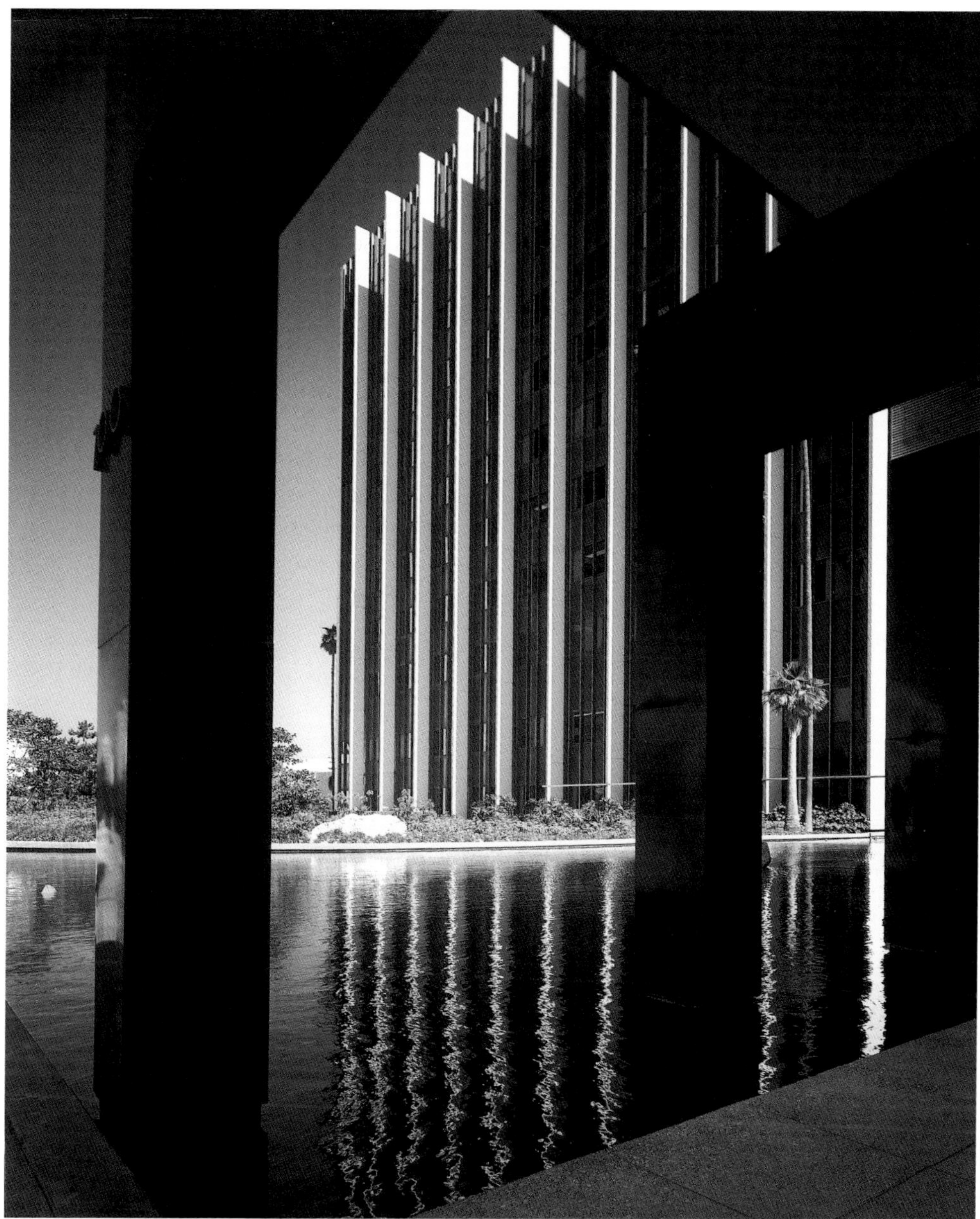

Neutra was passionate not only about aesthetics but about how architectural strategies could support – or thwart – the dispensation of justice. The walls behind judges were tilted forward so that their words could be heard by the lawyers clustering around the bench. The walls for the jury should be "zigzagged" with acoustically treated materials. He experimented with coatings for the window walls, not only to reduce solar gain but "so not to produce nervousness or straining relations ... so extremely important psychologically." The sophisticated Courthouse, with its vertical fins echoing classical Greek columns, continues to be one of Orange County's best examples of mid-century civic architecture.

EPILOGUE

The embodiment of a life's creativity, portrayed in the span of 64 years of photography, is abundantly expressed in my relationship with Richard Neutra from 1936 until his death in 1970. In retrospect, the fateful day of our first meeting in March 1936 marked my first introduction to an architect. Continuing until 1970, we created a thorough archive of the works of one of the world's most respected and most influential architects.

A question frequently asked after my lectures is: "How do you feel personally about Mr. Neutra's achievements?" My response: "How can I measure his work or personality in an objective manner?" As an articulate person, Neutra was brilliant. In frequent conversations, as we drove to distant projects, I was awed by his dissertations. I recall, in the spring of 1941 as we were on a trip to photograph his work in central and northern California, his evaluation of the international situations confronting the United States. He foresaw that we would be engulfed in World War II.

Later, becoming more familiar with his designs, I observed the logic of his thought processes, how his design projections were orderly structured. Although I admired his achievements, photography with Neutra created questions. He admired my first solo Vest Pocket Camera photograph of his Kun House in Los Angeles. His reactions were most favorable. As the years progressed, he insisted on literally pushing me away from my view camera: "Let me see," he would say as he pulled the focusing cloth over his head, directing my assistant what to do! Often, as he moved on to the next area with my assistant, if I preferred it, I would recover my original composition on film. Apparently, on viewing the finished product, he would not realize my camera's repositioning. Often his directions aimed at concealing elements, whereas my more objective statements resulted in photographs which became iconic in their worldwide acceptance.

A number of Neutra's clients had commented about drastic "alterations," changes between a finished plan and the final structure. The rationale for Neutra's (and other architects') "alterations" is evidence that the client-architect relationship could be an essential arm of architectural school training. It too often is a proprietary relationship, reminding me of a question from Frank Lloyd Wright when he asked how the architects I worked with "processed" their client's resistance. Pierre Koenig's role as professor at USC emphasized that students should learn how to structure a respectful and non-confrontational atmosphere with clients during the earliest stages. Neutra, I felt, was given towards a gentle, albeit quite persuasive, direction in confronting opposition from a client.

Generally, as I have recalled my Neutra-related life of scores of years, I cannot help but come away with an accelerated awareness of the significance of his primary role in my life's work: then, because of our meeting on March 5, 1936, I became an architectural photographer, and he was the first architect in my life!

Julius Shulman

PROJECT & NAME INDEX

PHOTO CREDITS

We thank the following institutions and photographers:

Loos-Archiv, Albertina, Vienna: 13

W. Boesiger, Richard Neutra 1950–60, Buildings and Projects (Stuttgart: Karl Krämer Verlag, 1960): 56

Archives-Special Collections, College of Environmental Design, California State Polytechnic University, Pomona, California: 18, 21, 29, 30, 68, 69, 72, 83, 149 top, 400–401, 403, 446, 447, 450 top, 451 top, 474–475, 477, 478, 479, 480–481, 482, 483, 484–485

Cal Poly Pomona / Hastings-Willinger photo: 344–345

Cal Poly Pomona / Martin Hesse photo: 448, 449

Cal Poly Pomona / Jordan Lagman: 503

Cal Poly Pomona / Chas A. Libby photo: 244–245

Cal Poly Pomona / Luckhaus photo: 74, 86 top, 91, 92–93, 94, 96, 100–101, 126, 129 top

Cal Poly Pomona / Klaus Meier-Ude photo: 450 bottom

Cal Poly Pomona / Bergen Patterson photo: 392–393

Cal Poly Pomona / M. S. Warren photo: 382–383

Cal Poly Pomona / Lawrence Williams photo: 426–427, 428, 429

David Glomb, Rancho Mirage, California: 222–223

David Glomb and Julius Shulman, Los Angeles, California: 185

Robert Hendershot, Los Angeles, California: 41

Don Higgins Photography, Santa Monica, California: 230–231, 236, 237, 505

Historical Archive Van Nelle, Rotterdam / E. M. van Ojen photo: 26

Historical Archive Van Nelle, Rotterdam / Kees van der Leeuw photo: 27

Walde Huth, Cologne / Schmölz-Huth photo: 496, 500 bottom, 501

Liška Archives, Vienna: 11, 12, 28

Tom Nagy, Hamburg: 497, 498–499, 500 top

Dion Neutra, Los Angeles, California: 61, 182

Julius Shulman Photography, Los Angeles, California: 4, 6–7, 24, 35, 36, 38, 42, 45, 47, 51, 54, 59, 64, 66–67, 70–71, 73, 79, 80–81, 82, 86 bottom, 87, 103, 104, 105, 106, 107, 109, 110, 111, 114–115, 116–117, 122, 123, 124–125, 127, 129 bottom, 146, 147, 150–151, 152–153, 154, 155, 160, 161, 162–163, 165, 166–167, 168, 169, 170, 171, 172–173, 174, 175, 176, 177, 178–179, 180, 181, 183, 184, 186, 187, 189, 190–191, 192, 193, 194, 195, 196–197, 199, 200–201, 202, 203, 204, 205, 206, 207, 208–209, 210, 211, 212, 213, 214–215, 216, 217, 219 bottom, 220–221, 224, 226–227, 228, 229, 232, 233, 234–235, 242, 243, 248–249, 250, 251, 252–253, 255, 258, 259, 261, 262–263, 265, 266, 267, 268, 270–271, 273, 274–275, 277 bottom, 277 top, 278, 279, 280, 281, 282, 283, 284–285, 286, 288–289, 291, 292–293, 294, 296–297, 298, 299, 300, 301, 302, 303, 304, 305, 306–307, 309, 310, 311, 312, 313, 314–315, 316, 317, 319, 328–329, 331, 332, 333, 334–335, 336, 337, 338–339, 340, 341, 342, 343, 346–347, 348, 349, 350, 351, 352, 353, 354–355, 356, 357, 358–359, 360–361, 362, 363, 368–369, 370–371, 372–373, 375, 376–377, 379, 380, 381, 386, 387, 388, 389, 394, 399, 404–405, 406, 407, 408–409, 411, 412, 413, 414, 415, 420–421, 422, 424–425, 434, 435, 440–441, 442, 443, 444, 445, 452, 453, 454, 455, 457, 458, 459, 460–461, 462, 463, 464, 465, 466, 467, 468, 469, 470, 471, 473, 486–487, 488, 490–491, 493, 494–495, 502

Tim Street-Porter, Los Angeles, California: 75, 76–77, 396–397, 398

Department of Special Collections, Young Research Library, University of California Los Angeles, Los Angeles, California: 1, 8, 16, 17, 19, 32, 39, 40, 62, 99, 102, 108, 128, 130, 131, 138, 142–143, 148, 149 bottom, 188, 198, 219 top, 247, 324–325, 327, 390, 391

Special Collections, UCLA / Beinlich photo: 2

Special Collections, UCLA / Harold Haliday Costain photo: 132, 133, 134

Special Collections, UCLA / Amir Farr photo: 436–437, 438, 439

Special Collections, UCLA / Luckhaus photo: 88–89, 97, 98, 112–113, 118, 119, 120, 121, 136, 137, 139, 140, 141, 144–145

Special Collections, UCLA / E. Marshall photo: 156–157, 158, 159